THE CHANGING BRITISH PARTY SYSTEM, 1945-1979

S. E. FINER

American Enterprise Institute for Public Policy Research
Washington, D.C.

S. E. Finer, M.A., D.Litt. (Oxon), is Gladstone Professor of Government and Public Administration and a Fellow of All Souls College, Oxford.

Library of Congress Cataloging in Publication Data

Finer, Samuel Edward.
    The changing British party system.
    (AEI studies ; 265)
    Bibliography: p.
    1.   Political parties—Great Britain.
I.   Title. II. Series: American Enterprise
Institute for Public Policy Research. AEI
studies ; 265.
JN1121.F56   329'.02'0941   79-25084
ISBN 0-8447-3368-7

AEI Studies 265

Printed in the United States of America

for
KATE

CONTENTS

3 THE LEVEL OF THE PARTY ORGANIZATIONS 72

4 THE PARTIES AND OTHER INSTITUTIONS 136

GENERAL CONCLUSIONS TO PART ONE 162

Part Two
THE APPRAISAL

PREFACE

In a foreword to a book about the changes in the British party system since 1945, I have, I fancy, three duties to fulfill: to justify the subject, to justify the year 1945 as my starting point, and to justify my treatment.

First, why do I think this subject worth writing about? To answer this, I must explain how this inquiry originated. It began when I was invited to join a western European team inquiring into the value and capabilities of political parties in western Europe in the closing years of the twentieth century: How had the parties changed since the end of World War II? Why had they changed? What functions were they meant to serve? How far were they still performing them, and how well?

I soon realized that my own part of this inquiry was not merely of interest to foreign observers of the British scene; it was of major importance to every British subject. We in Britain have no written constitution. Instead we have a sovereign legislature, to most intents and purposes unicameral, and we have two extremely powerful and highly disciplined national parties, either of which by dint of winning an election attains an almost despotic power over the affairs of the country. Political parties reshaped our medieval constitution to suit themselves, and nowadays the governmental system fits round them as the skin fits the human frame. Because they are integral to the governmental system, substantial change in their organization, membership, popular support, and power over other political, social, and economic institutions has vital consequences. It is a theme of grandeur. It might also be, as I found pursuing my research, a theme of servitude.[1] Be that as it may, whoever writes about the British party system writes about the British way and purpose.

We had set ourselves the task of starting in 1945 or thereabouts —the close of the war—and terminating at the moment of writing; we would compare the situation at the beginning and the end; and then we would see what changes and what trends, if any, had been developed during that time span. At first blush, the British party system looks exactly as it did in 1945 or 1950. It is, apparently, the same two-party system that every British and indeed every overseas student has been trained to believe is the very epitome of the British party scene. But on closer examination, it became clear that this is a façade. The extraparliamentary party organizations have not been static in this period. True, the elements of stability were there, and very powerful, but change had occurred in their organization, in their mode of policy making, and above all in their numbers. In addition, the relationship between the leadership and the rank and file had been questioned with some effect in both the Labour and the Liberal parties. Nor was that all. At the level of the general public, great changes had occurred which the electoral system had all but succeeded in masking. Some of these, like the decline in voter turnout and an increasing indifference to the two major parties, have their parallels in American experience, although one must be very wary indeed of suggesting that the causes are similar. The relationship of parties to nongovernmental institutions had clearly changed as well, and the parties visibly had much less control of organized forces in British society than in the past.

The detection of such changes would itself have justified writing this book. But there was more. It is my view—a little idiosyncratic, I know—that the numerous political scientists who specialize in parties fall into two main types: those who think of the parties as things that *do*, and those who think of them as things that *are*. The latter observe parties as naturalists observe larvae under a microscope. Every wriggle, every mutation is fascinating. It does not matter what they are about; what is important is how they behave. With this class of party watchers, changes in "party identification," "party space," "party fractionalization" are their food and drink. Others—I am among them—regard observation as instrumental to another inquiry altogether: What are these parties about? How do they relate to the machinery of government? And, at the end of the day, are they doing a good job or a bad one?

---

[1] See A. de Vigny, *Grandeur et Servitude Militaire* (Paris: Germain, 1965).

As I plodded through my mixture of documentary research and personal observation, I came to a dramatic conclusion. I call it dramatic because most of the facts I discovered were facts I had "known" all my professional life. What is more, the observations I made about them had often been made many times before me. Yet, one by one, they took on a novel significance. I concluded that since 1964 or thereabouts this party system, which I along with countless others had been accustomed to applaud, had become positively *dysfunctional* to the British system of government. At this point I began to think as what in the United States is called a "concerned citizen." Once I had reached this stage, nothing would content me but that I go back to the original report I had drafted for my colleagues in the research project and turn it into a book.

In 1964 my friend and colleague Antony Birch wrote a book called *Representative and Responsible Government*.[2] This excellent text about the government of Britain is the only comprehensive work I am familiar with on the relationship of the two concepts to one another and to the British system of government. In its last chapter, under the subheading of "The debate about representation," I found remarks so startling in the context of 1979 that in themselves they demonstrate the immense distance traveled by British opinion of its party system over a mere fifteen years.

Let me present a short inventory: "Some doctrines about political representation have never been seriously canvassed in Britain. Thus, there has been no support in this country for the Populist doctrine that representation is an inferior alternative to direct democracy." But now, in 1979, there is. Again: "It has occasionally been proposed that a referendum be held on a particular issue, but the proposals do not ever appear to have been taken seriously." We had one referendum in 1975 and two more in 1979. Again: "There has been no support at all for the idea that the initiative and the referendum should be adopted as permanent institutions of government as in Switzerland. . . ." True, as far as the popular initiative is concerned, but a number of leading Conservative politicians has come out in favor of the referendum.

Turning to the party organization, Birch was writing in 1964: "There has been no debate about the advantage of primary elections." Today this has been seriously advocated from such quarters as the Hansard society, and among the parties. And, finally, Birch was able to write in those halcyon days for the two-party system: "The electoral system is no longer a bone of contention; but . . . it is possible . . .

---

[2] Antony H. Birch, *Representative and Responsible Government* (London: Allen and Unwin, 1964), pp. 227–37.

that the case for proportional representation would become a serious issue." It *has* become a serious issue, and not merely because the Liberal party, which won nearly 20 percent of the 1974 votes, ended up with only 2 percent of the parliamentary seats, but because a large and growing number of Conservative politicians also are beginning to see its advantages, while a national Campaign for Electoral Reform has established itself to campaign on the issue.

All this suggests a prodigious change in the public perception of the nature of the political parties and the way they have carried out their functions. That change is part of the more subtle and half-concealed changes detectable once the façade of the parliamentary party duopoly has been penetrated.

This then was the justification for turning a research report into this book.

It is not hard to justify my choice of starting date, 1945. It has four things to be said for it. First, World War II ended in that year, and Britain was able to have its first elections in ten whole years. Second, 1945 marked the entry of the Labour party onto the political stage as the only serious competitor of the historical Conservative party—the Liberal party was finally consigned to the role of a minor. Third, that year marks the first accession of Labour to office with a parliamentary majority—an enormous one—and a successful program of nationalization and social reform, which places it among the three great reforming administrations of the post-1832 period. And, finally, that year ushered in the period of strict unmitigated two-partyism, which was not terminated until the elections of 1974, only to revert to two-partyism in 1979.

Finally, I must justify my treatment. I have divided this book into two rather unequal halves. The first half gives a factual account of the main changes that have taken place. I have tried very hard to keep my opinions out of this and to make it strictly factual. There is a technical fault in this first half, however; I have tried to order the facts in the most systematic way and to treat them at four levels: parliamentary, electoral, extraparliamentary, and social. But politics and society form a seamless web, and obviously what happens at one level relates always to what happens at the others. This is an artificial division, and sometimes it results in repetition. On the whole, though, I think it works, and it seems more logical and orderly than any other.

The second half of the book turns from a recapitulation of well-known facts to an appraisal. What functions do the parties perform, and how well do they carry them out? Obviously, an appraisal is likely to be more subjective than the inventory which is the first half.

Here again, I have tried to be objective, but the judgments are in the last resort personal ones. Only in the very last pages of Chapter 6, dealing with possible reforms of the party system, does the *brio* of my writing suggest, I think, my personal involvement. That was the point at which I became really "engaged." To make this quite clear, I have ended the book with a personal postscript in which I state what I like and above all dislike about the present party system and the reforms which I personally am prepared to campaign for.

ACKNOWLEDGMENTS

This book had its origin in the joint research project entitled "Recent Changes in the European Party Systems," established by the European Consortium for Political Research in early 1978 and funded by the Volkswagen Corporation. My long list of acknowledgments for help and encouragement starts from there. First, I would like to express my appreciation for a small research grant, via the Volkswagen funding, which enabled me to purchase materials and to cover certain clerical expenses in a way that made my mode of work less onerous. Second, I want to thank the authorities of two institutions who provided the research team with a venue for the conferences necessary to the project: the University of Mannheim and the European University Institute at Florence. The latter acted as the research team's headquarters, and we met there on three occasions to review our work and to plan future progress. Its support and assistance was essential to the pursuit of the project. And finally, of course, I wish to thank my colleagues in the research team itself for stimulus, constructive criticism, and active encouragement. Professor Hans Daalder of the European University Institute and Leiden University played a particularly important role; quite apart from organizing the various colloquia at Florence, it was he who acted as rapporteur to the team and was largely responsible for drafting the guidelines we followed in pursuing our research. To the members of the team themselves, my deep gratitude for their fellowship, their learning, and their valuable commentary: Professor Henrik de Wachter, Louvain, Belgium; Paolo Farneti, Turin, Italy; Henry Kerr, Geneva, Switzerland; J. P. Parodi, Centre d'études de la vie française, Paris; Mögens Pedersen, Odense, Denmark; Perrtti Pesonen, Helsinki, Finland; Gonnar Sjöblom, Copenhagen, Denmark; Henry Valen, Oslo, Norway; and Rudolph Wilde-mann, the Rector of Mannheim University, West Germany.

The book itself, which goes far beyond the work undertaken as part of the team project, has benefited prodigiously from the detailed comments of a large number of distinguished specialists, mostly British, in this field. They went through the draft from which this book is derived with the utmost attention. I am immensely grateful to them: Hugh Berrington, Newcastle-on-Tyne; Vernon Bogdanor, Brasenose College, Oxford; David Butler, Nuffield College, Oxford; Ivor Crewe, Essex; Nevil Johnson, Nuffield College, Oxford; Dennis Kavanagh, Manchester; Lew Minkin, also of Manchester; Richard Rose, Strathclyde; and also to Giovanni Sartori, Stanford, California; and Klaus von Beyhme, Heidelberg, West Germany. This book is vastly improved by their gadfly work. The errors that, alas, are likely to be found are all my own, and my personal predilection in the matter of reforming our party system is even more peculiarly individual.

As in so many other fields, I have derived immense stimulus from the intellectual vigor of the college to which I have the honor to belong. I have been helped by the indefatigable services of Codrinton's librarian, John Simmons, and Norma Potter and Barry Brittan, its assistant librarians.

I take this opportunity to express my appreciation of the generous support provided by the American Enterprise Institute for Public Policy Research, and in particular I want to thank Deborah Styles for her skilled editing and Cynthia Barry for her copy editing and production services.

And, finally, in a special place of honor, this is an opportunity to thank my secretary, Sally Rogers, who typed the entire manuscript accurately, rapidly, and not merely cheerfully, but—if I may say so—with a kind of gusto. Thank you!

S. E. FINER
All Souls College
August 1979

PART ONE
The Inventory

1

Parties at the Parliamentary and Governmental Level

The ritual of each party is rehearsed
Dislodging not one vote or prejudice;
The ministers their ministries retain,
And Ins as Ins, and Outs as Outs remain.

THOMAS HARDY, *The Dynasts*

Still a Two-Party System

Since the breakup of the wartime coalition in 1945 and the ensuing general election, parliamentary government in Britain has displayed two constant characteristics: a party *duopoly* of parliamentary seats and a party *monopoly* of the executive government. In 1950 the Conservative and Labour parties took 98 percent of the seats in the House of Commons; in October 1974 they still took 94 percent, and in 1979, they improved their share to nearly 96 percent as shown in Table 1.

The fractionalization of the parties is therefore very small. For all that, the number of M.P.s not taking the whip of the two major

TABLE 1

ALLOCATION OF COMMONS SEATS, 1950, 1974, AND 1979

Party	Number of Seats			
	1950	October 1974 (election)	April 1979 (dissolution)	May 1979 (election)
Conservative	298	277	282	339
Labour	315	319	307	269
Liberal	9	13	14	11
Other	3	26	28	16
Total	625	635	635[a]	635

[a] Includes four vacancies.

parties in April 1979 (forty-two,) represented the most serious inroad into the party duopoly since 1950.

The strength of the two major parties has fluctuated over time: Labour's seats have ranged from a low of 258 in 1959 to a high of 393 in 1945, while the Conservatives have ranged from a low of 213 in 1945 to a high of 365 in 1959. The strength of the Liberal party has fluctuated more narrowly, since its parliamentary strength has always been exiguous. Between the elections of 1945 and 1970, it never had more than twelve Members, and in four Parliaments (those of 1951, 1955, 1959, 1970) it had only six. Indeed, for a short period in 1957–1959, it had only five.

Table 1 does, however, draw attention to one striking difference: the rise in the number of "Other." While all of them represent peripheral nationalist movements, they have emerged as parliamentary parties in very different ways. Of the "Other," *ten* call themselves Ulster Unionists. Up to 1974, the Ulster Unionists had been associates of the Conservative party and had taken that party's whip in Parliament. The efforts of the Conservative government of Edward Heath (1970–1974) to force power-sharing upon the Ulster Protestants led to a Unionist revulsion, and in the February 1974 election they withdrew from the old relationship to form their own separate parliamentary group. Thus this particular component of the "Other" represents the breakup of the old Conservative and Unionist party, to give that party its full official title. By contrast most of the remainder, namely two Plaid Cymru and two Scottish National party, belong to parties that had previously never obtained more than one or two seats in any Parliament. Since all three parties—Unionist, Plaid, and Scottish Nationalists—were elected on an appeal to a cultural-ethnic cleavage in British society, it should be noted that apart from class this is the only social cleavage that has been overtly reflected in the postwar parliamentary party system. By the same token, insofar as Parliament is still dominated by the Labour-Conservative duopoly, it reflects the old and well-known cleavage between social classes: the Labour party being predominantly the party of the manual, poor, and urbanized, the Conservative the party of the nonmanual, the better-off, and suburbanized or rural members of the electorate. The extent to which they continue to represent these two contrasted sectors has altered, however, over the last thirty years.

Parties in Government and Opposition, 1945–1979

In current British constitutional practice, the sovereign sends for the leader of the majority party in the Commons to act as her Prime

Minister and form a government. In the event that there is no majority party, the Queen calls for the leader of the party that appears able in one way or another to "command a majority" in the House. This is usually the largest of the parties (though not necessarily). From 1946 until March 1974, either the Labour or the Conservative party had an absolute majority, so that the formation of a uni-party government was automatic. In February 1974 the Labour party became the largest parliamentary party but lacked an absolute majority. The sitting Conservative Prime Minister, Edward Heath, offered coalition to the Liberals in order to win their support. When they declined, he resigned, whereupon the Queen sent for Harold Wilson, the Labour leader, who formed a minority government. The second general election of October 1974 returned Labour with a narrow absolute majority, but this disappeared in November 1976. James Callaghan, who had replaced Wilson in April 1976 as Labour leader, thenceforward had to operate with a minority government, although between March 1977 and August 1978 he was supported by a legislative pact with the Liberals. At the May 1979 election, the Conservatives were returned with a clear majority. It follows that the pattern of government has been an alternation of uni-party Labour and Conservative governments, as shown in Table 2.

Trends in Parliamentary Government and Opposition. In the postwar period three trends in the alternation of the Conservative and Labour parties in Parliament are worth remarking.

The frequency of tiny majorities. As Table 3 shows, governments have come to power, for example, in 1950, 1951, 1964, 1970, and 1974 with very slender majorities; indeed, in February 1974, with no

TABLE 2

Turnover of Parties in Government, 1945–1979

Dates	Duration (Years)	Party Composition of Government
July 1945–October 1951	6	Labour
October 1951–October 1964	13	Conservative
October 1964–June 1970	6	Labour
June 1970–March 1974	4	Conservative
March 1974–May 1979	5	Labour
May 1979–	—	Conservative

TABLE 3

GOVERNMENT MAJORITIES IN THE HOUSE OF COMMONS, 1945–1979

Election	Seats in House	Seats in Government Party	Majority
1945	640	(Lab) 393	146
1950	625	(Lab) 315	5
1951	625	(Con) 321	17
1955	630	(Con) 344	58
1959	630	(Con) 365	100
1964	630	(Lab) 317	4
1966	630	(Lab) 363	96
1970	630	(Con) 330	30
February 1974	635	(Lab) 301	−33 (Minority)
October 1974	635	(Lab) 319	3
May 1979	635	(Con) 339	43

majority at all. The Table shows the absolute majority (or minority) the governing party held in the House of Commons, but this is not necessarily the same as its working majority. The reason is that four of the seats in the House (those of the speaker, the deputy speaker, and two committee chairmen) do not vote in party divisions, so the working majority of voting seats may differ from the absolute majorities shown in the Table.

The Labour government of 1950, with its tiny absolute majority of five was also much beset by internal dissension; this fact, rather than its small majority, accounted for its early demise. When the Conservatives were returned in 1951 with an absolute majority of seventeen, it was widely predicted that this would not be sufficient for it to pass its essential legislation and at the same time remain in power for very long. This prediction proved wrong, and the party was successful in passing its legislation and also living out most of its natural term. This was a result of the remarkable discipline of the two major parliamentary parties.

Since that date it has become clear, as Table 3 shows, that parties are able to carry on quite vigorously and for long periods of time with fractional majorities.

The party pendulum. As Table 4 shows, there is a marked difference in the swing of the pendulum between the two parties in the prewar period and the postwar period. In the prewar period the Labour and Conservative parties alternately lost seats and gained seats from one election to the other. To put this another way, a party that had lost seats at the first election gained seats at the next election, lost seats at the third election, and so on. But this pattern has not been repeated in the postwar period, as Table 4 shows. The Conservative party, after losing a massive number of seats in 1945, gained seats at the next election (1950), and continued to gain seats at the three subsequent elections of 1951, 1955, and 1959. By the same token, the Labour party continued to lose seats over these same four elections. Again, the Conservatives lost seats in 1964 and in 1966, while the Labour party gained seats in these two consecutive elections. The same pattern is repeated in the two elections of 1974. The conventional explanation for the characteristics of the prewar period was that voters became disillusioned with the party in office and subsequently withdrew support from it in the ensuing general election. If this explanation is true, then one must assume that in the postwar period after 1950, voters were on the contrary more pleased with the governing party's performance at the end of its tenure than they were at the period when they first elected it. One possible explanation for

TABLE 4

The Pendulum of Parliamentary Seats, 1922–1979

Election	Total Seats (Conservative)	± on Preceding Number of Seats	Total Seats (Labour)	± on Preceding Number of Seats
1922	345	—	142	—
1923	258	− 87	191	+ 49
1924	419	+161	151	− 40
1929	260	−159	288	+137
1931	473	+213	52	−236
1935	432	− 41	154	+102
1945	213	−219	393	+239
1950	298	+ 85	315	− 78
1951	321	+ 23	295	− 20
1955	344	+ 23	277	− 18
1959	365	+ 21	258	− 19
1964	304	− 61	317	+ 59
1966	253	− 51	363	+ 46
1970	330	+ 77	287	− 76
February 1974	297	− 33	301	+ 14
October 1974	277	− 20	319	+ 18
May 1979	339	+ 62	269	− 50

this phenomenon may be the increased ability of governments to manipulate the economy at the time of the election, a hypothesis that is explored later in this paper.

Increasing policy fluctuation. In the prewar period policy did not fluctuate significantly, since this was an epoch of Conservative hegemony. The Conservatives' hold on office was interrupted only briefly by the two Labour governments of 1923–1924 and 1929–1931; both of these governments were inherently feeble, and the second was overwhelmed by the effects of the economic crisis. From 1931 to 1940, the country was governed by the National Government, a coalition government in which Conservative party strength was all-powerful. It was, effectively, a Conservative party under a fancy name. From 1940 to 1945 the all-party wartime coalition was in office.

Thus, during this long period there was a very great continuity of personnel and policy.

The postwar period, however, has broken this pattern, and within this period itself there has been an acceleration of policy fluctuation. In the nineteen years from 1945 to 1964, there was only one change of government philosophy; that introduced in 1951 when the Conservative party took over from Labour. In the fourteen years since 1964, however, there have been four reversals of policy; the Labour victory of 1964, the Conservative victory of 1970, the Labour victory of 1974, and the Conservative victory of 1979. Furthermore, it is arguable that possibly since 1964, but certainly since 1970, the two major parties have adopted markedly antagonistic policies, so that the fluctuations in party fortune have brought about much greater dislocation in policy orientations than over the earlier postwar period and, unquestionably, than over the interwar period.

Majority vs. Minority Government. A government will claim a democratic mandate for the proposals contained in the (very detailed) manifesto on which it has fought the election that brought it to power, and it will *confidently* rely on the support of its backbencher M.P.'s to sustain it in power until the Prime Minister decides to request the sovereign to dissolve Parliament and call a new election.

Obviously a minority government such as the country witnessed after November 1976 is always liable to be defeated on a vote of censure or of "no confidence," to say nothing of day-to-day defeats on items of policy and administration. In the normal way, a government in this situation will seek a new election as soon as it feels it is confident of winning it, as Wilson did when he requested dissolution in October 1974, only seven months after becoming Prime Minister of a minority government. This option was hardly open to Callaghan, who took over as Prime Minister in April 1976, although he might have been forced to adopt this course in the absence of wider parliamentary support. In the event this was afforded by the Liberals, who in March 1977 formed a strictly legislative pact without entering the Labour cabinet. Its features were: the two parties established a consultative committee; regular meetings were held between the Liberal spokesman on economic affairs and the chancellor of the exchequer; Callaghan accepted a number of Liberal proposals for action (none of them very far-reaching); and the pact was limited in duration—indeed, it was formally renewed in September 1977. After an extraordinary Liberal congress meeting in January 1978, renewal or termination was left to the discretion of the parliamentary Liberal party. This arrangement enabled the government to cling to office, but did not ensure automatic passage of the details of all its measures. Indeed it suffered numerous defeats on items such as the devaluation of the "Green Pound," the taxation of petrol, income tax rates, the dock regulations, and the like. For its part Labour was unable to initiate a number of the more radical proposals contained in its election manifesto (for instance, introduction of a wealth tax and nationalization of ports, of mineral rights, and of a number of profitable sectors of private industry). The Liberals' announcement that they would terminate the pact by the end of the summer session of 1978 was widely regarded as making a general election in October 1978 inevitable. As it turned out, this assumption was incorrect: Callaghan decided to soldier on as a minority government.[1] This was finally brought down by a formal vote of no confidence, in March 1979. It was the first time a government had been so defeated since 1924. In the division, the Conservative Opposition was joined by a motley collection from the minor parties—eleven of the thirteen Liberals, eight of the ten Ulster Unionists, and all eleven of the Scottish National Party. The government was defeated by one vote, whereupon Callaghan declared that Parliament would be dissolved and a new election held.

Parliamentary Party Style

The central feature of parliamentary politics, which is party duopoly in seats and party monopoly of executive government, has its counterpart in party style. The two major parties alternately enact the roles

---

[1] A detailed account of the making and operation of the pact is given by A. Michie and S. Hoggart, "The Pact" (London: Quartet Books, 1978).

of government and of opposition. Nowhere except perhaps in New Zealand does the role of the minority vis-à-vis the majority party approximate that of the British party system. The opposition is concentrated in one major party, since there is no sizable or decisive block of third, fourth, or fifth party votes to take into account, as there is in Australia, or in Canada, or in practically every country in continental Europe except Austria and (perhaps) West Germany. Also, the opposition and the government parties are zero-sum competitive. In two-party America, or even in Austria and West Germany, the parties are involved in parliamentary collaboration as well as competition. In a final respect Britain may be said to be unique in Europe— a parliamentary election is *decisive* as to which party shall form the government.[2] Consequently, the goal of the opposition is simply expressed: it is, and is seen to be, *the alternative government*. As such it does everything in its power to turn the government out and put itself in its place. There is an old Spanish proverb that expresses this role exactly: *Dejame tu para ponermi yo*—"Get out so that I can get in."

The procedures of the House have been adjusted to this end. Legislative debate on the principles of a government bill takes place on the floor of the House. It is the arena of rhetoric. Detailed amendment of its clauses takes place in so-called standing committees, party replicas of the House as a whole, which are specially constituted for each bill as it comes from the House floor. Select committees, which also reflect the party composition of the House but which are traditionally nonpartisan in outlook, do exist, but as will be seen their role is subordinate. In short, the entire tradition of politics in the House is *adversary*. The two major parties confront one another *across* the House (which is rectangular in shape) as an organized government party consisting of ministers (frontbenchers) and supporters (backbenchers), and organized opposition, likewise consisting of "shadow ministers" on the frontbench and their supporters, the opposition backbenchers. This tradition is carried by extension into the standing committees on legislation, which meet upstairs in committee rooms shaped just like the House, where the party whips are put on to preserve party discipline, and where the politics are, as on the floor of the House itself, the adversary politics of confrontation.

Insofar as the sentiments of the House of Commons as such vs.

---

[2] Cf. Robert A. Dahl, *Political Oppositions in Western Democracies* (New Haven: Yale University Press, 1976), especially chapter 1 (A. Potter, "Great Britain: Opposition with a Capital O") and chapter 11 (Robert A. Dahl, "Patterns of Opposition").

the government as such are expressed at all, this occurs in select committees of the House. Like the standing legislative committees, these too must be constituted with "due regard to the party balance" in the House as a whole. Unlike them, however, the whips are not put on; members are expected to ignore party lines and, to the contrary, try to arrive at a unanimous report, supposedly representing the views of the House as a whole. These committees consist of backbenchers. The oldest and most influential, and the one with enough authority to influence government decisions, is the Public Acccounts Committee. The use of select committees to supervise the administration of government programs or individual departments has been advocated for the last fifteen years as a way to remedy the declining influence of the legislature as such vis-à-vis the executive, which in practice translates as the declining influence of backbenchers on government ministers. A number of such committees has been established; they do, on the whole, issue unanimous reports, but they have been remarkably unsuccessful in influencing government. As the late John Mackintosh put it, ". . . for Ministers, Shadow Ministers, and most MP's, the division that comes to mind is not between the executive and the House but between the government and Opposition."[3]

Until May 1979, at least, there had been no alteration in the hectoring attitude of the government toward the House for thirty years. In 1946, the then Labour government's leader of the House (in other words, the minister who is responsible for arranging the parliamentary program) claimed:

> Who is responsible for executive current administration, the Government or Parliament? I say it is the government that is responsible. . . . Parliament's business is to check the Government, throw it out if it wants to, go for it, attack it, criticize it by all means, for Parliament is not a body which is organized for current administration—not in this country. . . .[4]

In 1976, his successor (again, with Labour in power) stated to yet another select committee on procedure that government must govern, and consequently must be able to "secure from Parliament any necessary extension of their executive powers, and to implement their election pledges by legislation or otherwise (sic)."[5] The select com-

---

[3] John Mackintosh, *The Government and Politics of Britain*, 4th ed. (London: Hutchinson, 1977), p. 129.

[4] Lord Morrison of Lambeth, *3rd Report of the Select Committee on Procedure*, Session 1945–1946, (HC. 189-1).

[5] Quoted, *1st Report of the Select Committee on Procedure*, Session 1977–1978, volume I, p. viii (HC. 588-1).

mittees are so marginal because both government and opposition see the House as a battleground. The 1977–1978 Select Committee on Procedure, for instance, made this acknowledgment to the select committees: "One of (their) characteristics is their objectivity and freedom from party conflict." But the reason for this, it added, was that "select committees were not usually called upon to judge between the government and its political opponents." In short, these committees can be nonpartisan because the subjects they are permitted to handle are nonpartisan! And the moment partisan legislation came before them, the committee warned, "the party leaderships would have a natural and proper interest in influencing (their) proceedings." That is, the party whips would be put on.[6]

In short, adversary politics is the characteristic style of the major parties. Ever since the Balfour reforms of procedure in 1902, standing orders give the opposition wide latitude to select topics for debate, to put down motions of censure, and to elicit information, while for its part the government lays down the timetable and secures for itself sufficient time for its own business, which always has priority. The very amplitude of the opposition's opportunity to attack— and it is very ample—is predicated on the assumption, correct in majoritarian circumstances, that the opposition is incapable of pulling down the government.

In the minoritarian circumstances that prevailed between November 1976 and May 1979, the adversary style continued, but with a somewhat different effect: on a number of issues, some of great importance, the government was defeated. These defeats occurred mostly as a result of the defection of the Liberals and various nationalist groups, defections which were sometimes coupled with the defection of groups of government supporters.

The style of these minor parties was wholly tactical. It was governed by one or a combination of four intentions: to avert or alternatively to precipitate an immediate general election; to further special causes such as the devolution bills for Scotland and Wales; to trade support in return for concessions; to affirm some general policy that they would wish to pursue were they to wield effective power (for example, hostility to further nationalization of private industry).

It is desirable to draw a distinction, however weak, between the style of the nationalist parties in Parliament, which have little interest in anything beyond furthering their particularistic causes, and the Liberal party, which is a United Kingdom party and as such must take a position over the entire range of policy.

---

[6] Ibid.

The Left-Right Dimension

Persistencies, 1945–1978. Few British voters think of themselves as "left" or "right," although some 82 percent have been pressed into so identifying themselves.[7] One survey shows that 60 percent of the respondents did not recognize the terms at all, and another 20 percent gave them minimal recognition. Only 16 percent could elaborate, partially or fully, an ideological kind of interpretation.[8] The identification with "Left" or "Right" stems, in Britain, from voters' allegiance to the Labour or Conservative parties, which they have been taught to call "left" and "right" respectively. In short: British voters do not possess an ideological spectrum upon which they locate their political parties, but, on the contrary, have an allegiance to one or the other major party, which they call, respectively, the left and the right.

This is what one might expect if, following Miller, we postulate that the issues promoted by each of the respective parties were "linked together by a series of historical accidents in ways that were not logically necessary."[9] As he says, it is for this reason that they have been described as "non-ideologues."

Since the majority of British voters, however, support either the Labour party or the Conservative party, and since they are willing to call these left and right respectively, the way to proceed is to summarize the constant issues associated with each party and dub these, also, left and right respectively; but it will be a left and a right very much à l'anglaise.

Here again we can follow Miller as he discerns four issues that have a continuous life in the Labour party, and to these we ourselves would add a fifth. Miller calls his issues internationalism, socialism, class interests; and trade union power. We would add civil liberties. In varying shapes and forms all these themes have been repeated in all the party manifestoes since 1918.

Internationalism (in this definition, a very *English* and inward-looking internationalism). Internationalism has consisted of the three strands of *anticolonialism* (for example, decolonization in the 1950s, support for the Third World in the 1970s), *pacifism* (opposition to re-armament in the early 1930s, nuclear disarmament in the 1950s and 1960s, cuts in defense expenditure in the 1970s), and *international*

---

[7] Ian Budge, Ivor Crewe, and Dennis Farlie (eds.), *Party Identification and Beyond* (London: J. Wiley, 1976), p. 248.

[8] David Butler and Donald Stokes, *Political Change in Britain*, 2d ed. (London: Macmillan, 1974), pp. 238–334.

[9] William L. Miller, *Electoral Dynamics* (London: Macmillan, 1977), p. 22.

conciliation (support for the League of Nations in the 1930s, for the United Nations in the 1970s). This has not prevented Labour governments, with support from most of their M.P.s as opposed to mass-party sentiments, from taking hardnosed decisions to build and maintain a nuclear arsenal, to support NATO, and to reject the party's "Little England" opposition to the European Economic Community (EEC). It is noteworthy that the last issue still divides the party, both inside and outside Parliament, despite the results of the 1975 national referendum, which confirmed by a two-to-one majority the cabinet's recommendation to remain within the EEC. The committed antimarketeers reject the EEC as an obstacle to the full socialist planning of Britain and as too exclusive vis-à-vis the Third World.

Socialism (in this definition, nationalization of private industry and extensive controls over what is not fully nationalized). The party's 1918 demands for nationalization of the mines, transportation, and power were all achieved by Clement Attlee's Labour governments (1945–1951); the Bank of England was also taken over. The steel, shipbuilding, and aerospace industries have all been taken over since Attlee's time, and more is promised. There is a conflict between Clause Four of the party's constitution, which enjoins the full nationalization of production, distribution, and exchange, and the notion of a mixed economy. This conflict became open in the two years after the party's third successive electoral defeat in 1959. The party leader (Hugh Gaitskell) claimed that the party had lost votes through its identification with public ownership and the popular belief that the party wished to nationalize everything, and demanded that the hoary old Clause Four of the party's 1918 constitution be amended to say that Labour's goal was a mixed, not a fully socialized, economy. Gaitskell was defeated, and as the clause remains unamended to this day, there is still no established view nor any rationale as to where the limits of the public sector should be set. In Miller's words, ". . . the constant commitment to socialization implies even more extreme policies. . . ." *Labour's Programme 1973* and its successor, *Labour's Programme 1976*, both envisage massive extensions of the fields of public ownership and, in the private sectors that remain, of governmental direction.[10]

Class interest (in this context, special concern for the poor or for the manual working class). The capital levy proposals of the early 1920s have reappeared in the guise of the demand for a wealth tax

---

[10] For the development of *Labour's Programme 1973*, see Michael Hatfield, *The House the Left Built* (London: Gollancz, 1978), and further references below.

in the 1970s. The Labour party is the party of high public spending on social services: It advocates the so-called "social wage," achieved via direct and steeply progressive taxation.[11] In the words of the 1974 party manifesto: "Our objective is to bring about a fundamental and irreversible shift in the balance of wealth and power in favour of working people and their families." Like the open-ended commitment to socialism noted above, this equally open-ended commitment to egalitarianism leads to more and more extreme policies checked only by economic and/or financial crisis: for example, the sterling crisis of 1966, and, latterly, the sterling crisis of 1976. Even this had to be reinforced by the tough conditions imposed by the International Monetary Fund. For all that, the massive cuts proposed in the government's 1976 White Paper on Public Expenditure were resisted by the party's left-wing M.P.s, whose abstention brought about a government defeat on this issue in March 1976 and would have defeated it again, in March 1977, had the Liberals not formed their pact with the Labour party. The net effect was to check public spending and borrowing, while the universal revulsion to high direct taxation was recognized by Prime Minister Callaghan, who told left-wing M.P.s calling for increased public spending: "If you want to retain power you have got to listen to what people—*our* people—say, and what they want; and that is, to pay less taxes."[12]

Trade union power. The Labour party originated in 1900 as the Labour Representation Committee, composed of socialist societies and various trade unions. The organic connection between the unions and the party is the essential and unique characteristic of the party. The defense of trade union interests, and in particular their wide immunity from legal constraints on strike activities, is a perennial policy. In recent times the party has once departed from this line: in 1969, when the Labour government introduced the so-called "In Place of Strife" proposals in the shape of a bill which, among other things, introduced some legal regulation of the unions and, in particular, provided for the curbing of wildcat (in other words unofficial) strikes by court action. The opposition in the parliamentary party forced the government to withdraw the bill, but the attempt to enact legislation of this sort had created such resentment among the unions that the party promptly reverted to its traditional course. On its return to office in

---

[11] In 1976–1977 this social wage amounted to £1,460 for each member of the working population, while the wage packet averaged £3,207.

[12] James Callaghan to the parliamentary Labour party, March 13, 1978. Quoted in David Mackie, Chris Cook, and M. Phillips, *The Guardian/Quartet Election Guide* (London: Quartet Books, 1978), p. 75.

1974, it not only repealed the Conservative government's Industrial Relations Act (which had imposed legal regulation on the unions) but passed legislation protecting workers against unfair dismissal and providing for redundancy payments. The 1970s also witnessed a resurgence of the traditional concept of "workers control" in the shape of proposals for industrial democracy, and the party has commited itself to introducing some form of this.

Civil liberties. The Labour party's commitment to civil liberties is somewhat eccentrically expressed perhaps, since much of it appears as distaste for the police, sympathy with left-wing political refugees, and above all—in the context of the 1970s—a vigorous defense of the rights of non-white citizens: hence a reluctance to introduce immigration curbs, although Labour governments, in contrast to the rank and file, have done just this. Hence, too, the party's introduction of the Race Relations Act in 1976 and the Equal Opportunities Act in 1977.

The Conservative party likewise displays continuities of sentiment, but for very different things. They are notably patriotism, antisocialism, a property-owning democracy, law and order, and finally what may be described as possessive individualism, a concept that overlaps some of the categories above.

Patriotism. The Conservative party is the former imperial party. In the post-imperial era its commitment to the nation is evidenced in its priority for high defense spending and its dedication to the unity of the United Kingdom, which has caused it to oppose the establishment of local assemblies in Scotland and Wales by the devolution acts, which the Labour party, in alliance with the Liberal and nationalist parties, was able to pass through Parliament in 1978. It is manifested also in the party's early decision (1961) to seek membership in the European Economic Community, a decision made for purposes of foreign policy rather than of economics.

Antisocialism (in this context, opposition to the nationalization and state regulation of private industry). The party has ceaselessly though unavailingly campaigned in this direction and has continually pressed for a much more market-oriented economy. Its latest stress on monetary restraint as the weapon par excellence for curbing inflation and restoring economic dynamism follows this tradition.

16

The property-owning democracy. This is a traditional slogan of the party, but only recently has the promise been even partially substantiated. Earlier efforts to encourage wider ownership of stocks and shares faded in the bleaker economic climate of the 1970s, but the party has had great success in its dogged encouragement of individual home ownership. The Labour party's traditional attitude to housing is to provide municipally owned housing at subsidized rents, and some quarters of the party are still emotionally committed to this idea. The rise in disposable personal incomes together with favorable tax reliefs for home mortgages have encouraged private home ownership and at the moment of writing, some 54 percent of dwellings are privately owned as against only 32 percent in the public sector. Currently the Conservatives stand for selling off parts of the public housing stock to the sitting tenants—a further extension of this "property-owning democracy" theme.

Law and order. Conservative attitudes to law and order are reflected in concern for the level of police pay and recruitment; antipathy to lenient penal treatment, particularly of those convicted of violent crimes (a vocal section of the party favors the reestablishment of the death penalty for murder); hostility to extremist revolutionary groups; and demands for tougher action against terrorists in Northern Ireland.

Possessive individualism. At the root of the party's philosophy stands a concern for private property. This manifests itself in a variety of ways, of which property-owning democracy is only one. It is also exemplified in such themes as low direct taxation to generate incentives, in opposition to high public spending and to such taxes as the capital transfer tax and the proposed wealth tax, and to the confiscatory taxes that now apply to the profits made on land sold for urban development. The party does not oppose public welfare. On the contrary, it claims to have been the pioneer in public welfare because of its social welfare legislation in the nineteenth century and its claim that the massive welfare-state legislation of the Attlee Labour governments of 1945–1951 merely implemented policies worked out between the two parties during the wartime coalition of 1940–1945.[13] It differs from Labour on the way state benefits should be paid, favoring payment of benefits to those most in need instead of universal provision (the so-called "ladder and net" philosophy of public welfare provision).

---

[13] See Paul Addison, *The Road to 1945* (London: Cape, 1973) which persuasively argues their thesis. An important book.

Polarization, 1964–1978. Over a long period, during the 1950s and early 1960s, Labour and Conservative policy converged, in that differences in ideology on four of the above-mentioned themes became more muted than ever before or since. To begin with the Conservatives accepted the Labour government's 1945–1951 nationalization and welfare measures (with the exception of the nationalization of the steel industry, which it reversed on its accession to power in 1951). For its part the Labour party in 1959 renounced plans for further nationalization with the exception of steel, which it intended to renationalize. Second, during this period the Conservatives' relations with the trade unions were very good. Third, on international issues, after the desperately bitter conflict between the parties over the 1956 Suez expedition, the continued shrinkage of Britain's power so reduced possible options that there was little left to quarrel about. The disputes over class interest alone became the major distinguishing mark of the parties and hence of "left" and "right." But after 1966, disputes over the first three issues began to reemerge as exemplified by the interparty dispute over membership of the EEC, by the revival of Labour's nationalizing zeal, and, after 1970, by the issue of trade union power. In 1970 the Conservatives led by Edward Heath won the election and proceeded to regulate trade union powers by the far-reaching Industrial Relations Act (1971), while taking Britain into the EEC. The Labour party, which had itself tried to do both of these things during its 1966–1970 term of office, now opposed both policies and at the same time its policy organs began to develop extensive plans for sweeping nationalization and direction of industry. It also did an about-face on the need for a compulsory incomes policy, which it had hitherto both supported and implemented, at the very moment when the Conservatives (who previously had opposed Labour on this very issue) were themselves forced by economic events to introduce first a price and incomes freeze, and subsequently a full-blooded compulsory incomes policy. The unions opposed the Industrial Relations Bill, the incomes policy, and membership in the EEC. On all these issues the parliamentary Labour party actively supported the unions.

The election of February 1974 was precipitated by the miner's refusal to accept the government's guidelines for a pay settlement and their subsequent strike, which, coupled with the effects of the oil embargo, brought about the near shutdown of the economy in the winter of 1973–1974. The government introduced a three-day week for industry and proclaimed a state of emergency. Heath's failure to come to an accommodation with the unions led him to call the election, and to fight it on the cry of "who governs?". Although his party polled more votes than Labour, it received fewer seats in Parliament; Heath was forced to resign and Harold Wilson took office with a minority Labour government. In the course of the subsequent four years of Labour rule, almost every piece of Heath's legislation was repealed, from the Industrial Relations Act to the Fair Rents Act, while membership of the EEC only survived after a popular referendum in 1975 showed a two-to-one majority in its favor. The Labour government not only negated the preceding legislation but proceeded on a new burst of socialization by establishing the National Enterprise Board with money and powers to buy up or take stakes in profitable private enterprise, by the nationalization of the aerospace and shipbuilding industries, and by the establishment of the National Oil Corporation with wide control over the exploration and development of Britain's offshore oilfields by private licensees. It also strengthened trade union power by, for example, legalizing the closed shop and establishing the Advisory, Conciliation, and Arbitration Service (ACAS), which had considerable powers to force recognition of trade unions upon employers. The anti-EEC sentiment of the party, only temporarily stilled by the 1975 referendum, resurfaced on many occasions; for example, on whether to participate in direct elections to the European Parliament. Thus on the major themes of socialism, of trade union power, and of external policy, the gap between the two parties became wider than at any time in the pre-1970 period. *Labour's Programme 1976* took the party still farther along the first two roads, with corresponding threats of resistance from the Conservatives. Although the party manifesto of 1979 retreated from this document, as Prime Minister James Callaghan sought to move to the "middle ground," it stood pat on the party commitment to defend trade union power, and to extend socialism by means of enlarging the National Enterprise Board and nationalizing the seaports. But if this be deemed a move to the center, it did not close the gap between the two parties since the Conservative manifesto was described, even in the pro-Conservative *Daily Telegraph* as "a move to the Right in Conservative policies." It envisaged massive tax cuts and reductions in public spending, the curbing of trade union strike practices by law, and the selling off of portions of nationalized industry. The Conservative leader, Margaret Thatcher, quite ostentatiously rejected the politics of the "middle ground" and openly espoused direct confrontation with Labour policies.

19

The Social Representativeness of the Labour and
Conservative Parliamentary Parties

Neither the Labour nor the Conservative parliamentary parties is socially representative of the nation. Both have become increasingly middle-class, though this term means something very different in respect to each party. The Conservatives are socially more homogeneous and exclusive than the Labourites. The professions represented in the Conservative party tend to be the older and more prestigious ones, such as the bar, accountancy, medicine, and a very large proportion of the party's M.P.s are company directors. The characteristic Labour profession, in contrast, is some kind of teaching, which is a typical first-generation profession, indicating social mobility rather than descent from an acquired position of prestige and/or wealth. A similar distinction exists with respect to educational backgrounds. Despite the large and increasing proportion of Labour M.P.s with secondary school and university education, these tend to have come up from the state sector of education and then to have proceeded to the provincial universities and to London. The Conservative secondary-educated have characteristically come from the public schools, while the universities they have attended are more likely to be Oxford and Cambridge.[14] The Labour party has its quota of public school M.P.s also, but of the 619 Conservative public school M.Ps in the period 1945–1974, 165 had gone to Eton and 218 to the three top public schools; whereas of the 154 public school M.P.s in the corresponding Labour group, only 8 had gone to Eton and only 14 to the top three schools.[15]

Occupation. In the prewar period (1918–1945), 41 percent of the Conservative M.P.s came from aristocratic backgrounds. It had fallen to half that figure by 1951, and since then the major social components of the parliamentary party have been the professions and businesses. (A third, minor grouping, "miscellaneous" includes such diverse occupations as farming and journalism.) Since 1945 the professional sector has declined somewhat, while the business sector has expanded. Thus in 1945, the parliamentary party consisted of profes-

---

[14] In British parlance the public school is paradoxically a private fee-paying school, wholly independent of the state sector. The category includes quite humble establishments but also, at the other end of the scale, the prestigious and highly expensive schools like Eton, Harrow, Rugby, Winchester. The common characteristic, however, is that attendance at such schools is an indication of a relatively wealthy family background.

[15] C. Mellors, *The British M.P.* (London: Saxon House, 1978), pp. 52–56.

TABLE 5

Labour M.P.s by Occupation, 1945 and October 1974

(percent)

	1945	October 1974
Professional	34.6	50.8
Business	8.0	10.1
Miscellaneous	29.8	27.1
Workers	27.6	12.0

Source: Mellors, *The British M.P.*, p. 75.

sional 47.1 percent, business 36.7 percent, and miscellaneous 16.2 percent, whereas in October 1974 the proportions were professions 35.2 percent, business 46.2 percent, and miscellaneous 18.3 percent.

This understates the extent of change however, which is best seen by inspecting the social composition of new intakes at various times rather than the entire party at one time. Doing this, we see that among the pre-1945 cohort the professions make up 48.4 percent; in the 1950 cohort, 32.7 percent; and in the October 1974 cohort, 37.5 percent. The businessman component, however, which was only 34.8 percent in the pre-1945 cohort, had risen to 56.5 percent of the 1950 cohort and to 62.5 percent of the October 1974 cohort.[10]

Thus the route to the "bourgeoisification" of the Conservative party has been the decline of the aristocratic component and its replacement by businessmen; but in the Labour party it has been via the decline of manual labor and its replacement by the professions. This trend appears much more marked if, following Mellors (*The British M.P.*), we classify trade union officials as "miscellaneous" rather than as manual workers. In that event, the changing composition of the party can be seen in Table 5.

Indeed, whereas these manual workers formed 27.6 percent of the party in 1945 and only 12 percent in October 1974, the teacher/lecturer group formed 12.1 percent in 1945 and 28.1 percent in October 1974.

This change contrasts strikingly with the movement in the Conservative party. In Table 6, the expression "the talking professions" comprises the journalists and media workers, as well as the teachers and lecturers in the two parties.

---

[16] Ibid., pp. 60–74.

TABLE 6

THE "TALKING PROFESSIONS" IN THE LABOUR AND CONSERVATIVE PARTIES
1945 AND OCTOBER 1974

(percent)

	Labour 1945		Conservative 1945		Labour October 1974		Conservative October 1974	
Lecturers	20	5	5	2	52	16	3	1
Teachers	27	7	1	—	37	12	6	2
Journalists	38	10	5	2	25	8	17	3
Total	85	22	11	5	114	36	26	9

SOURCE: Compiled from data in Mellors, *The British M.P.*

These proportions shown in Table 6 changed significantly after the 1979 election. This was to be expected. The Labour party suffered a net loss of forty seats, and a disproportionate number of these were held by the "talking professions," since this had been the growth category in Labour's parliamentary candidatures, as the preceding analysis so clearly shows. The *Times House of Commons, 1979* gives figures which are not strictly comparable to those in Table 4, since definition of an M.P.'s principal profession is somewhat subjective. From the table in this reference work, however, it appears that the number of Conservative journalist-M.P.s in the 1979 House is thirty-one, and the number of teachers and lecturers fourteen. On the Labour benches, there are nineteen journalists and fifty-three teachers and lecturers. In percentage terms, then, in the 1979 House of Commons these "talking professions" make up only 13 percent of the Conservative M.P.s, but double that—nearly 27 percent—of the Labour members.

What is more, insofar as even 12 percent of the members of the parliamentary Labour party were manual workers in 1974, this was almost entirely a result of the trade union practice of sponsoring candidates. Most of the affiliated trade unions draw up a list of candidates they are prepared to help with their election expenses and the like; most of those who find nomination do so for a safe constituency.[17]

[17] For this somewhat curious feature of parliamentary representation, see Austin Ranney, *Pathways to Parliament* (London: Macmillan, 1965); Michael Rush, *The Selection of Parliamentary Candidates* (London: Nelson, 1969); and Peter Paterson, *The Selectorate* (London: Macgibbon and Kee, 1967).

Their proportion of the total M.P.s in the party is fairly constant—around one third—a proportion that rises when the party is defeated and falls when it is victorious (since by definition the safer seats are the ones retained and these are the ones in which the sponsored M.P.s are selected). For instance, as a consequence of the 1979 election, where Labour had a net loss of forty seats, the proportion of trade union sponsored M.P.s in the parliamentary party rose to more than 48 percent. But the trade unions themselves have progressively turned away from sponsoring manual workers, although some, like the National Union of Railwaymen, continue this tradition. Certainly compared with the rest of the party in Parliament, the sponsored M.P.s sector represents a higher proportion of members with the minimum of state education and by far the greatest proportion of manual workers. But a sample of the sponsored M.P.s for the 1966 Parliament shows that no less than 26 percent were journalists or professional persons. Nearly 23 percent were trade union officials. Only 35 percent were manual workers.

Education. The educational profiles of the two major parliamentary parties parallel the occupational ones. In the Conservative party there has been little significant change in educational background: the proportion of M.P.s coming from Oxford and Cambridge and from the public schools has hardly varied since 1951. In the Labour party, however, the transformation has been profound. In 1945, 43 percent of the parliamentary party had received only minimum state education and only 18.7 percent had attended secondary school followed by university. By October 1974, only 16 percent had received the state minimum of education, while 40.3 percent had proceeded to secondary school followed by university. And here again, the analysis by cohorts shows how rapid is this change. Of the pre-1945 intake, 49.3 percent had received only elementary education. This proportion fell to 38 percent in the 1945 intake, to 13 percent in the February 1974 intake, and to zero in October 1974. The university educated, however, who formed 30.5 percent of the pre-1945 intake, rose to 37.6 percent in 1945, to 56.2 percent in 1970, and to 72.7 percent of the newcomers in October 1974.[18] In the 1979 intake, the proportion who had received only an elementary education had risen to something like the February 1974 percentage—13 percent. The university educated, including those who had gone to colleges of technology and Ruskin College, Oxford, formed 66 percent of the total.

---

[18] Mellors, *The British M.P.*, pp. 50–51.

The Discipline of the Parliamentary Parties

It is a commonplace of British politics that the parliamentary party is there "to sustain the government," and indeed, constituency parties take it very badly if their members vote against the government in such a way as to jeopardize its hold on office. So for that matter do fellow M.P.s take a dim view of the dissident backbencher. Though revolts sometimes occur, the strength of party discipline can be gauged by the simple fact that governments have been able to govern effectively for quite long periods of time on razor-thin majorities, even as a minority, as Table 3 testifies. In the last resort, the party M.P. must ask himself whether he believes in his cause so strongly that he is prepared to see the government defeated on a motion of such importance that it will be bound to resign, thus letting in the opposition and/or precipitating a general election under an electoral system where a formally divided political party is so handicapped against the united front of its major opponent that it is almost mathematically bound to lose. (The great historic splits in British parties—the Tories in 1846, the Liberals in 1886, the Liberals in 1915, and the Labour party in 1931—were all followed by long periods of electoral weakness until the rift had healed.)

Since 1945 there has been certainly one intraparty issue of such gravity: whether or not to enter the EEC. Hence this is worth pursuing in some detail. After winning the 1970 election, Heath's Conservative government opened negotiations to enter the EEC, a course supported by most Conservative M.P.s. By October 1971, the Labour party—which in 1967 itself unsuccessfully sought to enter the EEC—had changed its mind. Entry, or at least entry on the terms proposed, was opposed by the trade unions, by the Labour party Conference and National Executive Committee (NEC), and by more than one-third of the parliamentary party. On the other hand it was just as uncompromisingly supported by almost as many M.P.s, of whom the most prominent were Roy Jenkins, Harold Lever, and Shirley Williams. Between October 21–28, 1971, the Commons conducted "the great debate" on the principle of entry. The government, whose majority was only thirty, had to reckon on the opposition of about forty of its members; thus it would suffer defeat without some help from opposition members. Although the opposition imposed a whip on their members, so that in principle all of them should have voted together against the government, sixty-nine Labour rebels voted for the government and against their party whip. The breakdown of the vote is shown in Table 7.

TABLE 7

DISTRIBUTION OF VOTE ON ENTRY INTO THE EEC

	For Entry	Against Entry
Conservative and Unionist	282	39
Labour	69	200
Liberal	5	1
Other	2	6
Total	358	246

Pursuant to this vote the government introduced its European Communities Bill, and the country formally entered the EEC on January 1, 1973.

The opposition Labour party became still more hostile to membership in the EEC, its antimarketeers demanding that the party commit itself to taking Britain out of the EEC once it returned to office; but this hostility was matched by the equal determination of the party's promarketeers to keep Britain within the EEC. When Labour unexpectedly returned to power, in March 1974, the government was threatened, whether it decided to keep Britain in or take Britain out, by the certain defection of one faction or the other.

In the nineteenth and earlier part of the twentieth century this split would have been one of those historical divides mentioned earlier, with disastrous consequences to the party at the ensuing elections. This tradition accounts for the novel formula adopted by Wilson on his return to the prime ministership: He seized upon the device of an advisory referendum—hitherto unknown at the national level—and in this way projected the locus of decision making from his parliamentary supporters to the general electorate. Since the government as well as the parliamentary party was split on the issue of the EEC, Wilson also conceded freedom to his ministers "to support and speak in favour of a different conclusion . . . during the campaign."[19]

The Scotland Act, 1978, to set up a Scottish local assembly, might be held to be a second example of an issue on which some M.P.s felt so strongly that they were prepared to defy their leaders

[19] Cf. Harold Wilson, *The Governance of Britain* (London: Weidenfield and Nicolson, 1976), pp. 194–97. The referendum was held on June 5, 1975, and the country endorsed Wilson's position for remaining inside the EEC by a massive 2-to-1 majority. Thus the split was avoided and the party enabled to continue in office.

even if it meant overturning their cabinet and precipitating a general election. The Scotland Bill had been very unpopular with many Labour backbenchers and only secured a second reading because the government agreed to insert a provision under which the act could not come into effect unless approved by a referendum of the Scottish electorate. Should the referendum say "no," then the government would be legally bound to place before the House of Commons an order for the repeal of the legislation.

During the committee stage of the bill in the Commons, however, a group of thirty-four Labour backbenchers (joined by the Conservative opposition) succeeded in making the government accept an amendment by which the government would have to lay the order for repeal if, in the referendum, less than 40 percent of the Scottish electorate voted "yes"; in other words a bare plurality of those actually voting would not suffice.

The referendum was duly held on March 1, 1979. Of those actually voting, 51.6 percent voted "yes," and 48.4 percent voted "no." But this fell far short of the statutory requirement that "yes" must attain 40 percent or more of the total electorate. On the contrary, only 32.85 percent of the electorate said "yes," while 30.78 said "no," and 36.37 percent did not vote at all. The result faced the Prime Minister with a dilemma. Since the demise of the Lib-Lab pact he was critically dependent on the eleven votes of the Scottish Nationalist party (SNP). If, in strict accordance with the terms of the act he laid an order for its repeal before the House of Commons and urged the parliamentary Labour party to vote for it (thus killing the act), he would lose SNP support. The alternative was to lay the order, as law required, but impose strict party discipline on the parliamentary Labour party to reject it; in this way the act would become operative, and, with the Scottish Nationalists in support, the Prime Minister could soldier on for a long time—possibly until the autumn, the time (it seems) he thought most favorable for a general election. But, despite the jeopardy into which their decision placed their parliamentary leaders, the thirty-four M.P.s who had forced the 40 percent requirement into the referendum made it clear that they would not support the Prime Minister in any vote to reject the order. The SNP now threatened that unless this was done they would table a motion of "no confidence." The Conservatives and Liberals made it clear that they would join forces behind a "no confidence" motion. Despite the threat to the government's survival, the Labour backbenchers showed no sign of relenting. The Scottish Nationalists duly tabled their motion and the Conservatives tabled one also. Under the rules of the House this took precedence, and it was on this motion of "no confidence" that the House voted on March 28, 1979 with the result already noted: a defeat for the government by one vote, consequent on which the Prime Minister was forced to resort to the dissolution of Parliament and a general election—an election which Labour lost.

The following general propositions can thus be expressed: one, backbenchers can defeat their own government on a major confidence motion only at the risk of destroying both that government and, temporarily, their own party also; and two, hence, save on an unusual issue of supreme importance such as the ones outlined above, dissident votes will be cast only under certain conditions, to wit:

> Votes intended to demonstrate discontent will be cast only when either the government majority is big enough to absorb this without the risk of defeat or when it is known that the opposition will sustain the government's position, either by abstention or by active support.
>
> Substantive votes to make a change in the bill or policy put forward will be cast only on minor issues, on issues the government can reverse later in the debate, or on issues that claim to represent a technical adjustment to the main principles put forward rather than a reversal of those principles.

These propositions are empirically confirmed by Norton.[20] While defiance of the party whip by M.P.s is, as he says, more prevalent than is generally realized, he agrees that for the period 1945–1970, it is correct that on whipped votes in divisions the votes "normally reflect complete intra-party solidarity." Rebellion—voting contrary to the wishes of the party whips—represented less than 12 percent of the total number of divisions in any one Parliament, save 1970–1974, when it rose to 20 percent. In 6,860 divisions (1945–1974), only 98 had more than 20 M.P.s in revolt, and only 22 had 50 or more in revolt.[21]

In conditions of minority government, however, the conventions as to what are and what are not confidence votes are highly relaxed, and effectively a government need not consider anything to be a confidence vote unless it itself states that this is how it will regard it (which is true by definition) or unless it is a formal vote of no confidence by the opposition. It follows, paradoxically, that a minority government is capable of sustaining many more adverse votes without having to resign than in a majoritarian situation, nor will it run

---

[20] P. Norton, *Dissension in the House of Commons 1945–1974*, (London: Temple Smith, 1978), pp. 609–13.
[21] Ibid., pp. 23–24.

the risk of a party split. Hence, in minority situations dissident votes are likely to be cast on all manner of occasions—as demonstrations or as substantive alterations, on petty issues and on the very gravest ones (for example on the Scotland Bill)—short only of votes of confidence. This proposition explains the heavy incidence of dissident votes cast against the Labour government of Callaghan after the government lost its majority in November 1976.

Empirical confirmation of this can be found in Table 8, which lists the major Labour party revolts in the 1975–1978 period. In every case where the revolt had only a symbolic effect, the reason is the same: that the government motion against which the Labour rebels were voting was supported by the Conservative opposition, thus guaranteeing the government's over-all majority in the House. In every case save one—the government's defeat on the public expenditure cuts of March 10, 1976, which was subsequently reversed—the effect of the government's defeat was to force it to amend its own policy accordingly. In all such cases, the government defined the vote as one that did *not* entail the resignation of the government; in other words did not consider them votes of no confidence. On those occasions where it did define the vote as one of confidence, the former rebels rallied back to the government to enable it to stay in office. There have been three signal occasions that illustrate this proposition and, incidentally, create precedents as to what is and what is not a vote of confidence.

The defeat on proposed cuts in public expenditures, March 10, 1976. The government was in a cleft stick as its left-wing members opposed any expenditure cuts at all, while the Conservative opposition maintained that they were not drastic enough. Hence the government's defeat, 284 to 256, as a result of Labour abstentions. The government staged a debate the very next day, on a technical motion for adjournment, which it declared a vote of confidence: If the government lost, it would resign. All the former abstainers except one returned to the fold and the government received its confidence vote by 297 to 280.

The confidence vote in Denis Healey, chancellor of the exchequer, June 14, 1978. Dissatisfied with the chancellor's handling of the economy, the Conservative opposition put down a motion to halve his salary, a traditional way for the House to express no confidence in a particular minister. Despite the Lib-Lab pact the Liberals made clear that, as the vote was directed at a particular minister, they too would vote for the Conservative motion. The Prime Minister's first reaction was to prepare for first one vote, on Healey, and if that was lost to bring forward a motion of no confidence for a second vote.

On the day of the debate, however, he belatedly recognized that (in his words) "an attack on the Chancellor . . . is an attack on the whole of government," and stated that the vote of censure on the Chancellor would be treated as a vote of no confidence. The Liberals who had no wish at all for an immediate election chose to abstain rather than vote against the government and they were joined by the three Welsh Nationalists, who also did not wish an election. The government defeated the attack by 287 to 282.

The "sanctions" vote, December 13, 1978. As part of its machinery to enforce a 5 percent wage norm, the government inflicted economic penalties such as loss of government contracts on managements that made wage settlements in excess of 5 percent; in particular, they were about to apply such sanctions against the British Ford Motor Company. The opposition put down a motion opposing the use of such sanctions as arbitrary. A number of Labour members were also unhappy at their use, because they disapproved in principle of government interference with free collective bargaining. The government was defeated, 285 to 279, with the assistance of five Labour abstentions. The very next day the government put down a formal confidence vote. All the Labour abstainers returned to its side, and with the assistance of seven Ulster Unionists the government obtained a confidence vote of 300 to 290.

These three examples adequately sustain the thesis that dissident votes will be much more frequent in minoritarian situations than in majoritarian ones, since in the latter case it is assumed that a defeat on an important issue is a matter of confidence; whereas in the former it is for the government to say that this is how it intends to treat it. Once it does so, the rebels return.[22]

Conclusions

1. Excepting 1974 to May 1979, the party system at parliamentary-governmental level is identical with that prevailing since 1945. The Labour and Conservative parties maintain a duopoly of parliamentary seats and alternate in a monopoly of the government where, by virtue

---

[22] This "lobster effect" is as true of the minority parties, which fear an immediate election, as of the government's own M.P.s. It will be recalled that in *Alice in Wonderland*, Chapter 10, "The Lobster Quadrille," the Lobster is described as follows:

> When the sands are dry he is gay as a lark
> And will talk in contemptuous tones of the shark
> But when the tide rises and sharks are around
> His voice has a timid and tremulous sound . . . .

TABLE 8
Major Labour Revolts, 1975–1978

Date	Occasion	Number of Rebels	Effect
Jan. 29, 1975	Relax earnings rule for pensioners	8	Government defeat
July 22, 1975	Incomes policy	34	Symbolic
Nov. 29, 1975	Prevention of Terrorism Bill	16	Symbolic
March 10, 1976	Public expenditure cuts	37	Government defeat
Oct. 12, 1976	Restriction of private beds in public hospitals	46	Symbolic
Dec. 21, 1976	Acceptance of IMF conditions for financial support	28	Symbolic
Jan. 12, 1977	Inadequacy of cuts in defense spending	72	Symbolic
Feb. 22, 1977	To approve closure (= "guillotine") motion on Scotland & Wales Bill	21	Defeat (and loss of Bill)
June 14, 1977	Additonal tax reliefs in Standing Committee on Finance Bill	Varied	Defeat (and acceptance of the amendments)
Jan. 25, 1978	To insert 40 percent vote requirements in referendum on Scotland Bill	34	Defeat
Feb. 14, 1978	Restrictions on timing of referendum	22	Defeat
Feb. 15, 1978	To delete 40 percent vote requirement in referendum on Scotland Bill	49	Defeat
Dec. 13, 1978	Condemnation of government's economic sanctions against firms in breach of pay policy	5	Defeat

of the disciplined support of their backbenchers, they wield the un-limited legislative, administrative, and financial authority that accrues to a British government via the axiom of the unlimited sovereignty of Parliament.

2. The alternation of these two parties in power was markedly more rapid in the post-1945 period than in the interwar period, and faster in the period 1964–1974 than in the period 1945–1964.

3. Since 1970 the policies of the two parties have become in-creasingly polarized and mutually antagonistic.

4. Between November 1976 and April 1979, the government party was in a minority as a result of which the government was able to retain office because of the reluctance of its backbenchers and of enough other parties to face an immediate general election; unlike the earlier period, this government had to give way on many important issues to the wishes of the House.

2

Parties at the Electoral Level

Vox populi may be vox Dei *but very little attention shows that there never has been any agreement as to what Vox means or as to what Populus means. In reality the devotee of Democracy is much in the same position as the Greeks with their oracles. All agreed that the voice of the oracle was the voice of a god; but everybody allowed that when he spoke he was not as intelligible as might be desired and nobody was quite sure whether it was safer to go to Delphi or to Dordona.* . . .

SIR HENRY MAINE, *Popular Government*

The party duopoly in the House of Commons does not reflect the distribution of the popular vote. It is the artifact of the electoral system. This is unique in Europe (though, of course, it is familiar to voters of the United States and Canada). Colloquially known as the "first past the post system," the electoral system has members elected in single-member constituencies (currently 635), in which the candidate with the most votes is declared elected regardless of the total number of votes cast for all the other candidates.

Changes in the Electoral System, 1945–1978

Until 1948 the system was governed by the Representation of the People Act, 1918. This act made local government officials (effectively) the responsible officers for listing persons legally qualified to vote. Some persons had more than one vote; owners of business property could vote in respect of their business premises as well as their place of residence, and university graduates were permitted an extra vote in one of the twelve university constituencies. Women aged over thirty were enfranchised in 1918, women over twenty-one (the minimum voting age for men) in 1928. Not all constituencies were single-member constituencies though, nor were all elections by the "first past the post" system. Thus, thirteen two-member seats persisted, while voting in the university constituencies was conducted by the method of proportional representation known as the Single Transferable Vote (STV).

The Representation of the People Acts, 1948 and 1949, abolished the university constituencies, the two-member constituencies, and the business vote, thus achieving "one man, one vote."

The electoral register is compiled on the basis of residence, as of October 10 of each year and comes into force on the following February 16 for a calendar year. This means that even the freshest register is four months out of date. Peers, the mentally deranged (unless it can be shown they are enjoying a lucid spell), and those serving prison sentences may not vote. Otherwise all British citizens may vote, but this category includes citizens of independent Commonwealth countries. Furthermore, by a legal anomaly, citizens of the Irish Republic may vote also.

Two major changes must be noticed. First, by the Representation of the People Act, 1969, the legal age for voting was reduced from 21 to 18. This added some 800,000 voters to the electorate, which numbered 39,345,000 at that time. Second, by the House of Commons (Redistribution) Act, 1944, separate permanent boundary commissions for England, Wales, Scotland, and Northern Ireland were established. Their task is to equalize the electorates of the constituencies subject to four qualifications: as far as practicable, administrative areas should not be divided between constituencies; Scotland, Wales, and Northern Ireland should be given special treatment; special geographical considerations could entitle the commissioners to depart from strict equality; and finally local community ties should be preserved insofar as possible.

Distorting Elements in the Electoral System

There are three types of distortion in the British electoral process: contingent, structural, and operational.

The Contingent Distortion. This type of distortion arises from the way the party vote distributes itself as between one constituency and another. It is not at all uncommon in Britain for one party to pile up

33

massive majorities in some constituencies, while losing others by the merest fraction. For instance, in the 1951 election, Labour won seventeen of the twenty seats won by majorities of more than 25,000, whereas the Conservatives won many suburban seats with majorities of 2,000–5,000. Thus, nationwide, the Conservatives polled 230,684 fewer votes than Labour but won twenty-six more seats.

Structural Distortions. There are three structural distortions, the first of which is the anomalous Irish vote. About 1,000,000 Irish citizens live in Britain. A 1970 survey showed that they divided their votes in the proportion of 84 percent Labour to 16 percent Conservative. If these proportions are applied to the Irish-born vote in the 1970 election, it seems that Labour definitely owed six seats to this vote, and might well have owed another five also.[1]

The second distortion arises from the underrepresentation of Northern Ireland and the overrepresentation of Scotland and of Wales in the House of Commons. If these three regions were each to enjoy the same ratio of seats to population as England, Northern Ireland would receive seventeen seats instead of its present twelve, Scotland's representation would fall from seventy-one to fifty-seven, and that of Wales from thirty-six to thirty-one.

The rationale for the underrepresentation of Northern Ireland is that after 1922 it possessed its own local assembly at Stormont. In 1972, however, the British government imposed direct rule on the province and so, consistently, the Labour government in 1978 announced its intention to increase the province's representation to seventeen. This was enacted in the House of Commons (Redistribution of Seats) Act, 1979, but not in time to take effect for the May 1979 election. As for Scotland and Wales, the reasons for their overrepresentation lie partly in the English desire to placate local Welsh and Scottish sentiment and partly in that the difficult mountain terrain in both of these areas makes difficult the amalgamation of constituencies.

The distortions, like the anomalous Irish vote, have partisan consequences. Wales is a Labour rotten borough, and the Labour party has consistently won a majority of seats in Scotland since 1964. Equalized representation of these two countries would reduce Labour party strength in the House of Commons: It has been calculated that this would probably have altered the party strength in the October 1974 election as shown in Table 9.

---

[1] David Butler and M. Pinto-Duschinsky, *The General Election of 1970* (London: Macmillan, 1971), p. 408.

TABLE 9

PARTY STRENGTHS IN THE OCTOBER 1974 HOUSE OF COMMONS
ASSUMING EQUAL SEAT/POPULATION RATIOS IN ALL FOUR PARTS
OF THE UNITED KINGDOM

(numbers)

	M.P.s Returned October 1974	M.P.s Who Would Have Been Returned under Equalization
Conservatives	277	279
Labour	319	314
Liberal	13	13
SNP	11	9
Plaid Cymru	3	3
N. Ireland	12	17
Total	635	635

SOURCE: Adapted from G. Alderman, *British Elections: Myth and Reality* (London: Batsford, 1978).

The third structural distortion arises from the unequal size of constituencies. The boundary commissions have not been able to change constituency boundaries fast enough to keep pace with population shifts, whose direction is away from the decaying urban centers into the suburbs. Despite extensive boundary changes in 1948 and 1954, the small urban centers continued to be overrepresented compared with suburbs and countryside. M.P.s, however, disliked a system that not merely exposed them to the hazards of an election every five years at least, but also to the alteration and often the very abolition of the constituencies they had to contest at the intervals prescribed for the commissions, namely every three-to-seven years. So, in 1958, the instructions to the commissions were amended. First, they were released from their obligation to keep seats within 25 percent of the "quota" (that is, the average-sized) constituency if they thought this necessary to respect local government boundaries. Second, the interval at which reviews were to be presented was lengthened to every ten-to-fifteen years. Hence, as the general election of 1970 loomed, the constituency boundaries still reflected the redistribution of 1954. So, the commissions presented an extensive revision in 1969. The home secretary at that time was James Callaghan. The proposed boundary changes were clearly going to eliminate many of the decaying urban constituencies, but these were largely Labour strongholds. Callaghan, arguing that it would be unwise to make these boundary changes

35

before the extensive reorganization of local government boundaries that was soon to be introduced, fulfilled his strict legal duty by putting the commissions' proposals before the House but advised it to vote against them, which it promptly did, despite an outcry from the opposition and the public.[2] Thus the 1970 election was fought on the outmoded boundaries of 1954. The effects may be gleaned from such statistics as the following: There were seventy-seven seats with fewer than 45,000 voters and ninety with more than 80,000; Labour won three-quarters of the former, the Conservatives seventy of the latter.

The Conservatives won the election despite this handicap. With the five years of office in front of them (in the event, this was curtailed to less than four), the interest of more equal constituencies and certainly their own political interest would now have been better served by following the Labour party's argument and waiting for the Local Government Bill to be enacted (as it was in 1972). Instead, with a consistency that served them ill, they immediately applied the boundary commissions' recommendations. True, the proportion of very large and very small constituencies was diminished; but there were still twenty-four English constituencies with fewer than 45,000 electors apiece, and twenty-nine with more than 85,000. The former were in the midst of dense conurbations, the latter were not. In the February 1974 election, Labour unsurprisingly won sixteen of the urban areas. Indeed, in England, Labour won two-thirds of the constituencies containing less than 50,000 electors apiece, but less than one-third of the fifty-two constituencies containing 80,000 electors apiece; the same pattern was repeated in Scotland and in Wales. Official figures for 1976 show that with a quota figure of 65,753 voters per constituency, twenty England constituencies were 39 to 51 percent above this norm, and another twenty were 32 to 63 percent below it. The 1979 election confirmed the anti-Conservative bias due to the unequal constituencies. Of ninety-eight seats with electorates of more than 80,000, seventy-six went Conservative, eighteen Labour, and one Liberal; whereas of the ninety-two seats where the electorates were fewer than 50,000, Labour won fifty-nine, the Conservatives twenty-seven, and the Nationalists or Liberals six. The boundary commissions are due to complete their next review before April 1984. This will be ahead of the latest date on which the next election must legally be held, May 1984; and it is calculated that the result of their work must be to increase Conservative representation by twenty seats and to reduce Labour's seats accordingly.

---

[2] Cf. Peter Bromhead, *Britain's Developing Constitution* (London: Allen and Unwin, 1974), p. 180, for a more detailed version of this complicated story.

Operational Distortion. Finally, the system produces three kinds of distortions that are inherent in its operation. They are first the distortion that is inherent between two parties in a two-party contest. This can be stated as the cube law, well known to students of British government. If two parties' votes are cast in the proportion A:B, then their parliamentary seats will stand in the proportion $A^3:B^3$. This also translates as the proposition that a 1 percent net swing from one party to another will cause the loss of $2\frac{1}{2}$ to 3 percent (fifteen to twenty seats) to one and a corresponding gain to the other party. Second, as between the two front-running major parties and the minor parties, parties that consistently run behind the majors in every constituency, even by wafer-thin margins, will win no seats at all. This is subject to the third distortion, that if the minor party's vote is regionally concentrated in a few constituencies, its likelihood of coming first past the post in such constituencies will be high, whereas if its vote is evenly distributed through the 635 constituencies, such a likelihood is very low indeed. This explains why the Scottish Nationalist party did fairly well in the elections of 1974, while the Liberal party did not. (Of course, inside Scotland itself, the second proposition holds: The SNP suffers compared to Labour and the Conservatives. This became very clear in the 1979 election. In October 1974 the SNP had run second to the Labour party and ahead of the Conservatives, with 30 percent of the Scottish vote. With this, it picked up eleven seats, some 16 percent of Scotland's parliamentary seats. But in the May 1979 election, it trailed both the major parties: the Labour party took 41.5 percent of the Scottish vote, the Conservatives 31.4 percent, while the SNP obtained only 17.3 percent. With this it picked up a mere two seats, that is, only 3 percent of the total Scottish seats.)

Disproportionality and the Electoral System

In Table 10, the number of seats won by a proportional system of representation is calculated as a pure arithmetical deduction from the proportion of votes cast; it would vary from this ideal figure according to the actual system of proportional representation in use.

Orientation Clusters of the Major Parties

Of the four types of social cleavage likely to be reflected in voting behavior,[3] only class cleavage is of major importance in Britain. Religion has long ceased to be a divisive or decisive factor in voting; the urban-rural cleavage can have little significance in a society in which only about $2\frac{1}{2}$ percent of the working population is engaged

37

TABLE 10

1979 General Election: Seats Won and Seats that Would Have Been Won under Strictly Proportional Representation

Party	Share of Vote	Seats Won	Seats under PR	Difference
Conservative	43.9	339	279	−60
Labour	36.9	269	234	−35
Liberal	13.8	11	88	+77
SNP	1.6	2	10	+ 8
Plaid Cymru	0.4	2	3	+ 1
Others	2.8	12	18	+ 6

Note: Because of rounding, percentage share of vote does not add up to 100%.

in agriculture. Although the ethnic-cultural cleavages manifested in the peripheral nationalisms of Northern Ireland, Wales, and Scotland have recently made a significant impact on the distribution of seats in the House of Commons, the entire number of votes cast for nationalist candidates in October 1974 was only 5 percent of the national total.

Both the Labour and the Conservative parties began life from a class-specific base. The Labour party was founded in 1900 specifically to increase working class representation in Parliament. It did not acquire a socialist orientation until it adopted its constitution of 1918; thereafter it also picked up from the declining Liberal party its legacy of internationalism and pacificism. By 1922 Labour's M.P.s were already becoming more middle class, and it tried so hard to extend its electoral appeal that its national leaders of the 1920s and 1930s, Philip Snowden and Ramsay Macdonald, are classic examples of would-be "catch-all" party leaders. In the economic crisis of 1931, Snowden and Macdonald continued to attempt a national appeal, but most of their parliamentary colleagues refused to follow them. In the debacle of the 1931 election the party lost all except the safest seats. Since these were the ones held by trade unionists and working class M.P.s, the party, in voting composition, in appeal, and in the social background of its M.P.s, was still in 1931–1945 predominantly a trade union and manual worker party.[4]

[3] Seymour M. Lipset and Stein Rokkan, *Party Systems and Voter Alignments* (London: Collier-Macmillan, 1967), pp. 1–65.

[4] Miller, *Electoral Dynamics*.

In its electoral triumph of 1945, a great many more middle class members were returned to Parliament, although 80 percent of its votes came from the manual working class. After the three electoral defeats of 1951, 1955, and 1959, it began to be argued that the party's lack of success was a result of its traditional "cloth-cap" image, and from 1964 its leader, Harold Wilson, deliberately set out to transform the party into "a party of government," a "natural governing party," similar to the supposedly "natural" majority of the American Democratic party. An emphasis was put on "modernization," "responsibility," the harnessing of the "white heat of the technological revolution," while the traditional definition of socialism as the public ownership of the means of production, distribution, and exchange was challenged, albeit not effaced, by the revisionist doctrine (of which Hugh Gaitskell and Antony Crosland were the theoreticians) that socialism was about equality and social justice. This broadening of its appeal was likely from time to time to bring the party into conflict with its trade union and working class core, as in the stormy debates over Clause 4 in 1959–1960, and again in 1969, when the Labour government of Harold Wilson tried to introduce legislation to regulate trade union status and to subject the freedom to strike in certain instances to legal restraints.

By contrast, the Conservative party, which antedates the extension of the franchise by one and a half centuries, was originally a landlord and business elite. In order to gain popular electoral support it had to reach down into the electorate and claim to be the national party. These objects were successfully achieved in the nineteenth century[5] and particularly so in the interwar period, which may be viewed today as an especially favorable time for the party, since it benefited from the Liberal party's disintegration on the one side and the infant Labour party's lack of credibility on the other. Its higher echelons were still largely aristocratic and connected to industry and to the administration of the Empire; it couched its appeal in terms of patriotism, tradition, and the great institutions (the armed services, the law, and organized religion). It successfully claimed to be the traditional ruling class in power, the only one in the circumstances that was fit to govern. After its defeat in 1945, which it regarded as an affront and which spurred it to massive rethinking and reorganization, the party was still able when it returned to office in 1951 for thirteen continuous years to offer the electorate a good counterfeit of its prewar image. The social characteristics of its leaders were still recognizably aristocratic, the Empire still a force, the armed services still very large.

---

[5] See Robert McKenzie and Allan Silver, *Angels in Marble* (London: Heinemann, 1968), chapters 1 and 2.

These characteristics appealed to large numbers of manual workers, and others were attracted by the party's emphasis on material self-advancement as reflected in the advocacy of private home ownership and the new affluence of consumer durables.[6] After 1959, however, some of these elements became tarnished and others were eroded. The Suez Crisis (1956) and the subsequent decolonization initiated by the Macmillan government after 1959 reduced the Empire and the armed forces at the same time, and adhesion to the EEC (in 1973) was a poor emotional substitute, if indeed it was a substitute at all. After 1970 the failure to make the economy grow faster cut away the party's appeal to material self-interest. And the leadership changed from aristocrat or big business to predominantly middle class. Finally, the national institutions with which Conservatism was identified, had lost their appeal: The vogue for "satire" in the mid-1960s, the denaturing of patriotism, and the widespread vogue for self-doubting and critical studies of the state of Britain, made them seem incongruous or unfashionable.

In short, if we look at the evolution of the two parties' respective orientation clusters, we find that both had had to move away from and outside their original and traditional bases into uncharted waters.

We can hypothesize thus: Since both the major parties have reached out beyond their respective cores—the manual working class for Labour and the nonmanual middle class for the Conservatives—and since, too, the average gap in the period 1945–1974 between the two parties' respective proportions of the national vote was only 3.5 percent one way or the other, it is logical to expect to find that voting was not entirely class-specific, even perhaps that it was not largely so. It is logical to expect to find that although Labour is a working class party it is not the party of the working class, and though the Conservative party is a middle class party it is not the party of the middle class. And this is precisely what we do find.

Social Determinants of Voting

The relationship between class and voting is set out in Tables 11, 12, and 13. The first two, based on Gallup Poll data, are presented here for their historical interest. It should be noticed that the fourfold categorization of the electorate adopted in Table 11, was abandoned after

---

[6] This thesis—contrasting "deferential" and "secular" (or, as some would call them, "instrumental") voters—is fully worked out in McKenzie and Silver, *Angels in Marble.*

TABLE 11

Class Differences in Voting Behavior, 1945–1966

(percent)

	Upper Middle Class (Average plus = 5%)						
Party	1945	1950	1951	1955	1959	1964	1966
Conservative	76	79	90	89	87	77	82
Labour	14	9	6	9	6	9	8
Liberal	10	12	4	2	7	14	10
Labour lead over Conservative	−62	−70[a]	−84	−80	−81[a]	−68[a]	−74[a]

	Middle Class (Average = 21%)						
Party	1945	1950	1951	1955	1959	1964	1966
Conservative	69	69	73	77	76	65	68
Labour	24	17	22	21	16	22	24
Liberal	15	14	5	2	8	13	8
Labour lead	−37	−52	−51	−56	−60	−43	−44

	Working Class (Average minus = 59%)						
Party	1945[b]	1950	1951	1955	1959	1964	1966
Conservative	32	36	44	41	40	33	32
Labour	57	53	52	57	54	53	61
Liberal	11	11	4	2	6	14	7
Labour lead	25	17	8	16	14	20	29

	Very Poor (= 15%)						
Party	1945[b]	1950	1951	1955	1959	1964	1966
Conservative	32	24	31	44	25	32	23
Labour	57	64	67	54	68	59	72
Liberal	11	12	2	2	7	9	9
Labour lead	25	40	36	10	43	27	49

[a] Liberals second to Conservative.
[b] 1945 figures in these columns are for working class and very poor respondents grouped together.

Source: Richard Rose, *Studies in British Politics*, 3rd ed. (London: Macmillan, 1976), p. 206.

1966 for the fivefold classification shown in Table 12. The change was made to adapt the classification to a much-altered social structure. A/B stands for the professional/managerial category, C1 for the lesser white-collar occupations, C2 for the skilled manual workers, and DE for the semiskilled and unskilled manual workers along with a residual category of "very poor" who in fact are mostly state-dependents.

Table 13 is derived from the MORI poll. The five socioeconomic

TABLE 12
CLASS DIFFERENCES IN VOTING BEHAVIOR, 1970–1974
(percent)

Party	Middle Class (A/B = 15%)		
	1970	February 1974	October 1974
Conservative	65	66	62
Labour	27	18	19
Liberal	8	16	19
Labour lead over Conservative	−38	−48	−43

Party	Lower Middle Class (Cl = 22%)		
	1970	February 1974	October 1974
Conservative	52	55	47
Labour	42	27	29
Liberal	6	18	24
Labour lead	−10	−28	−18

Party	Working Class (C2D = 56%)		
	1970	February 1974	October 1974
Conservative	35	33	29
Labour	57	51	55
Liberal	8	16	16
Labour lead	22	18	26

(Table 12 continues on the next page.)

TABLE 12 (continued)

Party	*Very Poor (E = 7%)*		
	1970	February 1974	October 1974
Conservative	29	32	35
Labour	64	56	53
Liberal	7	12	12
Labour lead	35	24	18

NOTE: Respondents preferring Nationalists and other parties as well as Don't knows are eliminated because of too few cases; votes for Conservative, Labour, and Liberals thus add up to 100 percent.

SOURCE: Richard Rose, *Studies in British Politics*, 3rd ed. (London: Macmillan, 1976), p. 207.

TABLE 13

CLASS AND OTHER SOCIAL FACTORS IN VOTING BEHAVIOR, 1974–1979

(percent)

1979 % of Voters		*Harris Surveys*		MORI	*Net Change (to Conservatives)*
		February 1974	October 1974	May 1979	October 1974– May 1979
100	All (Actual Result)	(N = 3,900)	(3,858)	(6,445)	
	Conservative	39	37	45	+ 3
	Labour	38	40	38	− 2
	Liberal	20	19	14	− 5
	Other	3	4	3	− 2
	Swing to Conservative		−2	5	
51	Men	(N = 1,873)	(1,795)	(2,889)	
	Conservative	35	32	43	+11
	Labour	42	43	40	− 3
	Liberal	19	18	13	− 5
	Other	4	7	4	− 3
	Swing to Conservative		−2	7	

(Table 13 continues on the next page.)

TABLE 13 (continued)

1979 % of Voters	Harris Surveys		MORI	Net Change (to Conservatives)
	February 1974	October 1974	May 1979	October 1974– May 1979
49 Women	(N = 2,023)	(2,063)	(2,783)	
Conservative	42	39	47	+ 8
Labour	35	38	35	− 3
Liberal	21	20	15	− 5
Other	2	3	3	0
Swing to Conservative		−3	5½	
12 18–24	(N = 394)	(377)	(697)	
Conservative	24	24	42	+18
Labour	46	42	41	− 1
Liberal	25	27	12	−15
Other	5	7	5	− 2
Swing to Conservative		2	9½	
21 25–34	(N = 688)	(780)	(1,193)	
Conservative	35	33	43	+10
Labour	40	38	38	0
Liberal	21	24	15	− 9
Other	4	5	4	− 1
Swing to Conservative		0	5	
31 35–54	(N = 1,412)	(1,486)	(1,764)	
Conservative	37	34	46	+12
Labour	40	42	35	− 7
Liberal	19	20	16	− 4
Other	4	4	3	− 1
Swing to Conservative		−2½	9½	
36 55+	(N = 1,402)	(1,239)	(2,018)	
Conservative	46	42	47	+ 5
Labour	33	40	38	− 2
Liberal	19	14	13	− 1
Other	2	4	2	− 2
Swing to Conservative		−5½	3½	

(Table 13 continues on the next page.)

TABLE 13 (continued)

1979 % of Voters	Harris Surveys		MORI	Net Change (to Conservatives)
	February 1974	October 1974	May 1979	October 1974– May 1979
35 ABCl	(N = 1,387)	(1,548)	(1,967)	
Conservative	57	56	59	+ 3
Labour	20	19	24	+ 5
Liberal	21	21	15	− 6
Other	2	4	2	− 2
Swing to Conservative		0	−1	
33 C2	(N = 1,299)	(1,292)	(1,907)	
Conservative	29	26	41	+15
Labour	48	49	41	− 8
Liberal	19	20	15	− 5
Other	4	5	3	− 2
Swing to Conservative		−2	11½	
32 DE	(N = 1,210)	(1,126)	(1,798)	
Conservative	28	22	34	+12
Labour	49	57	49	− 8
Liberal	19	16	13	− 3
Other	4	5	4	− 1
Swing to Conservative		−7	10	
30 Trade Unionist	(N = 1,053)	(1,059)	(1,715)	
Conservative	23	23	33	+10
Labour	55	55	51	− 4
Liberal	19	16	13	− 3
Other	3	6	3	− 3
Swing to Conservative		0	7	
70 Non-Trade Unionist	(N = 2,843)	(2,783)	(3,933)	
Conservative	45	41	50	+ 9
Labour	32	35	32	− 3
Liberal	21	21	14	− 7
Other	2	3	4	+ 1
Swing to Conservative		−3½	6	

SOURCE: MORI, Express/Standard, 1979.

categories are as in Gallup, but it should be noticed that it puts the ABC1 group at 35 percent of the population whereas Gallup (Table 12) puts it at 37 percent. But this difference will not affect the thrust of our analysis. Any of these tables give the lie to the notion that voting is based wholly or even primarily on class. While the Conservatives command a majority of the nonmanual votes, which form 37 percent of the electorate, in Table 12 they also take roughly one-third of the manual workers' votes. Confusion over the class interpretation of voting arises from two causes: the softness of the central concept of class and the detectable presence of a fair number of minor influences on voters that mitigate whatever effects class (however defined) may have.

Class Voting. If class is defined in occupational terms, then strict class voting is limited; conversely, if it is still argued that class is the key influence, then class must not be defined strictly. This is because there are many indicators of social class, such as occupation, self-rating, educational level, membership or nonmembership in a trade union, private home ownership as against rented accommodation; but they are not congruent. The ideal worker is a trade unionist with a manual occupation who has the minimum of state education, who rents municipal housing, and who thinks of himself as working class. But only 9 percent of the electorate conforms to this type! On the contrary, the ideal middle class voter would have more than a minimum education, would not be a trade unionist, would live in his own house or at least in a privately rented one, and would think of himself as middle class. Only 12 percent of the electorate conforms to this type. In all, no more than 21 percent, a mere fifth of the electorate, exhibit the undeniable and unmodified stigmata of class. It is no wonder then that as these stigmata are modified or withdrawn the voting behaviour of the elector is less class-predictable. This has been elegantly demonstrated in Table 14.

Note how 73 percent of the ideal worker-voters vote Labour, but how this proportion falls off to a mere 30 percent among those exhibiting only one characteristic. Now leaving his occupation aside, the average British voter has two middle class characteristics and two working class characteristics. As the table shows, this group makes up 28 percent of the total electorate. Another 17 percent of the electorate has fewer than two class characteristics that correlate with their occupation. Together this 45 percent of the electorate may be regarded as of indeterminate class.

TABLE 14

IDEAL CLASS CHARACTERISTICS AND PARTISANSHIP

(percent)

Number of Characteristics Exhibited	Conservative	Labour	Other	Total
Upper Middle Class				
Middle class characteristics				
Four	78	15	6	7
Three	67	25	8	5
Two	59	30	10	2
One	40	47	13	0.5
None	—	—	—	—
Lower Middle Class				
Middle class characteristics				
Four	69	22	9	5
Three	59	31	10	7
Two	47	43	10	6
One	35	57	8	3
None	21	69	10	1
Working Class				
Working class characteristics				
Four	19	73	8	9
Three	29	60	11	21
Two	42	47	11	20
One	59	30	11	10
None	67	21	11	3

SOURCE: Richard Rose (ed.), *Electoral Behavior, A Comparative Handbook* (Glencoe, Illinois: Free Press, 1974).

Furthermore, even the influence of class-correlated characteristics is declining. Using Tree-analysis (A.I.D., a form of computerized multivariate analysis in which each variable is in turn divided into two dichotomous variables) Richard Rose demonstrated that in 1959 such influences could account for 21.9 percent of the variance between the Conservative and Labour vote. In 1964 that proportion so accounted for had declined slightly, to 20.6 percent; but by 1966 it had fallen to 18.1 percent and in 1970 to a mere 12 percent. The method of analysis could not be used at all in the 1974 elections, because Liberals and others then formed so high a proportion of the votes that the simple dichotomization into two-class, two-party model was inappropriate. Furthermore, the influence of the different class-related characteristics fluctuated during this period. Whereas occupation explained 12.5 percent of the variance in 1959, it explained none by 1970; conversely, home ownership vis-à-vis council tenancy explained 7.1 percent of the variance in 1970, as against only 5.6 percent in 1959; and possession of a telephone, which explained nothing in 1959, explained 1.6 percent of the variance in 1970.[7]

Another indicator, pointing in the same direction, is the response to a questionnaire asking the respondent to assign himself to a social class. It is of great significance in itself that even in 1964 one-half of the respondents refused to assign themselves to any class at all. The proportion (50 percent) who did so in 1964 had declined to 44 percent by 1970 and then, despite the revival of class as an election issue, declined further to 43 percent in 1974.

There is yet another approach to this question. What follows is based upon the findings, fully reported in their article, of Dr. Ivor Crewe and his associates of the Essex University British Election Study team.[8] The time series extends from 1964 to 1974. The data base consists not of voters but of party-identifiers, a distinction made because a voter can identify with one party but, for any number of reasons, desert it in a particular election.[9]

Crewe and his colleagues report the following. First, from 1964 to October 1974, the manual classes identified themselves with Labour and Conservatives in a constant fashion. In 1964, 32 percent identified with the Conservatives, 68 percent with Labour; in October 1974 the respective proportions were 33 percent with the Conservatives and 67 percent with Labour. Party-identification of the nonmanual classes, however, did not follow a similar pattern. This distributed itself in 1964 in a ratio of three Conservatives to one Labour; in October 1974 this had changed to a ratio of only two Conservatives to one Labour. In brief, the decline in class alignment over this decade was not due to the Conservatives increasing their share of the manual workers party-identification but, conversely, to increased Labour-identification among the nonmanuals, usually referred to as "the middle class."

Second, this arithmetic can be revolved to show the class compo-

---

[7] Richard Rose, *The Problem of Party Government* (London: Penguin, 1976) pp. 464–68.

[8] Ivor Crewe, Bö Svarlik, and Jim Alt, "Partisan De-Alignment in Britain 1964–1974," *British Journal of Political Science*, vol. 7, part 2 (April 1977).

[9] See the section in this chapter, "Party Identification and Voting."

sition of Labour- and Conservative-identifiers. The makeup of the Conservative-identifiers at the end of the period was almost identical with that at its beginning: 57 percent came from the nonmanuals and 43 percent from the manuals. Not so for the Labour-identifiers. In 1964 these broke into the proportions of 17 percent from the nonmanuals to 83 percent among the manuals, but by October 1974 the respective proportions had altered to 27 percent from the nonmanuals to 73 percent among the manuals. This can be translated thus: if we look at one (or the other) of these two classes—the nonmanuals or the manuals—and ask, what is the size of the gap between the proportions in such a class identifying with Labour and those identifying with the Conservatives, we find that in 1964 the gap was 40 percent. In October 1974 it had shrunk to only 30 percent. The reason is as before: the growth of the nonmanual component of Labour-identifiers.

Third, in the two cases above, the authors of the article proceeded by ignoring those who identified with parties other than Labour or Conservative. Identifiers were simply dichotomized into these two categories. This excluded the very large proportion (25 percent of the total voters) who did not vote for these two parties in 1974. Suppose that Liberal- and other party-identifiers were taken into account? In that case, the proportion of manual workers identifying with Labour in 1964 was 58 percent, but in October 1974 it had fallen to 54 percent. On the other hand the proportion of nonmanual classes who identified with the Conservative party fell from 58 percent in 1964 to 48 percent in October 1974. This permits of an alternative way of measuring class alignment; take the Conservative proportion among nonmanuals, the Labour proportion among manuals, and average these. When this is done it shows that the percentage of the electorate who identified with "their" party—that is, the class-consonant party—was 58 percent in 1964 but had fallen in October 1974 to only 51 percent.

Were these trends continued in the 1979 election? Unfortunately the Essex 1979 British Election Study data are not yet available. Fieldwork is continuing, after which the punching, checking, and computing of data must be undertaken. It is possible, however, to construct a sort of "dummy." The series will not be precise but will serve to indicate the broad trend of development since 1974. The data base for this exercise is the BBC/Gallup Election Day Survey. The survey did include a question on party identification which is only slightly different from that used in the Essex surveys. Unfortunately, however, the social class categories used by BBC/Gallup are not the same as those used in the Essex surveys. BBC/Gallup categorizes 64 percent of the electorate as working class, whereas the Essex surveys put this at only 56 percent.

This means that BBC/Gallup must include among its working class some grades of routine white-collar workers or foremen; therefore the BBC/Gallup working class will contain a higher proportion of Conservatives, and by the same token its middle class will contain a smaller proportion of Labour-identifiers, quite irrespective of any real shifts in allegiance since 1974.

In what follows, then, the figures will underestimate Labour-identifiers among the middle class and overestimate Conservative-identifiers among the working class. For all that, the results indicate a broad, indeed, startling, trend which is wholly consistent with the actual voting behavior of the public mentioned above.[10]

First, how did the manual class-identifiers distribute themselves in 1979 as compared with the nonmanual classes? Did the swing to Labour among the nonmanuals continue, while the manuals continued to distribute their favors in their ten-year-long constant fashion? The nonmanuals identified 69 percent Conservative and 31 percent Labour. This is lower than the 65 percent/35 percent split of October 1974 but not very much lower. It is still much higher than the 75 percent/25 percent split of 1964. And futhermore, as we have stressed, the nature of the sample is bound to underestimate Labour-identifiers among the middle class. We would not be far wrong in concluding that the proportions in 1979 were much the same as in October 1974. (It can be noted that if we have regard only to actual voters, as contrasted with identifiers, Table 13 suggests a slight 1 percent swing towards Labour in 1979.) But when we turn to the way the manual classes behaved, the change is striking. Even allowing for some overestimation of Conservative-identifiers among the manual classes, the 1979 election shows no less than 40 percent of the manuals identified with the Conservatives, while only 60 percent identified with the Labour party. Compare the proportions of actual voters swinging from Labour to Conservative in Table 13.

Next, we can ask the reciprocal of the preceding question, namely, what proportions of the Conservative- and Labour-identifiers were drawn from the manual and nonmanual classes respectively? Whereas in 1974 the Conservative-identifiers came 57 percent from the nonmanuals and 43 percent from the manuals, in 1979 the proportions had altered to 48 percent from the nonmanuals and 52 percent from the manuals; on the Labour side their nonmanual identifiers had fallen from 27 percent in 1974 to 21 percent in 1979, while their proportion

---

[10] This method of continuing the Essex time series, as well as the calculations, are derived entirely from Dr. Ivor Crewe. I am most grateful to him for his generous and indispensable assistance.

of manuals had jumped from 73 percent in 1974 to 79 percent in 1979. The size of the gap between nonmanuals (or manuals) identifying with Conservatives and Labour respectively in 1979 was, then, 48 percent Conservative nonmanuals *minus* the 21 percent Labour nonmanuals; or alternatively, the 52 percent Conservative manuals less the 79 percent Labour manuals. In short the gap is only 27 percent as compared with a gap of 30 percent in 1974 and 40 percent in 1964.

Finally, we can complete the exercise by taking into account those who identified with Liberals and other parties. If this is done in the same way as previously, then the Conservative proportion of the nonmanuals is 49 percent, while the Labour proportion of the manuals is 54 percent. If, as before, we average these two proportions we find that this index of class alignment (that is, the percentage of each class identifying with "their" class-consonant party) has fallen from 58 percent in 1964, to 51 percent in 1974, to only 47 percent in 1979.

In brief, the overriding explanation of the "decline in class voting" is to be found in a simple statistical artifact—that "class voting" is measured in: (a) terms of *occupation*, more specifically, in terms of a dichotomization between blue-collar and white-collar employment, the first of which is normally supposed to be working class and the second, middle class; and (b) the measurement of the *ratio* between the proportions of working class who vote or identify with the Conservatives and, conversely, the proportion of the middle class who vote or identify with the Labour party. From this, two facts have so far emerged. The first is that since 1964 the proportion of middle class voting for or identifying with the Labour party has increased. The second is that from 1964 to 1974 the proportion of working class voting for or identifying with the Conservatives remained constant, but between 1974–1979 it made a huge jump forward. Can these two trends be explained?

The middle class labourite. If there were independent evidence that the middle class of twenty years ago is still the same animal but has become radicalized, has somehow changed its opinions, then we might truly speak of a decline in class voting. But there is no such evidence. On the other hand there is strong and positive evidence of the emergence of a new sector of white-collar workers in a new, grossly expanded white-collar sector. For in the period 1961–1974, employment outside industry increased by 33.9 percent in Britain. This is unparalleled in the western economies: the comparable figures for the United States, France, and West Germany were 15.4 percent, 18.6 percent, and 14.2 percent. Furthermore, nearly all this increase went to swell the public sector. Central government employment rose by 9.4

percent and local government employment by no less than 53.7 percent in this period, compared to only 13.2 percent for services such as banking and insurance. White-collar employment in education rose by 76.1 percent, in health services and the like by 45.1 percent, and in public administration by 21.2 percent.[11]

Many, perhaps most, of these new recruits to white-collar work come from working class homes. Thus in the Department of Health and Social Security it is reported that half the staff members are aged under 30 and are the "sons and daughters of blue collar workers."[12]

At the same time there has been rapid and extensive unionization in this public sector. For instance, the National and Local Government Officers Association climbed from 240,000 in 1965 to 600,000 ten years later; the National Union of Public Employees, which numbered 257,460 in 1967, had reached 600,000 by 1977; and the Confederation of Health and Social Employees had nearly doubled, from 89,550 in 1970 to 166,000 in 1975. All these unions, such as the National Union of Teachers and various civil service unions, have also become highly militant and have adopted the strike as a weapon, just like the industrial unions.

The identification of this new sector of white-collar workers with the rise in the Labour middle class vote is as yet not quite certain, but it appears very probable. Three separate pieces of evidence combine to support it.

First, white-collar trade unionists form a high proportion of all trade unionists, and a large number of them voted Labour in 1979. According to the MORI poll, 1979, they formed 29 percent of all trade unionists. And as many as 39 percent of them voted Labour, as compared with 45 percent who voted Conservative. Next we know that the young Labour middle class voters of the post-1950 cohorts favor trade union power and increases in public-sector spending more than do their manual worker counterparts. These are precisely the attitudes we should expect of these new recruits to the public sector. They are ill paid, hence they militantly favor unionism; and they are in the public sector, hence they favor more public spending.[13] Finally, the social profile of this Labour middle class provides the required linkage

---

[11] Roger Bacon and Walter Eltis, *Britain's Economic Problem: Too Few Producers* (London: Macmillan, 1976), pp. 10–15.

[12] Robert Taylor, *The Fifth Estate* (London: Routledge and Kegan Paul, 1978), p. 315. Further evidence is provided in pp. 312–17.

[13] Crewe, Svarlik, and Alt, "Partisan De-Alignment in Britain 1964–1974," pp. 154–56. Note that support for traditional Labour policies flagged between 1964–1974 among *all* sections of Labour supporters, but less among the white collar than among the core.

between the growth of public sector employment on the one hand and the attitudes of young, middle class Labour voters of the post-1950 cohorts on the other. The profile is derived from as yet unpublished data from the Essex University British Election Study:

> It is fairly clear that the growth of the Labour middle class has occurred not amongst the petit bourgeosie, clerical workers, or traditional professions, but amongst the 'new' middle classes in other words, those who are (1) professionally qualified, and usually graduates, (2) employees rather than self-employed, (3) employed in large bureaucratic organizations, especially in the public-sector, for example local and central government, nationalized industries, quangos, universities, hospitals etcetera, (4) slightly younger than average, (5) the children of skilled working class and lower middle class parents, in other words, those who have entered the middle class through the higher educational system rather than through the possession of capital and "contacts."[14]

Working class conservatives. Why did such a large proportion of the manual classes vote Conservative after a decade during which the Conservative-Labour proportions of the manual vote remained static? At the superficial level, the answer must surely be that the Conservatives offered the more attractive policies. This can easily be seen from Table 15. Furthermore, that table does not contain one Conservative policy which was salient in the election campaign: the pledge to cut income tax even if this meant that Value Added Tax would rise, or even if it meant a cut in public spending. The MORI survey, for instance, found that 75 percent of its respondents favored reducing income tax by reducing government spending, and only 17 percent opposed this (8 percent "did not know"). Furthermore, of those polled 49 percent correctly perceived this to be a Conservative rather than a Labour policy. The following table sufficiently summarizes voters' preferences on the issues they thought to be the "most important," and it is obvious that while Labour was ahead on prices and unemployment—the two most salient issues—the Conservatives were much further ahead on the next two important issues, namely, taxes and law and order.

It is likely, however, that there were more longstanding and deeply rooted causes for the hemorrhage of Labour's manual voters. The clue to this is to be found later in "Party Identification and Voting" in this chapter. There it is demonstrated that in 1974 Labour lost support to the lesser parties as the consequence of a long-term decline

---

[14] Private communication from Professor Ivor Crewe.

TABLE 15

WHEN YOU DECIDED WHICH WAY TO VOTE, WHICH TWO ISSUES DID YOU YOURSELF CONSIDER MOST IMPORTANT?

Issue	Percent Mentioning Issue as One of Two Most Important in Influencing Their Vote					Party Preference on Issue (Those Citing Issue as Important)
	All	Conservative recruits	Labour defectors	1974 Liberals	Aged 18–34	
Prices	42	39	40	42	43	Labour +13
Unemployment	27	20	21	27	31	Labour +15
Strikes	20	30	29	24	18	Conservative +15
Taxes	21	28	23	37	26	Conservative +61
Law and Order	11	13	10	8	7	Conservative +72

NOTE: This was an open-ended question. No prompt card was given to respondents. The five issues were the most frequently mentioned.
SOURCE: BBC/Gallup Election Day Survey, published in the *Economist*, May 12–18, 1979.

in the attractiveness of its quintessential and key policies to the Labour-identifiers. The misfit between its election pledges and the aspirations of its identifiers grew ever wider over the decade 1964–1974. That misfit seems to us to have been even greater in the 1979 election, and we shall present evidence to support this view. In 1974 the Labour vote drained away because of this long-term disaffection, but—as is shown below—the Conservative vote drained away for short-term reasons only. Hence, in 1979 the Conservative vote rebounded, while Labour's remained almost the same as in October 1974, albeit in a larger electorate, and in the face of a reduced third-party vote. If this analysis turns out to be correct in the light of the research currently undertaken by the Essex University British Election Study team, then Labour's narrow victory in 1974 will have to be regarded as a short hiccup in the long-term alienation of Labour supporters from Labour policies.

Other Determinants of Voting. Finally, a multiplicity of minor differences have a differential effect upon voting behavior. Once again we are indebted to Professor Rose for this demonstration. His method is as follows: Let us suppose that X percent of a given occupational stratum votes for a class-typical party when it has a certain social characteristic C; and equally suppose that Y percent of that stratum votes for the class-typical party when it does not possess characteristic C. Then the difference between X and Y may be said to be the *effect* of possessing characteristic C. When, in Table 16 the sign is "+," it signifies that possession of the characteristic increases class voting independent of occupation; if it is "−," it signifies that it decreases class voting.

Women are more conservative than men. Older persons are more likely to vote Conservative than younger voters. Voters who live in a predominantly class-specific constituency are more likely to vote for the party that stands for that class: in a Conservative safe seat more voters vote Conservative than could be accounted for by their objective class characteristics, and conversely in Labour safe seats. By the same token, council house tenants are more likely to vote Labour and private home owners more likely to vote Conservative. Rural voters favor the Conservatives. Religious loyalties in areas where these are strong, as they are in Ulster for instance, will alter the pattern of class voting; this is confirmed from Clydeside, where a high proportion of voters are Catholic and vote Labour for that reason. Differences are detectable between the voting behavior of Anglicans and Nonconformists, but these are very slight indeed.

TABLE 16

Socioeconomic Influences on Party Allegiance

	Conservative	Labour	Other	Effect of Difference
Trade union membership				
UMC: Nonmember	73	20	7	+15
LMC: Nonmember	57	33	10	+12
WC: Member	31	60	9	+16
Life style				
a. Ownership of motor car				
UMC: Has car	74	20	6	+17
LMC: Has car	57	33	10	+ 8
WC: No car	33	56	11	+10
b. Ownership of telephone				
UMC: Has telephone	76	18	6	+18
LMC: Has telephone	63	29	7	+15
WC: No telephone	35	54	11	+18
Education				
UMC: Above minimum	72	20	8	+ 6
LMC: Above minimum	59	31	9	+11
WC: State minimum	35	54	11	+10
Sex				
UMC: Female	71	21	8	+ 1
LMC: Female	54	34	11	+ 1
WC: Male	35	56	10	+ 8
Age				
UMC: Older (age 50+)	78	15	7	+ 4
LMC: Older	64	29	7	+15
WC: Younger (below 35)	35	52	13	+ 1
Community influence				
a. Housing				
UMC: Home owners	74	19	7	+19
LMC: Home owners	63	29	8	+20
WC: Council tenants	27	63	11	+20
b. Constituency				
UMC: Safe Conservative	73	19	8	+ 4
LMC: Safe Conservative	64	25	10	+12
WC: Safe Labour	29	63	9	+18
Urban/Rural				
UMC: Rural areas	77	15	7	+ 9
LMC: Rural areas	63	30	7	+12
WC: Cities above 50,000	38	53	10	+ 3

Note: UMC—upper middle class; LMC—lower middle class; WC—working class.

Source: Richard Rose, *The Problem of Party Government*, Pelican Edition, 1976, pp. 36–37.

Finally, nationality makes voting diverge from the class-pattern. This is demonstrated by the rise of the Scottish National party vote and the Blaid Cymru vote. These parties draw their support from all classes equally. Furthermore, the Conservative party is preeminently the English party. If national elections were decided in England alone (which accounts for 85 percent of the electorate), the Conservative party would have won all elections, including the October 1974 election, with the exceptions only of 1945, 1966, and February 1974.[15] Britain has few peasants; those who exist tend to deviate from the class pattern of voting. Thus, in the 1974 general elections, the Liberals and the SNP obtained an average of 34 percent and 29 percent of the vote, respectively, in seven Highland constituencies, a substantially higher proportion than they obtained in the Lowlands. Similarly, in nine rural seats in Wales, the Liberals averaged 24.2 percent of the vote and the Blaid Cymru, 18.4 percent.

Some 2-2½ percent of the British population is non-white; the presence of these people in large numbers in urban constituencies appears to cause further deviations from the class pattern, but the evidence is so far mixed.

Finally, it is very clear that immediate economic circumstances have a marked effect on intraparty competition. The hypothesis has received support from a study showing how party preference, as measured in the opinion polls, is strongly correlated with shifts in unemployment, price inflation, balance of payments, and changes in personal income.[16] It is generally agreed that favorable circumstances at election time will benefit the incumbent party, and the notion that governments create an artificial pre-election boom is a standard feature of political journalism.

Two points remain. When the numerous variables are taken into account, they blur still further the already hazy contours of class voting. Rose's "compositional" approach to voting behavior and the fact that almost half the electorate falls outside the ideal working or middle class together constitute an adequate explanation of the social correlates of voting and show that the two classes-two parties hypothesis is incorrect.

The second point is that the fluctuation in voting between the two major parties, 1945–1974, is lower than in any European country

---

[15] That is, by seats won in the Commons. If we look at the share of the English vote, however, the Conservative party led the Labour party in all elections except 1945, 1950, 1966, and October 1974. In 1951 the parties tied.

[16] C. A. E. Goodhart and R. J. Bhabsali, "Political Economy," *Political Studies*, vol. 18 (1970), pp. 43–106.

except Switzerland. If we add together the change in the percentage of the poll obtained by the two major parties in the eleven elections since 1945 and divide by this number, the *mean* change in percentage obtained is only 3.5 percent. Of course this represents only net change; the switching of votes among all parties and between voting and nonvoting is more like one-third. Now this 3.5 percent net fluctuation is not a highly significant figure, nor does it follow a trend. If we turn from competitive party change to noncompetitive party change, however, the trend in the period 1945–1974 is striking, linear, and most important.

Noncompetitive Party Change, 1945–1979

Noncompetitive party change since 1945 has been marked by three features: a decline in turnout; a desertion of the two major parties; and increased volatility of the vote.

Nonvoting. Table 17 shows that turnout hovered in the 80 percent bracket between 1950 and 1964, and has sunk to the 70 percent bracket since 1966. The decline has been persistent, and, although smallish in percentage figures, its significance is appreciated if other statistics are presented. First it must be remembered that over the

TABLE 17

ADJUSTED TURNOUT IN BRITISH GENERAL ELECTIONS, 1945–MAY 1979
(percent)

Election	Adjusted Turnout
1945	73.3
1950	83.9
1951	88.4
1955	83.2
1959	85.0
1964	83.3
1966	77.4
June 1970	75.1
February 1974	79.1
October 1974	78.7
May 1979	78.6

NOTE: Adjusted by the formula of Richard Rose.
SOURCE: Rose, *Electoral Behaviour*, p. 494.

period 1945–1979, the absolute number of electors has risen from 33,240,391 to 41,093,264. While there were 8,154,413 nonvoters in 1945, therefore, there were 9,871,579 in May 1979.

The decline in the percentage of votes is striking in view of a number of other factors. First, it has taken place against an increased number of candidates and hence increased voter choice. The number of candidates rose from 1,868 (in 1950) to 2,135 in February 1974 and to the postwar record of 2,756 in May, 1979. Second, media coverage of the elections has expanded greatly, particularly since 1959. Indeed, it was so extensive in the elections of 1974 that it provoked widespread complaint from the public. Third, the decline in the percentage of Britons voting contrasts with almost every other western European country. Of the four countries that show a declining trend (all others are either stable or have shown an increasing turnout), only Switzerland shows a steeper decline than Britain: between the first two postwar elections and the last two elections turnout declined by 16.1 percent in Switzerland compared with the decline of 8.6 percent (unadjusted) in Britain. Turnout in Austria declined by 3 percent over the period and in Luxembourg by 2 percent. In addition, Britain's level of turnout is all but the lowest. Whereas the average turnout for Austria and Luxembourg was more than 90 percent, the average (unadjusted) turnout in Britain is considerably less than 80 percent over the period, and is almost the worst in Europe, exceeded only by Switzerland's.[17]

Who are the nonvoters, and why do they abstain? Crewe measured nonvoting by the number of times a person claimed to have voted in the four elections 1966–1974. There were almost no consistent abstainers; only 1 percent voted in none of these elections. Social variables bear no relationship to the propensity to vote, with the exception of residential mobility, type of housing, and age. Mobility and housing are clearly related to the legal residence requirement for being enrolled in the register, and housing may also be a result of the relative lack of pressure to vote on solitary renters as compared to council tenants. Only age is likely to be genuinely independent; in general, older people tend to vote less regularly than younger persons. But the usual background variables that relate to voting—income, class, education, and sex—appear to have no bearing on the propensity to vote.[18]

---

[17] Derived from Karl Dittrich and Lars N. Johansen, *A Preliminary Note on Voter Turnout* (Florence: The European University Institute, 1978; mimeo).

[18] Ivor Crewe, Tony Fox, and Jim Alt, "Non-Voting in British General Elections 1966–October 1974," *British Political Sociology Yearbook*, vol. 3 (London: Croom, Helm, 1977), pp. 38–109.

The distinction between voters and nonvoters is not social but attitudinal; compared with the nonvoters, voters show stronger attachment to a party, more interest in politics in general and the election in particular, and a higher degree of exposure to the media or to friends' opinions.[19] This amounts to little more than saying that those who vote do so because they believe in the act of voting, while those who do not believe in voting do not vote. It would be very surprising if this were not the case! (Whether nonvoting can be related to a weakening in partisanship will be discussed below.)

The Desertion of the Two-Party System. Even more striking is the decline in the two major parties' share of the total vote. In 1951 the respective shares were Conservative + Labour, 96.8 percent, Others 3.2 percent. In 1970, Labour + Conservative took some 90 percent of the total vote and Others 10 percent. But in October 1974, the Labour + Conservative share was down to 76.9 percent; Others took 23.1 percent. Over the period 1951–1970, the decline is steady and more or less continuous; in the period 1970–1979, it is very sharp and dramatic.

The degree of this desertion appears more striking, however, if the drift away from the two major parties is combined with the general decline in turnout. This is shown in Table 18.

By 1979, even if we adjust for turnout, only about six voters in every ten were casting a vote for the Conservative and Labour parties.

It is worth noting that this desertion of the two-party system accords with other indicators. Labour and Conservative reaction ratings to the two major parties' political broadcasts have steadily declined since 1959.[20] Polls show that the number of respondents desiring a coalition government, which stood at only 30-40 percent in the 1960s, rose to 60-66 percent in February 1974. An Opinion Research Centre special survey in April 1977 indicated that majoritarian party government was deemed "good for Britain" by only 32 percent of the respondents, while 55 percent thought it bad.[21] Further evidence is provided by the proportion of voters who see "no significant difference" between the two major parties. In 1964, 51 percent of Conservative- and Labour-identifiers perceived a "good deal of difference" between their parties. By 1970 the proportion had sunk to only 36

---

[19] Ibid.

[20] Budge, Crewe, and Farlie, *Party Identification and Beyond.*

[21] But this was not the sentiment in the 1979 election. Respondents were asked whether they wanted another "hung Parliament" or a clear-cut decision, and the latter was preferred by an overwhelming majority.

TABLE 18

ELECTORAL SUPPORT IN GREAT BRITAIN FOR THE CONSERVATIVE AND
LABOUR PARTIES, 1950–1979

(percent)

Date of General Election	Share of Poll Obtained by:			Share of Electorate[a] Obtained by:		
	Con- servative[b]	Labour	Con- servative and Labour Combined	Con- servative[b]	Labour	Con- servative and Labour Combined
1950	43.0	46.8	89.8	36.2	39.3	75.5
1951	47.8	48.3	96.1	39.5	40.8	80.3
1955	49.3	47.3	96.6	37.9	36.4	74.3
1959	48.8	44.6	93.4	38.5	35.3	73.8
1964	42.9	44.8	87.7	33.1	34.6	67.7
1966	41.4	48.9	90.3	31.5	37.2	68.7
1970[c]	46.2	43.9	90.1	33.2	31.6	64.8
February 1974	38.8	38.0	76.8	30.7	30.0	60.7
October 1974	36.7	40.3	77.0	26.8	29.3	56.1
1979	43.9	36.9	80.8	33.3	28.0	61.3

[a] These figures are based on the registered electorate in Great Britain (in other words, Northern Ireland is excluded), which will have included people who died or moved out of the constituency by the time the election took place. Adjustment for the age of the register at the time of the election would raise the figures (by 4 percent on average) but would not alter the scale of the trend over the period. This table makes no adjustment for the number of Liberal and other minor party candidates. Their steady increase since 1955 partly accounts for the decline in the major party vote but partly results from it, too.
[b] Includes votes for National Liberal and Conservative candidates.
[c] The voting age was lowered from twenty-one to eighteen in 1969.
SOURCE: Crewe, Svarlik, and Alt, "Non-Voting in British General Elections," p. 130, amended for 1979.

percent and there—despite the class and ideological polarization of the parties in the 1974 elections—it remained at 35 percent.[22]

Although the drop in the two major parties' electoral support is reflected in the corresponding rise in support for the Liberal party and the various nationalist parties, it is not necessarily caused by it. Whether that is so or not depends on how far the rise of such parties can be regarded as a protest vote against the Labour-Conservative duopoly.

[22] Crewe, Fox, and Alt, "Non-Voting in British General Elections," p. 156.

The answer is not the same in all cases. It is best approached by way of the two concepts of issue voting and dissatisfaction voting. The Ulster Unionist vote is specifically issue-oriented. It is directed against power-sharing with the Ulster Catholic minority, and it expresses a revolt against the power-sharing formula espoused by both the Conservative and the Labour parties. Indeed, all that needs to be said is that in February 1974 it was the Conservative party that had changed its opinions on this issue, not the Ulster Unionists. Here then is a specific, issue-oriented vote, not a vote of general protest against the duopoly. Something of this appears in the Scottish Nationalist vote also, where the specific issue concerns autonomy for Scotland. But in 1974 it also seemed to express a more diffuse dissatisfaction. This may be demonstrated by contrasting the survey findings. The percentage of respondents favoring autonomy was a constant 20–25 percent during the period 1964–1974, whereas the percentages of the Scottish vote cast for the SNP soared over the 32 percent mark in October 1974 and went even higher for sometime after that, before dropping back to 17 percent in 1979.

In contrast to the specific issue vote of the Ulster Unionists, stands the great bulk of "other party" voting in 1974 and 1979: that is to say, the Liberal vote, which amounted to something like one-fifth of the votes cast in the election of February 1974, and still almost 14 percent in 1979.

Hitherto we have said little about the Liberal party. This is an appropriate place to provide more details. We have already noted that the parliamentary representation of the Liberal party has never exceeded fourteen seats. This is why the party, for all its quite distinctive programs, could never place them on the national agenda. It has vacillated between two goals. It could present itself as the moderate, middle-of-the-road party, seeking a balance-of-power position, and this, broadly speaking, was its stance into the mid-1950s; or it could claim to be a radical alternative to an allegedly conservative Labour party. This was its posture in the 1960s. In practice neither position served, and the Liberal party has always had to react to the agendas set by the two major parties rather than impose its own. Hence, whatever its self-image, its public image was the middle party, somehow posed between two extremes. In the February 1974 election its leader, Jeremy Thorpe, openly adopted this stance, claiming it to be the moderate party standing between the party of capital and the party of labour, and survey evidence shows that the great bulk of its new supporters did indeed see it thus, as a center party. In the 1979 election the Liberal leader David Steel was if anything even more specific. He made it clear that he hoped for another "hung" Parliament and pledged himself, should that situation arise, to enter a coalition with one or the other of the two major parties.

In the 1945 and 1950 elections the party obtained a respectable 9 percent of the national vote, but it was all but destroyed in the 1951 election, obtaining only 2.6 percent of the vote, a total it virtually repeated in the 1955 election. The 1959 election saw a modest revival to nearly 6 percent, and in the 1964 election the party's total rose to more than 11 percent. Then the vote declined again, to 8.5 percent in 1966 and 7.5 percent in 1970. But in February 1974 it soared to 19.3 percent, and although it dropped back in the October 1974 election, it still reached 18.3 percent. In large measure this was because the party fielded more candidates than it did in 1970: 619 as opposed to 332. For all that, there was a genuine increase in its popularity, since the average vote for the Liberal candidate was nearly 19 percent in 1974, compared with only 13.5 percent in 1970. In 1979, the party suffered a setback rather than a defeat. Its share of the vote fell from 18.3 percent (October 1974) to 13.8 percent. This was partly accounted for by a drop in the number of candidates, from 619 (October 1974) to 576. The average vote per candidate was down, correspondingly, from its 19 percent level in 1974 to 15.2 percent. Yet this still represents a considerable advance on any election from 1945 to 1970.

Survey-based research for the 1960s showed three things: The Liberal vote was volatile, with a remarkably high traffic of voters into and then out of the ranks of supporters; the Liberal vote was socially representative, without social or economic variables to distinguish it sharply from the rest of the electorate; the Liberal vote was basically a negative vote, a rejection of the duopoly rather than a positive endorsement of distinctive liberal party policies.[23]

The 1974 pattern was remarkably similar. The vote was still volatile: only one in five of the February 1974 voters had voted Liberal in 1970; less than half had voted Liberal in either 1970 or 1966; one-quarter of the vote came from persons who had not voted at all in 1970; and half of the February voters did not vote for the party again in October, while half of the October voters had not voted Liberal in February. The vote remained socially representative: The survey distinguishes between "core" Liberal voters who were more middle aged and more middle class than the electorate as a whole, and the newcomers who, as in the 1960s, were a cross section of the electorate.

[23] David Butler and Donald Stokes, *Political Change in Britain*, 1st ed. (London: Macmillan, 1969), chapter 14 (this chapter is omitted in the second edition).

On the question of the motivation of the voters, the survey distinguished between the core voters and the rest. The core voters were Liberals by conviction and voted for the party's policies. They were, on the whole, not dissatisfied with the general state of society, and were highly engaged in political activity. But the bulk of the Liberal voters were more dissatisfied with the state of society than the core voters, they were not highly interested in politics, and their vote was essentially a negative vote. When it came to issues, most of them preferred the Labour or the Conservative stand to that of their own party, and indeed, when five issues were put to them, fully half failed to name any one on which they preferred the Liberal stand to that of the two great parties. One study[24] demonstrated that the former Labour voters who voted Liberal in 1974 did so because they had specific policy differences with the Labour party—and the same was true for the ex-Conservative Liberal voters. In short, apart from the core voters, the Liberal voters voted for contradictory reasons, but concurred in one major matter—they rejected the two major parties. The conclusion must stand that the bulk of the Liberal surge of 1974 was a negative vote, a vote of no confidence in the duopoly, a vote therefore of *protest*.[25]

For the 1979 election we must wait for the results of research into the attitudes of the Liberal voters, but their volatility and their social representativeness stand confirmed. As to the former, only about half the 1974 Liberals voted Liberal again in 1979. The defectors split three to one in favor of supporting the Conservatives against Labour. The trend was pronounced among the white-collar Liberals, who split five to one in favor of the Conservatives, whereas the manual class Liberals only split in the proportion of two to one. In return for the drain of half their vote to the two major parties, the Liberals picked up 10 percent of those who had voted Labour in 1974, and 4 percent of those who had voted Conservative. Most of the Liberal loss was from its younger supporters; the party neither held the bulk of its former young people nor attracted the new voters. One effect of these differential gains and losses was to make Liberal support more an all-age and all-class party than before. Finally, insofar as protest is concerned, we do have one significant datum, at least. The MORI poll for the 1979 general election establishes that

---

[24] Peter H. Lemieux, "Political Issues and Liberal Support in the February 1974 British General Election," *Political Studies* 25, no. 3 (1977).

[25] Cf. also Jim Alt, Ivor Crewe, and Bö Svarlik, "Angels in Plastic: the Liberal Surge in 1974," *Political Studies* 25, no. 3 (1977).

26 percent of the Liberal voters (including 45 percent of the young Liberals) voted "against" the other parties rather than "for" their own.

The Volatility of the Vote. Accompanying the decline in turnout and the desertion of the two-party system has been a third trend, which is unmistakable and continual: Shifts in support for Labour and Conservative have become increasingly volatile, whether measured by by-election results or by the fluctuations in opinion poll ratings, as Table 19 indicates.

The table can be continued into the present. Thus, the two-party swing in 1979 was no less than 5.2 percent—an all-time record. And the range of the monthly opinion polls veered about thus: 1975, 21 percent; 1976, 31 percent; 1977, 21.5 percent; and 1978, 15.5 percent. Again, whereas only 10 seats registered swings of more than 7 percent in February 1974—of which 5 were more than 10 percent swings—the number of seats to register double-figure swings in the 1979 election reached 13, while the number in which the swing exceeded 7 percent was no less than 150. Crewe suggests yet another indicator of volatility when he aggregates the respective changes in parties' general share of the total vote (excluding Northern Ireland). In 1979 the Conservative vote was +8.4 percent, Labour —4.6 percent, Liberal —2.3 percent, and others —1.5 percent. Together, these changes add up to 16.8 percent. In February 1974 the total was even higher: 25.8 percent. But the 1979 figure exceeds that for any election, apart from February 1974, since 1945.[26]

Party Identification and Voting

The tiny median fluctuation in intraparty aggregate votes and the narrowness of the net two-party swing (which is the crucial measure used in the analysis of voting in Britain) disguise the very large dimension of the ebb-and-flow of voting support. In the five intervals of change that Butler and Stokes observed in the 1960s, never more than two-thirds of the electorate positively supported one party at any two successive moments. In 1979, for instance, 73 percent of those polled said that they had made up their minds how to vote "long ago"; 13 percent said they had done so two or three weeks before; and only 12 percent said that they had decided in the last few days. Again, according to the BBC/Gallup survey, 87 percent of

[26] Ivor Crewe, *The Voting Surveyed, The Times House of Commons May 1979* (London: Times Books, 1979), p. 250.

TABLE 19

Indicators of Volatility of Support between the Conservative and Labour Parties in General Elections, By-Elections, and Opinion Polls, 1950–1974

(percentage)

Year	National Two-Party Swing[a]	Percent By-Elections in Which Support for Government Party Fell by over 20 Percent Compared with Previous General Election[b]	Mean Fall in Support for Government Party in By-Elections	Range in Monthly Opinion Polls[e]
1950[d]	+1.1	0.0 (N=14)	2.0	8.0
1951				13.0
1952				11.0
1953	+1.8	0.0 (N=43)	1.9	6.0
1954				9.0
1955				8.0
1956				8.0
1957	+1.1	10.0 (N=50)	8.8	18.0
1958				16.0
1959				12.5
1960				9.5
1961				12.0
1962	−2.9	16.5 (N=61)	13.5	11.5
1963				9.5
1964				12.5
1965[e]	−3.1	0.0 (N=13)	1.8	18.0
1966				18.0
1967				27.0
1968	+4.7	34.2 (N=38)	16.8	19.0
1969				17.5
1970				12.0
1971				20.5
1972	−0.8	35.3 (N=18)	13.1	10.5
1973				15.0
1974 (Feb)	*[f]	*[f]	*[f]	
1974 (Oct)				23.0

the Conservative voters said that they had voted Conservative in 1974, and 75 percent of the Labour voters said that they had voted Labour in that election. It may be argued, therefore, that such percentages are very high and show fixed predispositions among the voters. Certainly, but does this give any support to the "party identification" model of voting as understood by the Michigan school and applied to Britain by Butler and Stokes?[27] Briefly, the model postulated that the majority of the electors possess a partisan self-image; this image is the most enduring feature in their electoral comportment; and it is the strongest single predictor of their party choice at the actual election, the stability of their vote, and their turnout. In respect to the last three variables it is argued that the stronger the identification the higher the probability that they will vote "regularly" at a given election, repeat their vote at successive elections, and turn out to vote on the day.

In fact, this model not only does not "explain" the recent evolution of the vote in Britain, it is completely contradicted by it. Butler and Stokes predicted that party identification would increase, since the most important variable associated with it was parental partisanship, and as the old fashioned Liberal-party identification of parents declined, so the new generation would increasingly identify with the Labour party and to a lesser extent with the Conservative party. This

---

[27] Butler and Stokes, *Political Change in Britain*, 2nd ed.

TABLE 19 (continued)

[a] Swing is defined as the average of the Conservative percentage gain and the Labour percentage loss.
[b] Calculations for by-elections between 1970 and February 1974 exclude the Speaker's seat, Southampton Itchen, and those cases (N=12) where there was a non-trivial redistribution of constituency since the previous general election such that meaningful swing figures would not be calculated.
[c] Range is measured by the difference between the highest and the lowest support for the Conservatives in any one month *plus* the difference between the highest and lowest support for Labour in any one month.
[d] Northern Ireland is included in the general election figures, excluded in the others.
[e] In the 1950–51 and 1964–66 parliaments, Labour was in office but with only a tiny majority. Both periods continued to experience the electoral trends of the previous few years.
[f] There was only one by-election between February and October 1974.
SOURCE: Budge, Crewe, and Farlie, *Party Identification and Beyond*. The figures for [c] are calculated from David Butler and Jennie Freeman, *British Political Facts 1900–1968*, for the period until 1968; and from the *Gallup Political Index* (London: The Gallup Poll), for 1969–1974.

prediction has proved correct. But as a result, one would expect attachment to the two major parties to have increased or remained steady at least; yet it has fallen.

The model would explain the fall in turnout by a general weakening of partisanship among the most recent electorates, but the evidence does not point to this. Nor can the model explain the increased volatility of party support.

A recent article throws light on the factors, immediate and underlying, that seem relevant to this fall in turnout and the desertion of the two-party system.[28] The first point to notice is that party identification ("a more stable and enduring form of party support than voting preference and . . . the better guide to the electors' long-term partisan allegiance")[29] remained pretty well constant in the period 1964–1974; it stood at 81 percent of those polled in 1964 and 76 percent in October 1974. On the other hand its intensity had declined: the proportion of "very strong identifiers" fell from 40 percent in 1964 to only 24 percent in October 1974. *But*—and this is a most important finding—this collapse occurred entirely after 1970! The proportion of "very strong identifiers" still stood at 39 percent in 1970—virtually the same as for 1964, especially after allowing for sampling error. It was between 1970 and 1974 that the fall to a mere 24 percent occurred.

One inference may be drawn immediately: The two major parties still have vast reserves of loyalty and habit.

The research referred to goes much farther, however, in its efforts to ascertain the reasons for the decline in turnout and desertion of the duopoly, especially in the four years 1970–1974. One much canvassed hypothesis is that youth was disillusioned with the two parties. The study contradicts this. It finds that partisan decline was uniform across the entire electorate.

A second and fairly obvious hypothesis in the light of the preceding analysis of the decline of class alignment with the parties is that this factor will explain the desertion of the two parties. The study finds this highly probable. The elections of 1974 were bitterly fought on class issues. Yet, the voters' response to these politics of class was tepid among all classes. This is vividly illustrated by electors' response to a standard question on class identity: "to which class—if any—did the respondent assign himself?" In 1964, 50 percent assigned themselves, without prompting, to one class or another. In 1970, only 44 percent did so, and in February 1974 the proportion was almost the

---

[28] Crewe, Svarlik, and Alt, "Partisan De-Alignment in Britain."
[29] Ibid., pp. 141–42.

same—43 percent. Therefore, though the parties revived class politics, the electors did not respond to it. Earlier it was shown that the decline in class alignment to party up to 1974 was not the result of a greater attachment of the working class to the Conservatives, but to an increased identification of the nonmanual classes with the Labour party and that this in turn was related to the emergence of a new stratum among the white-collar workers: the "new" minor professional workers whose numbers burgeoned after 1961. It is therefore significant that the support for major Labour policies—such as trade union power, more public spending, and more nationalization—declined far less among post-1950 voters belonging to this new Labour middle class than among the hard-core Labour supporters in the manual working class.

There remained a third possible hypothesis: that the desertion of the two-party system was a temporary disillusion brought about by the dramatic events of 1973–1974. This hypothesis was confirmed; it is consistent with the fact that the decline in turnout was a fairly gradual and continuous process between 1945 and 1974, whereas the desertion of the two party system was abrupt, most of it taking place between 1970–1974.

There was, however, an important difference between the nature of the Labour and Conservative disillusion. Conservative disappointment marks a return to quite normal levels of dissatisfaction as found before the exceptionally high morale of 1970, the year of the Conservative victory. In the Labour case, however, it manifests a terminal reaction to a long precedent period of dissatisfaction with the party's policies. There is often a wide divergence between Labour party policy as set out in its program and manifestoes and the views of its identifiers. The Labour manifesto of February 1974 was no exception to this. According to this study, this is the reason for the withdrawal of Labour support in the 1974 elections. For instance, Labour-identifiers with "at least one dislike of the Labour party" numbered only 36 percent in 1964. By October 1974, this proportion had risen to 51 percent.[30] A striking clue is provided by contrasting the fit between Conservative-identifiers' attitudes and party policies and the Labour-identifiers' attitudes and party policies. During the period 1964–1974, there is no trace of any widening divergence between the Conservative-identifiers' views and their party's policies. Among the Labour-identifiers the gap became wider and wider, as shown in Table 20.

Could this slow alienation of Labour-identifiers from Labour policies

---

[30] Crewe, Svarlik, and Alt, "Partisan De-Alignment in Britain."

TABLE 20

SUPPORT OF PARTY POLICIES AND ATTITUDES TOWARD TRADE UNIONS AND
BIG BUSINESS AMONG LABOUR-IDENTIFIERS, 1964–FEBRUARY 1974

(percent)

Labour-Identifiers	1964	1966	1970	February 1974
Favor nationalizing more industries[a]	57	52	39	50
Favor spending more on the social services[b]	89	66	60	61[c]
Favor retaining close ties between the trade unions and the Labour party	38	27	32	29[d]
Sympathize generally with strikers	37	32	16	23[c]
Do not believe that trade unions have "too much power"	59	45	40	44[c]
Believe that big business has "too much power"	80	75	78	83[e]

[a] In other words, saying that either "a lot more" or "only a few more" industries should be nationalized.
[b] Excludes those who said that only spending on pensions should be increased (coded separately in 1970 and February 1974, but not in 1964 or 1966).
[c] Taken from 1970–February 1974 panel sample.
SOURCE: Crewe, Svarlik, and Alt, "Partisan De-Alignment in Britain."

explain why the manual classes deserted the party in the 1979 elections? This is precisely what we suggested earlier. The presumption can be established only by the continuation of the time series in Table 20, and this must wait until the Essex University British Election Study research is completed. But to our mind, the answer to one batch of questions in the May 1979 public opinion polls does suggest to us that the slow decline shown in Table 20 must have continued into 1979. This batch of questions confines itself, effectively, to Labour voters' perception of the trade unions. The BBC/Gallup poll shows that 38 percent of Labour voters supported the very drastic proposal to stop social security payments to strikers' families; 63 percent of them preferred trade union activities to be regulated by law rather than by voluntary self-regulation; and no less than 83.4 percent favored a legal ban on secondary picketing. All of these had been vigorously opposed by Labour in the 1979 campaign.

Conclusions

1. The party duopoly at the parliamentary level is an artifact of a system of disproportional representation, which discriminates severely against parties whose national vote may be large but are unsuccessful in coming first past the post in the majority of constituencies—in this case, the Liberal party. The system does not discriminate as heavily against parties with a heavy regional concentration of votes, for example, the nationalist parties.

2. Both major parties have had to appeal beyond their class nuclei, and their votes have become more class indeterminate in the process.

3. Class is still the most important social determinant of voting, but its importance has declined since 1945, and its influence is modified by a large number of individual variables.

4. Competitive party change is far less significant a phenomenon than noncompetitive party change, which has manifested itself in a secular decline; that is a basic long-range decline in turnout, the desertion of the two-party system, and increasing volatility of the vote.

5. Although identification with the two major parties has remained constant, its intensity has declined.

3
The Level of the Party Organizations

. . . The strong disposition I observed in them towards news and politics; perpetually inquiring into Public Affairs, giving their judgments in matters of state; and passionately disputing every inch of a party opinion.

Dean Swift, *A Voyage to Laputa*

The party—the mass, extraparliamentary party—is the link between the parliamentary level and the electoral level, and in all that follows it is essential to remember that parties fight elections on manifestoes and that these manifestoes contain highly specific commitments. If the party is elected to office, it regards the fulfillment of the commitments as a right and also as a duty, a view to some extent shared by significant proportions of the electorate and certainly by the party members. The electoral efforts of the parties are dedicated to mobilizing the maximum number of votes behind party candidates. The candidates must commit themselves to accept unmodified the manifesto on which the party is campaigning. The object is to produce a parliamentary majority of seats and thus the call to form a government. It is necessary, therefore, to examine first the size, coherence, and resources of the party, for these govern its ability to win; to analyze its mode of selecting candidates and its internal policy-making processes, since these govern its election program and team; and finally to consider the manifestoes of the parties to determine how representative they are of the party leadership, the party rank and file, and the party voters.

Party Structures

The structure of the two major parties is substantially as it was in 1945. In the following analysis, such changes as have occurred will be treated as they arise.

The Labour Party. It should first be noted that in theory the parliamentary Labour party is a sort of coalition of the Labour party proper and the Cooperative party. The Cooperative party sponsors a number of candidates, the maximum number (currently thirty) fixed by agreement with the Labour party. Once elected these M.P.s take the Labour whip and in all major respects are indistinguishable from other Labour M.P.s.

It is not unusual to find parties whose policies are oriented toward the claims and interests of trade unions and which derive electoral and financial support from them—the Australian and the New Zealand Labour parties for instance, and a number of the European socialist parties (Sweden is particularly relevant). The relationship between the Labour party and its affiliated trade unions, however, is unique as far as our knowledge goes, and it is essential to outline this if the party's structure and performance is to be understood.

First of all, the party is widely considered by its members to be only a part of a wider "Labour Movement." Clause 4.2 of its constitution (framed in 1918) states that one of its objects is, precisely, to "co-operate with the General Council of the Trades Union Congress, or other kindred organizations in joint political and other action in harmony with the Party Constitution and Standing Orders. . . ." Indeed, in 1922 an advisory National Joint Council of the party and the trade unions was set up, which the Cooperative Union subsequently joined also, and in the interwar period acted as a high council of "the Movement." It ceased to be influential in the 1950s and was last convened in 1971 to consider the party's pension proposals. Nowadays the relationship between the party and the Trade Union Council (TUC), or the Cooperative Union, is bilateral. For instance the most important channel between the Trade Union Council and the party since 1972 has been the TUC-Labour party "Liaison Committee."

The party began in 1900 as a mere Labour Representation Committee, to secure "the representation of working-class opinion" in the Commons by "men sympathetic with the aims and demands of the Labour movements."[1] In 1906 the committee changed its name to the

---

[1] Statement of the founders, at the Memorial Hall meeting, 1900, quoted in Robert Mackenzie, *British Political Parties*, 2nd ed. (London: Heinemann, 1964), pp. 456–57.

Labour party, but until 1918 it did no more than coordinate the political activities of the organizations—seventy-six trade unions, the Independent Labour party, the Social Democratic Federation, and the Fabian Society—that were affiliated with it. Thus during the first eighteen years there was only one class of membership—affiliated. There were no direct members. Direct membership was created under the 1918 constitution. An individual member simply joins his constituency branch party and pays his dues to it.

What then is an "affiliated" member? Any union may take the decision to affiliate to the Labour party—or to any other party for that matter—but this does not legally authorize it to give money to that party. A general ballot of the membership is required to authorize the establishment of a "political fund," and some unions have established such funds although not affiliated to the Labour party. In 1977, however, fifty-eight trade unions, each with its political fund, were affiliates of the Labour party. From the political fund they pay party dues for each union member who has contributed. The contribution is known as the political levy, and the union will collect it automatically, except from those who have signed a form which, in official jargon, "contracts them out" of paying it. (From 1927 until 1946 the unionist had to "contract-in" to signify his assent—a more meaningful political gesture.) Thus, the member of a Labour party-affiliated union who pays the political levy thereby becomes an affiliate member of the Labour party. What this means in terms of partisan commitment is very doubtful indeed. For the moment it is enough to note that each affiliated union will pay the Labour party an annual sum of party dues, equal to the annual subscription multiplied by the number of affiliated members—or, to be more accurate, the number the union *declares* to be affiliated, which tends to be either less or more than the true number, as we shall see later on.

Such affiliated members of the Labour party outnumber the individual members by at least ten to one; some 85 percent of the income received at the party headquarters derives from the dues paid by the unions on members' behalf; the general election fund is almost entirely donated by the unions from their political funds, which also go to help support the constituency Labour parties and to assist candidates whom a union is prepared to sponsor. 131 M.P.s currently sit as such union-sponsored candidates, equivalent to 48 percent of the entire parliamentary Labour party. One of the questions that will have to be confronted, therefore, is to find out who leads whom; unions the party, or the party the unions?

Returning now to the Labour party structure, this consists (see

Figure 1) of two major components: the parliamentary party, composed of candidates selected by the constituency parties and duly elected on the Labour manifesto by the electorate; and the party conference, composed of elected delegates. The parliamentary Labour party annually elects a leader who to date has automatically become the leader of the national party. It also elects a deputy leader. When the party is in opposition it elects a parliamentary committee, from which the leader selects a shadow cabinet, the opposition equivalent of the cabinet itself. When the party is in office, it elects a liaison committee which represents the backbench M.P.s as against the cabinet, which of course is personally selected by the party leader, who has now become the Prime Minister.

The Annual Conference, widely regarded as the party's "parliament" where policy is made, has four main functions: to debate and make policy; to consider the report of the parliamentary party; to elect a National Executive Committee (NEC) to direct and administer the national party in between conferences; and to consider the report of this committee. It consists of delegates from the socialist associations affiliated to the party (a trivial element); from the constituency parties; and from the affiliated trade unions. These delegations are bound or mandated by their electors' instructions, and the number of votes cast by a delegation depends on the number of affiliation fees paid by the organization. No constituency party is permitted to affiliate with membership of fewer than 1,000, although this is grossly in excess of the average number of members per local party. By the same token the affiliated trade union casts votes according to the number of fees it pays, but this may be higher or lower than the number of the trade unionists who, by virtue of not exercising their option to refuse to pay the political levy are considered for the record as members of the Labour party.

Some unions have been naming the identical approximate membership figure for years. At one time (before 1961, when the union was under Communist influence) the Electricians Union (ETU) affiliated on a very low membership figure, because its leaders chose to spend most of their political levy on other political activities. Similarly, in 1954, when it was believed that the next party conference would see a very close left-right contest for the office of party treasurer, the right-wing Transport and General Workers (TGWU) and the General and Municipal Workers (GMWU) raised their affiliations from 800,000 to 1,000,000 and from 400,000 to 650,000, respectively, to increase their voting strength.[2] And the TGWU, whose affiliation

[2] Lew Minkin, *The Labour Party Conference* (London: Allen Lane, 1978), p. 25.

FIGURE 1

THE ORGANIZATION OF THE CONSERVATIVE PARTY

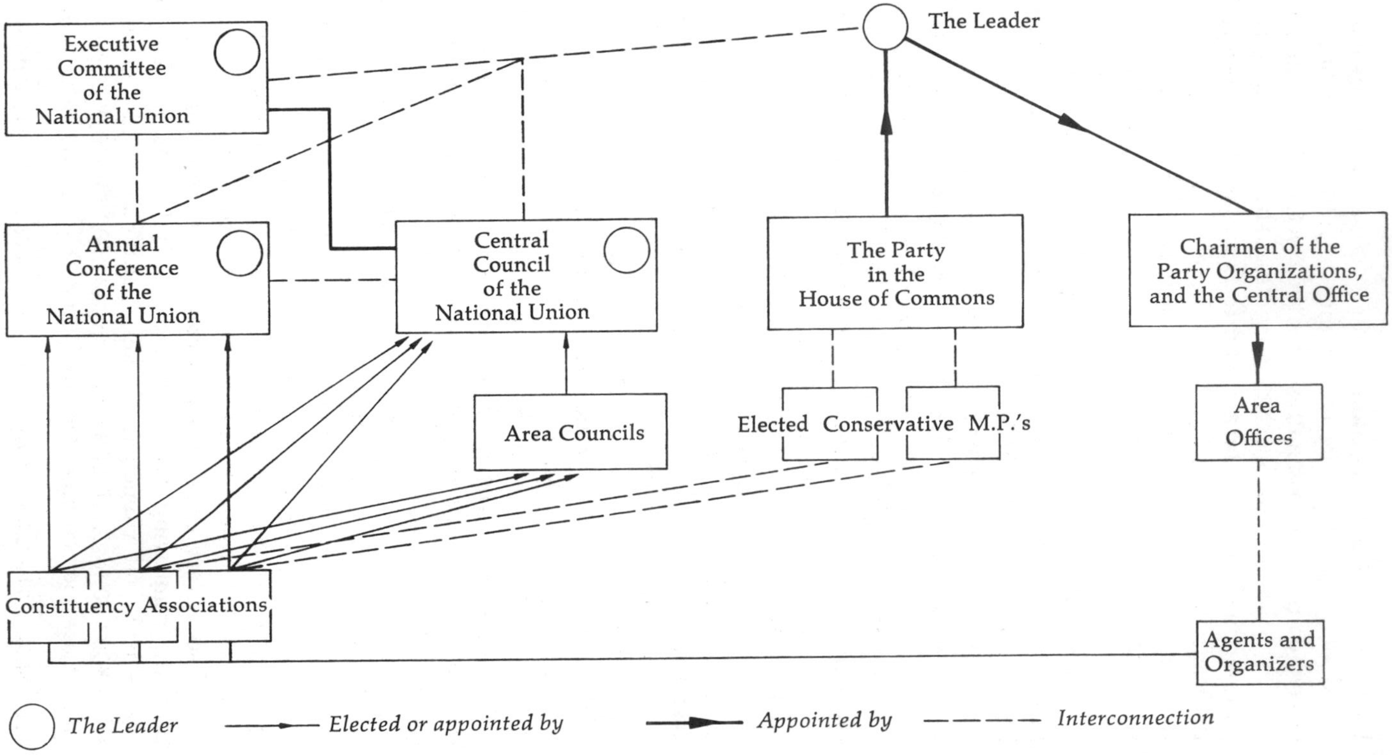

The Leader

Chairmen of the Party Organizations, and the Central Office

Area Offices

Agents and Organizers

The Party in the House of Commons

Elected Conservative M.P.'s

Central Council of the National Union

Area Councils

Executive Committee of the National Union

Annual Conference of the National Union

Constituency Associations

——— *Elected or appointed by*

———▶ *Appointed by*

— — — *Interconnection*

◯ *The Leader*

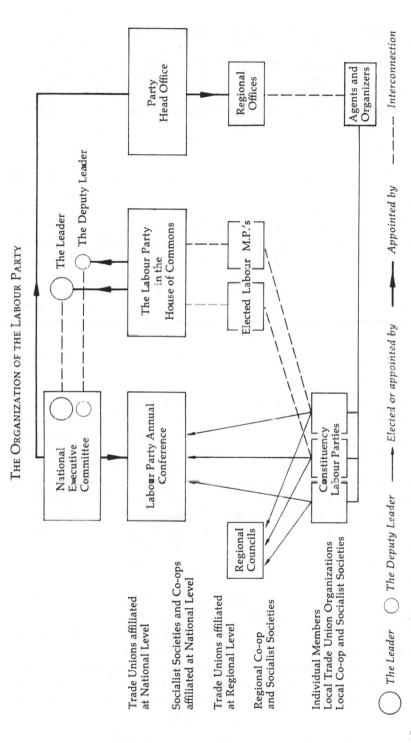

The Organization of the Labour Party

Party Head Office

Regional Offices

Agents and Organizers

The Leader

The Deputy Leader

The Labour Party in the House of Commons

Elected Labour M.P.'s

National Executive Committee

Labour Party Annual Conference

Regional Councils

Constituency Labour Parties

Trade Unions affiliated at National Level

Socialist Societies and Co-ops affiliated at National Level

Trade Unions affiliated at Regional Level

Regional Co-op and Socialist Societies

Individual Members
Local Trade Union Organizations
Local Co-op and Socialist Societies

◯ The Leader   ◯ The Deputy Leader

⟶ Elected or appointed by   ⟶ Appointed by   - - - - Interconnection

SOURCE: Roy Macridis, ed., *Modern Political Systems: Europe*, 4th ed. (Englewood Cliffs:: Prentice-Hall, 1979).

has stood at 1,000,000 since then, is about to raise this figure to 1,200,000, ostensibly to generate more central income for the party.

The overwhelming balance of voting strength always was and still is the trade union membership as against the constituency party membership. In 1951 the trade union vote at the party conference was 4,937,000 as opposed to 876,000 constituency party votes, a ratio of 5.2:1. In 1978 the figures were 6,061,000 trade union votes to 633,000 constituency party votes, a ratio of 9.57:1. This is almost double that of 1951.

The National Executive Committee's composition is designed to modify this grave imbalance. The leader and deputy leader sit ex-officio, and so does the representative of the Young Socialists. One member is elected by the votes of the socialist associations alone—usually a member of the Cooperative party, (although this tradition was broken in 1978)—but seven members are elected solely by the constituency Labour party vote, while twelve are elected solely by the trade union delegation votes. The remainder—the treasurer and five women representatives—are elected by the entire conference. Thus the constituency parties are guaranteed at least seven places on the executive committee. The trade unions are the decisive voice in electing their own representatives, the women representatives, and the treasurer—in all, eighteen places.

The National Executive Committee directs the party organization. It enforces party discipline by (in extremis) expelling individuals or disaffiliating organizations. Although it cannot force the choice of candidates on constituency parties (except at by-elections), it can veto candidates who in its opinion are inappropriate. It acts as a court of appeal over procedural disputes when local M.P.s or candidates are in contention with their local party. It controls the party bureaucracy ("Transport House"). Its two major policy committees (the International Committee and the Home Policy Committee) are the chief policy-formulating organs in the party. The Research Department works to them, and they in turn report to the full NEC; the party manifesto must be drawn up in a joint parliamentary party-NEC committee on which the NEC has a majority.

Frequently tension arises between the big battalions of the trade union delegations and the outnumbered constituency party delegates at the Annual Conference. There is also periodic tension between the parliamentary party and, if not the conference itself, then the NEC representing the conference, since the party constitution is obscure as to the precise relationship between them. Is the parliamentary party autonomous or is it bound to follow the mandates of the conference? Serious crises on this issue arose between 1959 and 1961, and again ever since 1974. The important thing to note here is the incompleteness of the leader's control of the party: the NEC is independent of the leader, the party machine is independent of the leader, and—as in the issue of maintaining an incomes policy (in 1978)—the conference may be hostile to the leader, too.

The Conservative Party. By contrast the Conservative party's structure does not invite or institutionalize the collisions found among the components of the Labour party. By and large power and influence reside in the parliamentary Conservative party and, within this, in the party leader.

The party has three components; the parliamentary party, the Central Office, and the National Union of Conservative Associations. The first consists of the Conservative peers and of the M.P.s, who of course have been nominated as candidates by the local Conservative associations but elected by the public, so the parliamentary party would regard itself as responsible in the last resort only to the electorate. The Commons party elects the party leader. Until 1965 the selection was made by a clandestine process of consultations, which continued until such time as, to use the language of that era, the leader "emerged." The emergence of Lord Home in 1963 by such a process split the party, and since 1965 the leader has been elected. The electoral procedure was modified in 1975, and the sentiments of local associations are to be ascertained and conveyed to the M.P.s before they get down to balloting.

If the party is in office the leader will have become Prime Minister, of course, and as such will select a cabinet. In opposition, the leader nominates the members of the shadow cabinet (whose official title is the Consultative Committee). Only backbenchers form the "1922 Committee" when the party is in office; when the party is in opposition this committee includes the entire membership of the party in the Commons.

The Central Office is the central bureaucratic organization of the party founded by Benjamin Disraeli in 1870. It is the leader's office; he appoints its chairman and deputy chairman, the two vice-chairmen, the treasurers, and the chairman and vice-chairmen of the policy committees. In practice the leader's choice is likely to be constrained, his relationship with the chairman is apt to be distant, and occasionally his line may be different from the one proposed by the chairman and/or the head of the Conservative Research Department. But this does not and cannot give birth to a formalized opposition

79

faction as in the Labour party; in the last resort the Conservative leader's decision is final.

Finally, the constituency parties (associations) are federated into the National Union, founded in 1867. Its governing body is the Central Council, but this numbers some 3,600 persons and meets twice yearly, so it is a sort of demi-conference. This council elects the Executive Committee (150 persons), which in turn elects the General Purposes Committee (56 members), a body that meets frequently and makes most of the day-to-day decisions. The most important of its activities is compilation of an agenda for the Annual Conference. At this level are found a number of often highly influential advisory committees. The Committee on Candidates is responsible for interviewing would-be candidates and putting them on an approved list, although in practice this function is usually left to a vice-chairman of the party. Local associations select their own candidate; and although the committee may not wholly approve, the local association is almost certain to be able to get him endorsed if it is adamant enough. But the National Union does have the power to disaffiliate local associations. It is only used in extremis; for example, it has been exercised to prevent some branches from admitting members known to belong to the National Front.

The Annual Conference of the National Union differs signally from that of the Labour party. First, each constituency party is entitled to send as many as seven delegates, irrespective of branch membership. Next, these are representatives and not mandated delegates. Finally, in constitutional status the conference is only "advisory," so much so that until the last decade the leader used to arrive to address the conference after it had concluded its labors. Nowadays he arrives for the conference debates but still reserves his address for the end of the conference. The resolutions of the conference are apt to be orthodox and supportive of the platform, but in any case they are conveyed to the leader on the understanding that in the last resort the choice of policy is his.

The Cooperative Party. Nearly 11,000,000 persons are members of the Cooperative Union, which federates retail, wholesale, and social cooperative societies. This of course is a business organization. There are, however, 200 cooperative societies affiliated to the Cooperative party (founded in 1917), representing some nine-tenths of the Union's membership. They pay affiliation fees to the party. The party holds as Annual Congress, which makes national agreements with the Labour party, formulates policy, and decides on affiliation fees. Local cooperative societies can and do affiliate to the constituency Labour parties, thus ensuring themselves a say in candidate selection. By agreement with the Labour party, these societies may sponsor up to thirty candidates, much as the trade unions also sponsor candidates. In the 1979 election the party put up twenty-five candidates who ran as "Cooperative and Labour," of whom seventeen were elected. Once in Parliament they take the Labour whip.

The Liberal Party. The Liberal party is federal; there are separate organizations for Northern Ireland, Scotland, Wales, and England. The basic unit is the constituency association; each constituency association is represented by a regional association. The highest governing body is the Assembly, composed of some 800 representatives from the constituency associations, members of the parliamentary party, and the senior officers. The Council is principally charged with expressing party views on current issues as they arise. It comprises the senior party officers, representatives of the parliamentary party, and the Liberal peers, representatives of the constituency associations elected by the regional association, and representatives of ancillary bodies such as the Young Liberals and the Women's Liberal Federation. The Standing Committee is really a kind of liaison body between the parliamentary party and the Liberal party organization; it prepares the agenda for the Council, but in addition it is the body the leader must consult (along with the Liberal Candidates Association) when he draws up the election manifesto. Twelve of its members are elected jointly by the Council, the Candidates Association, and the parliamentary party; there is one representative each from the Irish, Welsh, and Scottish parties, and five senior officers sit on it ex-officio, including the party leader, the chief whip, and the leader of the Liberal peers.

The National Executive Committee, according to the party's constitution, "directs the work of the party." It too is broadly representative of the various party institutions: It contains the senior officers, ex-officio; representatives from the regional associations in proportion to their strength; representatives from the Irish, Welsh, and Scottish parties and from the party's ancillary organizations; and eight Council representatives. It may be that this body "directs the work of the party," but this is by no means the same as "directing the administration of the party . . . employing staff . . . and running the party headquarters through the Head of the Liberal Party Organization and . . . raising and administering the finances of the party."[3]

---

[3] Section J6 of the Constitution.

On the contrary, this key responsibility rests in the Finance and Administration Board. When this body was orginally conceived in 1969, it was wholly elected by the NEC; such a simple line of responsibility would be a refreshing anomaly in a constitution so cross-patterned as the one so far described. But this board too has been turned into a composite without a clear-cut responsibility to any other organ except, in the last resort, the Assembly. The treasurer is elected to the finance board by the Assembly; two members are nominated to the board by the organization's Staff Association; four more are appointed to it from the NEC. This body appoints the secretary general of the party organization, who then sits as the eighth member of the board. Through him it controls the four divisions (organization, policy, finance and administration, and communications) of the headquarters staff, but there is controversy over the precise relationship of the board to the NEC, and it is certainly not unambiguously responsible to it.

The 1969 constitution was designed to ease communication between the parliamentary party and the organization, which had been very strained. It has not succeeded. The Standing Committee, designed as the link-organ, was never attended by the leader and his chief whip while Jeremy Thorpe led the party (1967–1976). Relations between the two parts of the party have been strained over long periods. One participant-observer argues that the vital chance of a post-February 1974 coalition with the Conservatives misfired because Thorpe failed to take the Assembly into his confidence.[4] The organization is in very poor shape. True, it suffers terribly for lack of money. Additionally, it has had to move its offices. Furthermore, in the last few years one director resigned, and it was some time before his successor was appointed. But until recently at least, the party was expressing strong dissatisfaction with the administration, and revelations about financial muddle made at the 1978 Assembly also reflected on the efficiency of headquarters.

Finally, the extraparliamentary organization has resented the M.P.s' authority to select the party leader. In 1967, when the National Executive Committee bitterly criticized the election of Thorpe, the party was rent by recrimination for many months. By 1975, new arrangements were under discussion, and after Thorpe resigned in January 1976, a special party conference adopted an entirely new procedure. The candidate must be a Liberal M.P. and is elected by a

---

[4] M. Steed, "Foreword," in A. Cyr, *Liberal Party Politics in Britain* (London: Calder, 1977), p. 29. But contrast Cyr's somewhat different interpretation of these events on p. 171.

special convention of the constituency representatives according to their strength in voters and the like. Furthermore, these associations must themselves ballot their members and allocate their votes in the electoral convention in accordance with the preferences they have expressed for the candidates. This was the process by which the present leader, David Steel, was elected in 1976, by 12,451 votes to his opponent's 7,032.

The Nationalist Parties. The justification for describing the somewhat intellectualized organization of the Liberal party is that this is still a natural third choice for voters disaffected from the two major parties and, indeed, this is an important reason that it picked up nearly one-fifth of the national vote in 1974 and managed to hold on to some 14 percent of the vote in 1979. But although the nationalist parties only won a little more than 3 percent of the national vote in 1979, they had won some 6 percent of it in the 1974 election; at least one of them, the Scottish Nationalist party, which polled some 17 percent of the Scottish votes, may well expand back to the strong position it obtained in October 1974 when it took 30 percent of the vote and won eleven of Scotland's seventy-one seats. In the 1974–1979 Parliament it was the nationalist parties that, along with the Liberals, held the balance of power, and it was the vote of the members of two of these—the SNP and the Ulster Unionists—that, along with the Liberals, brought the government down on the Conservative "no confidence" vote of March 28, 1979. Another "hung" Parliament is by no means inconceivable. Hence the desirability of examining these parties.

Plaid Cymru. This party was founded in 1925, but it never contested a parliamentary seat until after 1945. It elected its first M.P. in 1966 but lost the seat again in the 1970 general election. Yet in that year its share of the Welsh vote rose to 11.5 percent. Although in 1974 (October) its share of the vote dropped somewhat, to 10.7 percent, the party won three seats.

Its electoral weakness is that its vote is heavily concentrated in the Welsh-speaking areas, which is not surprising in view of the central role of language in Welsh nationalism. But four out of every five Welshmen speak only English and evince less than a desire to have to speak Welsh. Hence the dilemma: If a Welshman is a Welsh-speaker, what is the national status of the English-speaker? And conversely, if they are each of equal national status, what special significance attaches to the Welsh tongue? Significantly in 1974 the

Blaid polled less than one-eighth of the total votes cast in twenty-three of the principality's thirty-six seats.

These questions were put to the test on March 1, 1979, when the Welsh electorate voted in a referendum on whether to approve the Wales Act, 1979, to establish a local Welsh Assembly. Welsh voters rejected the act by the overwhelming majority of 79.7 percent to 20.3 percent. Significantly, the highest proportion of "yes" votes was cast in the most Welsh-speaking of the counties—in Gwynedd, ancestral home of the last kings of independent Wales many centuries ago; even there the electors rejected it by two to one. The rebuff was reflected in the general election of 1979. True, the Blaid's total vote fell from 10.7 percent to only 8.4 percent of the Welsh vote, and it lost only one of its three seats and held the other two with bigger majorities; but everywhere else its vote fell away. More significantly than anything else for the future, it was beaten into third place by the Conservatives in a number of South Wales industrial seats where it had previously run second to the Labour party. The importance of this development is that hitherto it had been generally assumed that the Blaid was the natural heir of the Welsh radical tradition, which was once borne by the Liberals and then by the Labour party. Instead the Conservative vote in Wales increased in 1979 from some 20 percent of the electorate to 32.2 percent.

The branches, each of which has a minimum of twenty members, are the base of the party structure and form part of the constituency associations, whose principal task is to select the parliamentary candidate. The constituency associations are grouped into eight district organizations, one for each of the Welsh counties.

The national machinery consists first of the Conference: each branch and each constituency sends a representative who sits along with the membership of the council and with the party officers. The Conference elects all officers. Its decisions are carried out by council: the officers, the M.P.s, two representatives from each constituency, and four other elected members. Finally the National Executive Committee is the governing body of the organization: its fourteen voting members include the six senior officers plus a representative from each provincial committee. The directors of the organization also sit but have no vote.

Because the party is so small, decision making is in practice concentrated in a few individuals at the apex, and the structure is in practice very centralized, with the NEC much the most powerful organ—it claims nineteen full-time officials, which is a very large figure by comparison with the three United Kingdom parties, and especially with the Liberals who in 1977 had only seventeen. Furthermore, perhaps because the M.P.s numbered only three (now, only two), they have been unassertive and have chosen to follow the party rather than to lead it.

The Scottish National party. This is altogether more significant than the Blaid. In 1974 it had eleven M.P.s; its share of the Scottish vote was three times that of the Blaid's share of the Welsh vote; and its potential for advance was and still is considerable.

It was formed in 1933 by the merger of two nationalist parties. It won its first seat in April 1945, but lost it at the ensuing general election. It won a by-election in 1967, lost that seat at the 1970 general election, but in compensation won one seat (Western Isles). In February 1974, however, it won seven seats and increased this number to eleven in the October election. Its share of the Scottish vote had advanced very steadily. In 1955 it presented fifteen candidates to win 2.4 percent of the Scottish vote. In 1966, with twenty-three candidates, it took 5 percent; in 1970, with sixty-five candidates, it secured 11.4 percent; in February 1974, it fielded seventy candidates and took 21.9 percent of the Scottish vote, and in the following October with a candidate in every Scottish constituency (seventy-one) its total soared to 30.4 percent of the vote, making it the second largest vote-getter in Scotland. Public opinion polls subsequently showed that proportion rising still higher until 1977, when it began to return to the 1974 level.

The party's long-term policy is to secede from the United Kingdom. In the short term, it supported "devolution," that is, the establishment of a local Scottish Assembly with considerable autonomy in a wide range of domestic affairs. In 1974 and subsequently, therefore, its ranks contained both secessionists and strongly anti-secessionist "devolutionists."

The so-called devolution issue, as embodied in the Wales Bill and the Scotland Bill, took up a great deal of Parliament's time from the end of 1976, through enactment of both measures in 1978, up to the fateful day of March 28, 1979, when the SNP precipitated the fall of the Callaghan government and the subsequent election.

While the Labour party was pursuing its devolutionist course, the Conservative party, led by Margaret Thatcher, shook off its previous commitment to a Scottish Assembly. SNP support was in a decline. The Scotland Act, 1978, depended for its implementation on a positive vote of not less than 40 percent of the total Scots electorate, in a referendum slated for March 1, 1979. Significantly, the Labour party refused to share a platform with the SNP in the "yes" campaign, in order to disassociate itself from secessionism. In any event, although

52 percent voted "yes" in the referendum, this amounted to not quite 33 percent of the eligible electorate, too far short of the statutory requirement for the government to press on with implementing the act. When it prevaricated, the SNP tabled a vote of "no confidence," and, as already described, it was this which, with the support of Liberals, Conservatives, and Ulster Unionists (but not the Blaid Cymru), defeated the government in the March 28 vote; thus preparing the way for the May 3 election.

This proved a disaster for the SNP, which lost nine of its eleven seats—two to Labour and seven to the Conservatives. Labour clearly benefited from its devolutionist stance, and, indeed, ended up with a positive 0.7 percent swing in its favor in Scotland as opposed to the 5.2 percent average swing against it for Great Britain as a whole. This result, however, is more likely to spell electoral eclipse than demise for the SNP. Scottish nationalism is by no means dead. The Conservative party has not made it clear what solution if any it has for Scottish devolution, and the SNP vote, although only 17.3 percent of the Scottish vote as compared with its 1974 peak of 30.4 percent, is still much higher than its 1970 share, which was only 11.4 percent.

The party is highly decentralized. Its basic unit is the branch (minimum twenty members). Headquarters leaves them to themselves. At the national level, the supreme body is the Conference, which discusses branch resolutions and elects the officers and the members of the Council. It meets twice a year and consists principally of representatives of the constituency associations (which incorporate the party branches). Between conferences the governing body is the Council, which meets every quarter. It has wide powers to amend the rules of the party and to fill casual vacancies among officers, but it is too large to be effective: it is 500 strong, made up of representatives of the area organizations, the constituency associations, the branches, and fifteen members elected to it by the Assembly. Hence its role is for the most part taken over by the twenty-four member National Executive Committee. This is often styled "the cabinet of the party." It is headed by the national secretary (elected by the Assembly), and in 1977 had four sections, which in 1978 employed ten full-time staff members. Extra volunteer labor is fully available at election time, and finance seems to present no problems: the branches are very successful money-raisers, and their subsidies keep the headquarters organization adequately funded.

The "center," as it is called, plays a purely administrative role. The decentralization of the party creates a heavy administrative load. It also fosters a certain self-sufficiency in the branches, which indeed sometimes leads them to react against the party center. Finally, because the M.P.s spend their time shuttling between their constituencies and Westminster, they have little opportunity to maintain more than intermittent contact with the center. The SNP M.P.s have nothing like the authority that M.P.s have in the Labour, Liberal, or Conservative parties. For instance, it is often the officers who make the official party political broadcasts, rather than the M.P.s. Again, when M.P. Douglas Henderson contested the post of vice chairman with Margot Macdonald (an officer), he was soundly defeated. In truth it would seem that the M.P.s are somewhat disliked: They are remote, and the rank and file distaste for Westminster, where of course M.P.s must perform, rubs off on them. There is therefore continual tension between the party and the M.P.s.

The Ulster Unionists. The Unionist party (parties) at Westminster faces two ways: inside Ulster to the local assembly, the Stormont Parliament which from 1922–1972 governed internal affairs, and outward toward Westminster, where Ulster is represented by twelve M.P.s. The former face only concerns us in so far as it affects the party's strength and role at Westminster.

Two points deserve attention. First, the Ulster Unionists, who in 1923–1970 provided the Conservative party at Westminster with never less than eight and as many as twelve of Ulster's twelve seats, ceased to take the Conservative whip in 1974; some are currently as likely to vote with the Labour party as with the Conservatives. The second point is that the formerly united Official Ulster Unionist party has disintegrated since 1970 and no longer presents a united front inside Ulster or at Westminster. What follows briefly presents the sequence in which this disintegration occurred along with the reasons for it.

After the establishment of the local Stormont Parliament in 1922, the local Catholic minority suffered a variety of civil disabilities. A civil rights campaign launched in 1969 degenerated into violent disturbances, and, as the Irish Republican Army (IRA) joined in, into terrorism; so that in 1972 the British government suspended the Stormont Parliament and took Ulster under direct rule. The first repercussion felt at Westminster occurred when one of Ulster's parliamentary seats was captured in 1970 by a dissident unionist, the Reverend Ian Paisley, campaigning under the banner of the Democratic Unionist party.

The Conservative government of 1970–1974 adopted the formula of power-sharing between Protestants and Catholics as the basis for the future government of Ulster and persuaded the Catholic leaders and Brian Faulkner, the leader of the Ulster Unionists, to accept a new constitution. As the proposed new assembly was to be elected by proportional representation, the Catholic minority would at last be adequately represented, while the Cabinet (called the Executive) was to be drawn from this assembly by the Secretary of State for Northern Ireland. A revolt occurred among the Unionists, and in the elections to this new assembly in June 1973, Faulkner's faction secured only twenty-two seats, while a Vanguard faction, which opposed the new arrangements, together with other dissidents and Paisley, secured twenty-seven among them. Nineteen seats went to the largely Catholic Social Democratic and Labour party (SDLP). In December 1973, the Conservative government held talks with the assembly and concluded the Sunningdale Agreement. The Executive was to consist of six Faulkner Unionists, four SDLP, and one representative of the middle-of-the-road Alliance party.

For the Ulster Unionist party this proved the breaking point. Its members rejected the agreement, and Faulkner resigned its leadership. Almost immediately afterward, with Faulkner's supporters in disarray, the general election of February 1974 was announced. Faulkner's Unionist antagonists formed the United Ulster Unionist Coalition (UUUC), sweeping up eleven of Ulster's twelve parliamentary seats. (Its representation was reduced to ten seats in the October election.) Seven of these were the official Unionist party (led by Harry West); two belonged to the Vanguard party; and the last was Paisley, as "the Democratic Unionist party." These ten members did not necessarily vote together in Westminster. Indeed, in a critical vote of confidence in the Labour government of December 1978, the official Unionist M.P.s voted with the government while the three unofficial ones voted against it. In what was to prove the decisive vote of March 28, 1979, only eight of the Unionists voted against the government and two voted for it.

The 1979 election splintered the Unionists still further. The Official Ulster Unionists lost two seats directly to the more extreme Democratic Unionist party of Paisley, and its leader (West) thereupon resigned. Two M.P.s of the former official Ulster Unionist party are really independent of it, going under the titles of Ulster Unionist and United Ulster Unionist Party respectively.

Antisystem Parties. No antisystem party is currently represented in Parliament.

Left-wing antisystem parties. The Communist party is the largest antisystem party, but its strength has fallen to the all-time low figure of 20,000. The Socialist Workers' party (until 1976 the International Socialists) is one of the many Trotskyite parties. It claims 4,600 members. The International Marxist group is another such, but it claims only 800 members.[5] Although these parties do very badly in elections, they are by no means unimportant. For one thing their members are active in the trade union movement, often rising to high office and influential positions on the shop floor. In 1974–1975, for instance, the Communist party was represented on the main committees of the largest unions as follows: the Mineworkers (NUM), six Communist members on the twenty-seven member executive board; the Transport Workers (TGWU), at least ten Communist members of the thirty-nine member general executive council; Scientific Technical and Managerial Staffs (ASTMS), seven seats on the twenty-three member-strong executive board; National Union of Teachers, three members on the executive; and its members also sat on the executives of the Local and National Government Officers (NALGO) and the Shopworkers (USDAW). For some time the Amalgamated Engineering Union (AEUW) was under the influence of Communists and other left-wing socialists in the "Broad Left," and this alliance secured the election of Hugh Scanlon (a former Communist) as general secretary in 1968. Over the next five years such Communists as Arthur Gill became general secretary of the union's white-collar section (TASS) and another party member went on to the executive committee where he could draw support from Reg Birch, a Maoist, and so forth.[6]

The strength of these antisystem parties among the shop stewards and the rank and file is not known exactly, but a current estimate is that "about ten percent of all union officials are Communist and there must be a higher proportion of stewards and lay 'activists.' More important is the emergence of the 'broad left alliance' under which Communists and Labour Party militants unite to keep Labour moderates from office."[7] The influence of such broad left alliances reaches beyond industrial disputes to affect Labour party policy itself. The union delegations at the Labour party conference arrive with mandates to vote for or against certain resolutions. These mandates are taken in union branches, then in the superior echelons, until they reach the supreme policy-making organ (which differs among the different unions): in this way they are highly influenced by the views

[5] A good survey of all these parties is to be found in Peter Shipley, *Revolutionaries in Modern Britain* (London: Bodley Head, 1975).

[6] Shipley, *Revolutionaries in Modern Britain*, pp. 50–57.

[7] John Torode, "Unions that Began to Shout," *The Guardian*, February 7, 1979.

of these left-wing militants, who are far more active than the rank and file, and may not be members of the Labour party at all.

Another reason for not ignoring such antisystem groups is that they have infiltrated the Labour party Young Socialists, now largely dominated by the militant faction of Trotskyite Marxists,[8] and they also dominate the National Organization of Labour Students.[9] And of course insofar as trade union branches and Young Socialist branches are affiliated to Constituency Labour parties, they are vehicles for leftism in these, as well.

Right-wing antisystem parties. The National Front (NF) is the result of the merger of certain neofascist groups in 1967. Its current membership is estimated at between 10,000 and 12,000, mostly from poorer working class youth, and it has a very high rate of turnover.

Stridently and overtly neo-Nazi and racist, hating Jews and non-white immigrants alike, the party has thrived best in constituencies where there are high concentrations of non-white immigrants. Its 1979 manifesto, entitled *"It's our country—let's win it back,"* stated among other things: "The policy of the National Front on coming into office will be to place all coloured immigrants on a register of persons liable to be required eventually to leave the country. . . ." The NF fielded ninety candidates in October 1974 but collected only 0.4 percent of the total British vote. Encouraged, however, by its success in a 1977 by-election at Stetchford, which has a large number of non-white immigrants and where it polled 8.2 percent of the local vote, as well as by some flattering local government polls, it fielded 303 candidates in the May 1979 election. It fared disastrously. Admittedly its total votes rose from 113,000 (October 1974) to 191,000, but the average vote per candidate dropped from 2.9 percent (October 1974) to only 1.3 percent. It failed to run third in any constituency contested by the three main parties. Its best results occurred in the East End of London (as in the October 1974 general election), where it obtained 7.6 percent of the local vote in Hackney, 6.2 percent in Newham South, and 6.1 percent in Tower Hamlets; but in all three the vote was down compared with the previous general election.

Persistencies in the Structure of the Two Main Parties

Apart from the general structural frameworks so far described, three specific structural characteristics have persisted over the last thirty years.

---

[8] More will be said about this group, or faction, in a later section on factions and tendencies in the parties.

[9] Shipley, *Revolutionaries in Modern Britain*, pp. 91–102.

Policy-making Hegemony of the Parliamentary Leadership. In examining this feature, five preliminary considerations must be borne in mind. It is essential to conceptualize party more sharply, so as to distinguish between the parliamentary party, the government when that party is in office, and the extraparliamentary party. A party-government makes policy, although the extraparliamentary, policy-formulating organs may continue to make proposals. Generalizations about the Labour party must all be qualified to recognize that after 1970 the extraparliamentary party took a leftward turn that put it on a collision course with the parliamentary leadership. The policy-making organs of the extraparliamentary party come into their own when the party is in opposition, and the techniques by which policy is formulated in these conditions have been greatly developed and elaborated upon since 1945. In very broad summary, when the party is in office, the government makes policy. In opposition the parliamentary party remains the locus of decision making. The Labour party does, however, admit two qualifications to this rule. The first is that the hegemony of the parliamentary party rests on an accord with the more powerful among the affiliated union delegations to the conference, and hence operates within the constraints so imposed. Second, this accord held good until 1970 (despite a bumpy ride in 1960–1961), but with the leftward drift of the major unions after 1968 it ceased. (The reasons for this leftward shift, how it occurred, and its effect on the political weight of different elements in the party structure are more appropriately described in the later sections that analyze factionalism inside the two major parties.)

The formal position differs between the two parties. In the Conservative party, policy is in the last resort the prerogative of the leader, who is the leader of the parliamentary party. In the Labour party, the formal position is that for a policy to become part of the program, a two-thirds majority vote at the Annual Conference is required, although the timing and application of this policy by the parliamentary party is left to the discretion of its leaders. In many cases party policy has waited years before being executed, and some policies are still waiting. The party manifesto is drawn up by a joint meeting of the NEC and the parliamentary committee—in other words, the shadow cabinet or, if the party is in power, the Prime Minister and his colleagues. Thus, in either event even the formal position ensures the parliamentary party at least parity in the case of the Labour party, while the parliamentary party is paramount in the Conservative party.

This hegemonic position of the parliamentary leaders is at its maximum when the party is in power where such concessions as they may make to the national party is, at the best, a concession from a position of considerable strength. This is true even for Labour governments which, quite unlike Conservative ones, must confer with the NEC, which runs the party organization and is the custodian of the decisions of the Annual Conference. This is strikingly evident in the shaping of the party manifestoes of 1966 and 1970, and, above all, in 1979. In 1966 the NEC members of the joint NEC-Parliamentary Party Committee were "overawed by the occasion and situation," and the drafting was monitored throughout by Prime Minister Wilson.[10] In 1970 the Prime Minister and his colleagues were faced by a strong NEC team, which had prepared a set of policies much to the left of what the parliamentarians were prepared to accept; the parliamentarians omitted many of them and reformulated the others in bland and unspecific language.[11]

In the formulation of the 1979 manifesto, Prime Minister Callaghan and his parliamentary colleagues were confronted by the very left-wing NEC. The Prime Minister vetoed the most extreme of the NEC's proposals as contained in the *Labour's Programme 1976* document, fudged phraseology dealing with their more moderate proposals, and, effectively, did little more than to endorse a program of "more of the same." Admittedly this did include proposals for a wider role for the National Enterprise Board, more public spending on social services, and a limitation on the powers of the House of Lords. But the headlines of the *Daily Telegraph*, "*Left yields to Callaghan,*" or of the *Financial Times*, "*A Triumph for Mr. Callaghan,*" give the essence of the matter.[12] It is precisely this that has generated the current struggle between the NEC and the parliamentary leadership over who should draft the manifesto in future, as will be recounted below.

When either party is in opposition, however, the divergence between their loci of decision making is wider. Opposition has been the major occasion for reformulating policy, and in both parties the Research Department plays an important initiatory role (this will become evident when the actual techniques of policy making, as contrasted with its locus, is described below). In the Conservative case, the major lines of policy will have been approved by the shadow cabinet and, in the last instance, the leader, and will then usually be incorporated

---

[10] Minkin, *The Labour Party Conference*, p. 293; and R. Crossman, *The Diaries of a Cabinet Minister*, vol. I (London: Hamish Hamilton and Jonathan Cape, 1975), p. 471.

[11] Butler and Pinto-Duschinsky, *The General Election of 1970*, pp. 59–60, 149–51; Minkin, *The Labour Party Conference*, pp. 293–94.

[12] *Daily Telegraph*, April 7, 1979; *Financial Times*, April 7, 1979.

in some rather bland policy document and submitted to the conference for general approval, which can be taken for granted.

In the Labour party, too, the conference followed the parliamentary leadership on most major issues until 1970, the historic exception being the notorious encounter of 1960 when Hugh Gaitskell, the Labour party leader, openly defied a vote of the conference that committed the party to the unilateral nuclear disarmament of Britain. As the conference reversed itself in the following year, however, congruence was restored. It is also true that from 1960 onward the conference passed a number of resolutions against the wishes of the parliamentary leadership, but with the parliamentary party in office (1964–1970) Prime Minister Wilson simply ignored these. "Conference does not dictate to the Government" was an unanswerable riposte in the light of British constitutional convention.

But the congruence of parliamentary leadership and the party conference, even in the total harmony that existed in the period 1946–1960 (when no hostile resolutions at all were passed), rested implicitly on the support of the large trade unions. Their delegations arrive at the conference with mandates that have already been evolved in union meetings (sometimes more than one year in advance). Furthermore, the delegations cast the total of their affiliate membership's votes in one block, ignoring the minority opinion within the union. The two largest unions (the TGWU and the AEUW) cast two million (nearly one-third) of the total conference votes between them. Somehow union assent must be secured if the congruence of parliamentarians and the extraparliamentary party is to be assured. And on the whole it is. These delegations tend to defer to the parliamentary leadership or are persuadable or even manipulable except where policy affects their corporate self-interest, this imposes a constraint on the parliamentary leadership.

In short, the parliamentary leadership must anticipate union reaction in cases involving the unions' internal procedures, the unions' legal status and immunities, wage restraint and income policy, or superannuation.[13] If it fails to do so or does so incorrectly, it may be defeated. The unions resisted the Labour government when it tried to regulate the status of the unions and to impose restraints on unofficial strikes in 1968–1969, and they forced the party to drop that policy. Ten years later, the same fate overtook Callaghan's insistence on a 5 percent wage norm, although he even hinted that he would resign if defeated. But the 1978 conference, which means the unions' vote,

---

[13] Minkin, *The Labour Party Conference*, pp. 53–54.

rejected this policy in favor of free collective bargaining (by a massive five-to-two majority), and then within weeks swept on to press and to win wage increases of at least 15 percent.

After 1968, however, some of the largest unions moved leftward on policies well wide of corporate self-interest, and this general movement was communicated in time to the NEC, whose political complexion moved leftward in sympathy. Hence the 1974 manifesto was considerably to the left of the party's previous programs, despite resistance from the Prime Minister and his senior colleagues.[14]

To summarize: In both parties policy is made in the parliamentary party, but whereas in the Conservative case this is unequivocal, in the Labour party it is circumscribed by constraints imposed by the affiliated unions' perception of their corporate self-interest.

The technique of policy formulation must be understood inside these policy-making contexts, and here there has been a steady evolution. Before 1945, the opposition had been seen, variously, as the critic of the government, as the group responsible for examining and criticizing legislation; or as a check on the executive. In the postwar period, however, it has been regarded as the alternative government.

Such a role requires the opposition party to prepare and publish concrete policies as alternatives to the government's. In the Conservative party the usual process has been for the influential Research Department to generate policy suggestions which are then reworked by policy committees of the parliamentary party assisted by outside experts, then by the Standing Advisory Committee on Policy, and finally by the shadow cabinet and party leader. The expansion of the Research Department is itself significant: The full-time officers numbered five in 1947,[15] twenty-five in 1963, thirty-one in 1973, thirty-eight in 1978–1979.

The first major incidence of the opposition as an alternative government occurred in 1947, in the wake of the Conservatives' defeat in 1945. During the next period, 1964–1970, the Conservatives' exercise of that role was altogether more substantial. Whereas in 1947 only three committees had been established, by the 1960s there were more than thirty. The impressionistic policy documents of 1947 were replaced in the 1960s with statements that were highly detailed, especially those concerned with industrial relations, housing, finance, tax reform, and the structure of central government. Again, whereas in

---

[14] A detailed account is given in Hatfield, *The House the Left Built.*

[15] Including the Parliamentary Secretariat, at that time a parallel department. It was amalgamated with the Research Department in 1948.

1947 no outsiders were consulted, the pattern in 1964–1970 consisted of a frontbench M.P. as chairman of a committee composed of about six backbench M.P.s and an equal number of outside experts. All these committees were serviced by the staff of the Research Department. Their completed reports went via the Advisory Committee to the shadow cabinet, where policy was decided. The 1975–1979 exercise followed similar lines. The general direction of the research was set by the Advisory Committee on Policy. There were even more policy-making groups than previously, though their structure remained similar, but they were given wider rein and encouraged to take a broader approach. As this process threw up a large number of policy suggestions, the committees' reports passed to a policy subcommittee, which selected the ones to go to the shadow cabinet.[16] The Conservative pattern, then, is unequivocally centered on the parliamentary party, or, even more, on the shadow cabinet. The Conservative Research Department is responsible to the shadow cabinet through the party leader, who controls it and appoints its head.

Although the Labour Party Research Department has played a similar role (at least since 1960), it is a different animal from its Conservative counterpart. In the first place it is the creature of the NEC, which is not necessarily the catspaw of the parliamentary leadership and at the present time is its rival. Second, it is highly politicized; since 1960 it has been to the left of the parliamentary leadership and often on acrimonious terms with it. It got off to a slower start than its Conservative counterpart—its significance in policy making can be said to have started only in 1959—and it is not as large. But the stages in its expansion parallel the Conservative department; it grew from only two principal officers in 1940, to twelve in 1963, and to nineteen at the present day.[17]

The NEC has two policy-making committees, the Home Policy Committee and the International Committee. The NEC authorizes the establishment of study groups and special committees, and lays down their terms of reference. Each is allocated a research officer, and the chairman is usually the NEC's spokesman (which is not at all the same thing as the parliamentary spokesman) for a particular area. Subcommittees of these committees invite outside experts to participate, and the extent of this is impressive. (In the 1970–1974 exercise, nearly 1,000 individuals served on more than 80 committees.)[18]

---

[16] For a general account, see R. Malcolm Punnett, *Front Bench Opposition* (London: Heinemann, 1973), pp. 264–78.

[17] Ibid.; Richard Rose, *Politics in England* (London: Faber, 1965), p. 47; and Richard Rose, *Politics in England Today* (London: Faber, 1974).

[18] Hatfield, *The House the Left Built*, p. 17.

The Research Department has managed to arrogate to itself some potentially influential privileges. It drafts a committee's agenda before the committee has chosen its chairman, for one thing. It also initiates the draft policy proposals. How effectively such action can preempt a committee's options can be seen from Michael Hatfield's detailed account of the framing of party policy in the period 1970–1974.[19] Its drafts are discussed and suitably amended by the subcommittee or study group, then go to the home policy committee for further discussion and finally reach the NEC itself. When the party was in office, ministers inevitably, if sometimes acrimoniously, dominated discussions in the NEC, since, in the last resort, the minister could simply ignore the draft policy document and proceed to run his department according to his own lights. In opposition this was never necessarily so; and in 1970–1974 it was not so at all.

Until 1959 the Labour Party Research Department showed little initiative, and for its part the NEC was content with intermittent ad hoc policy documents. In the ideological confusion of the 1959 defeat, the new research director, Peter Shore, persuaded the NEC that nothing less than a comprehensive policy document was required. With the party's general secretary he drafted a document, *Labour in the Sixties*, for the 1960 conference, and this formed the basis for discussion by a special policy subcommittee. Redrafted and then modified by the NEC, this became *Signposts for the Sixties*, which was adopted by acclamation at the 1961 conference and formed the basis for the party manifesto (a somewhat unspecific but very highsounding one) in 1964.

Under a new and left-wing director, Terry Pitt, the Research Department continued to formulate policies during the period of Labour government, 1970–1974, often critical of the government's actions, notably on race relations and immigration. In 1969 it opposed its "In Place of Strife" proposals to curb unofficial strikes.[20]

In 1970, the ministers became ex-ministers. Shorn of their authority—and in the case of the right-wing leaders unmindful of their responsibilities[21] they did not perceive the radicalization of the NEC until too late. Under the chairmanship of the active, energetic, left-wing Tony Benn, the Home Policy Committee inaugurated a sweeping review of party policy. This culminated in *Labour's Programme 1973*.[22] Although Wilson and his colleagues were able to delete some of the more far-reaching proposals for public ownership and control from the

[19] Ibid.

[20] Minkin, *The Labour Party Conference*, pp. 307–11.

[21] Hatfield, *The House the Left Built*.

[22] Ibid.

1974 manifesto, they had to swallow a great deal. After their return to office in 1974, the government faced an NEC that became more left-wing every year and that, fed by the Research Department, poured out a stream of policy documents critical of, incompatible with, or openly opposed to government policy. For instance, it opposed direct election of M.P.s to the European parliament and dragged its feet over whether even to contest them (reluctantly concluding that it had no alternative but to do so); opposed the public expenditure cuts of 1976; and opposed the government's policy of a 5 percent pay norm in 1978. By the same token, it proposed policies going far beyond what the parliamentary leadership found acceptable, notably the extension of the scope of the National Enterprise Board, the imposition of mandatory planning agreements on private corporations, the takeover of the country's twenty-five largest firms, the reduction of tax relief on house mortgage interest payments, and the nationalization of the construction industry. These policies were the despair of the government, and a red rag to the center-right wing of the parliamentary party, which represented two-thirds of the parliamentary party's membership. In 1977 some members of this persuasion tried to contest left-wing influence at the grass roots by setting up an organization, "The Campaign for Labour Victory." This says that the Research Department is:

> a short cut to the House of Commons, full of frustrated party candidates who are not interested in making the party organization effective, but simply in becoming MP's. Instead of building up a proper party they are spending their time researching rubbishy pamphlets for one or two members of the NEC.[23]

Importance of the Periphery. In both major parties only policy making, research, and publicity are centralized; campaigning, finance, and the selection of the candidate are highly decentralized.

Finance. During the period 1975–1977 the constituency Labour parties raised 59 percent of the total party income, while the local Conservative associations raised 80 percent of party revenue.

Candidate selection is even more completely local. The central party organizations maintain lists of approved candidates, which many constituency parties make use of. Occasionally party headquarters is able to persuade a local party that it would prove helpful if a certain

---

[23] Times, October 1, 1977. Cf. the incident in November 1973, when Callaghan "told the Home Policy Committee that Transport House was making too many policies and not devoting energies in getting across the ones already agreed." To this Pitt rejoined that "it was their job to provide policies for discussion." Hatfield, The House the Left Built, pp. 224–25.

candidate were selected. More often, however, such well-intentioned efforts are counterproductive, as witness rebuffs experienced by Prime Minister's Callaghan's political assistant, Tom McNally, in his search for adoption.[24] In any case the lists contain more names than the number of vacancies and unlisted persons are free to come forward. By the same token both party headquarters have powers to disqualify candidates for technical or political reasons, but they are used very rarely indeed. In general, it is enough if a would-be candidate is a party member in good standing who undertakes to subscribe to the party program and to present the party's views and policies during the election.

Those conditions fulfilled, the choice is the local party's, and here selection resides in a tiny group. In the Conservative associations vetting is carried out by the chairman and some half-dozen senior officeholders. The list (some three or four names) goes to the Executive Council, which may have as few as twenty-eight or as many as 400 members. It will comprise the officers, a representative from each ward, from each Young Conservative branch, and from each affiliated Conservative Club, with some coopted members. This is the body that chooses the candidate. The candidate must then be adopted by a general meeting of the association, so in principle the entire membership participates, but only in rare instances has a general meeting overturned the council's choice.

Labour practice is likewise restrictive. A would-be candidate must be nominated by some constituent element of the local party, and such nominations are then validated by the NEC, in London. (None appear ever to have been referred back.) The governing body of a constituency Labour party is its General Management Council (GMC), served by an Executive Committee, which it elects. The Executive Committee reduces the list of candidates, and the GMC then transforms itself into a selection conference to select among them. (It can happen, however, that the GMC itself nominates a candidate who has not been included by the Executive Committee.)

The structure of a constituency Labour party, which is more complex than that of a Conservative association, has a bearing on candidate selection. Individual members form into ward parties, while the affiliated membership, which is much more numerous, is represented to the extent that its union, cooperative party branch, or socialist educational association affiliates itself to the local party and pays dues on a declared number of members. The number of affiliates declared and

---

[24] Cf. *The Guardian*, July 29, and September 13, 1978.

paid for determines the size and voting strength of the union's delegation on the GMC, though normally an upward limit of five or six delegates per union branch is set. This limit is evaded where a union has more than one local branch, a loophole particularly relevant where the National Union of Mineworkers is concerned, since they consider each pit a separate branch.

Consequently a typical GMC will consist of about half a dozen officers, the secretaries of each ward committee, a women's section, and Young Socialist branches, together with delegates from all these according to their membership and delegates from the affiliated organizations. A party rule permits entitled organizations that have hitherto neglected to affiliate or have affiliated on a low membership to rectify such omissions when it is a question of selecting a parliamentary candidate. As a result, the size of a GMC is apt to expand remarkably on such occasions as these organizations affiliate on "backwoodsmen" to increase their vote on the selection conference. These conferences vary from 20 to as many as 120 members, and it is they that select the candidate.

The matter may be further complicated by the Labour party tradition of trade-union sponsored candidates. A sponsored candidate is financially attractive to a local Labour party, since the union will pay up to 80 percent of the candidate's election expenses. Such unions are most tenacious of any historic right to nominate the candidate. A union's nomination, which is drawn from the union headquarter's central list of such candidates, is made by its local executive committee— not by any special ballot of the affiliated members. While the weight of union votes is a factor in all selection conferences, in the trade-union sponsored constituencies it is decisive, and in many of them it reflects conflicts or alliances among the different union delegations.

Summing up, then: In the Conservative association a body averaging 110 persons makes the selection,[25] which is subject to veto (unlikely) by a general meeting. In the Labour constituency party, the selection conference, a group of between 20 and 120 persons, makes the decision.

These groups form the "selectorate"[26]; and *these selectorates effectively decide the nature of the parliamentary party, because, in the overwhelming majority of cases, nomination is tantamount to election. For the majority of parliamentary seats are safe: between 1955–1970,*

---

[25] Michael Rush, *The Selection of Parliamentary Candidates* (London: Nelson, 1969), p. 36. This gives the membership of executive councils in sixteen selected constituencies; their average membership, calculated by myself, is as above.

[26] The phrase was coined by Paterson, *The Selectorate*.

*470 seats (75 percent) of the 630 parliamentary seats remained in the
control of one party.*

One consequence, in the Labour party, is the encouragement of
that "entryism" by left-wing elements already noted. That this has had
some successes is undeniable: Prime Minister Callaghan himself declared, "There are too many of these people who have infiltrated this
party already. Get them out!"[27] His words were echoed the next day
by his predecessor, Sir Harold Wilson, who spoke of "an unrepresentative caucus" and of "the calculated actions of what we in Yorkshire
call 'comers-in'."[28] The most notorious of such cases was that of
Reg Prentice, a former Labour minister whose views had moved
increasingly to the right, and whose constituency party voted, twelve
to eight, to drop him as their candidate at the next general election. In
the subsequent struggle, the constituency party decision was confirmed
by the GMC after its left-wing members had been returned with increased majorities. This particular story had a mordant sequel, when
two Oxford graduate students in their turn infiltrated this local party
and proceeded to turn the tables by challenging its procedures in frequent appeals to the courts. The incident shows how easily such small
bodies can be infiltrated, whether by left or right.

Other moderate Labour M.P.s, such as Frank Tomney (Hammer-
smith North district) and Neville Sandelson (Hayes and Harlington
district) also found their readoption challenged by left-wing executive
committees; there has been a noticeable tendency for the constituencies to select left-wing candidates in recent by-elections.

The extent of this infiltration is questioned, however, some experienced academic observers thinking it exaggerated. One of them
has commented, for instance, that for the left-wing activists to try to
alter the balance of the parliamentary party by these one-shot efforts
would be a "sisyphaen task." This is certainly true, but would it remain true if the readoption of all sitting M.P.s were automatically
challenged by their parties instead of such M.P.s enjoying a presumption that they will be automatically readopted, as at present? If the rule
were so changed it would permit a concerted nationwide push from
left-wingers throughout the constituency parties. And, as will be seen
later, a sizable minority in the party is currently trying to change the
rule in this sense, and for this reason.

Smallness of Party Bureaucracy. The party bureaucracy is as large
nowadays as at any time in the past, but how small it is still can be

---

[27] *Times*, December 6, 1976.
[28] *Sunday Telegraph*, December 7, 1976.

discerned from Table 21. The constituency-level staff mentioned therein are the political agents. Britsh law requires each candidate to appoint an election agent. The agent is legally responsible for authorizing all expenditure on behalf of a candidate, and at the end of the campaign he must send a statement of election expenses to the election return officer. A candidate may act as his own election agent, and independent candidates sometimes do this, but more often they will secure the services of a sympathizer. But the two major parties have encouraged their constituency parties to appoint full-time agents; these are styled "political agents," for they also act as professional managers and organizers at the local level. Their presence or absence is widely regarded as an indicator of the efficiency of the local party machinery. Agents are (nearly always) paid by the local party, but they are trained and certified and, where relevant, promoted, by party headquarters. A recent study of Conservative agents[29] stresses their real independence of the Central Office. It also demonstrates that their role varies greatly. In some constituencies they play a formative part in the running of the association; in others they are little more than administrative assistants to the party chairman. In no way, however, can they be regarded as a bureaucracy that runs or controls the association by imposing choices on the activists. To the contrary; the Michels model of bureaucratic control of the rank and file is wholly inappropriate.

(Table 21 does not include the support staff—secretaries, messengers, and others—except in the Liberal party column. If the support staff were added in, the total personnel at Conservative headquarters would stand at about 200 instead of the 95 shown, and the Labour figures would have to be inflated accordingly. Even so, it will be seen that the total bureaucracy is a very small proportion of a party's membership.)

A Note on Eurocandidates

As a member of the EEC, Britain, like the other members, has sent M.P.s to the European Parliament. These M.P.s were selected by the parliamentary parties from among their own members—in other words they were indirectly elected. In 1979, throughout the member-states of the EEC, all were to be directly elected. In Britain these elections were set for June 7, 1979. The country is divided into eighty-one Euroconstituencies, each comprising about eight of the existing parliamentary

---

[29] Michael Pinto-Duschinsky, *The Limits of Professional Influence: a Study of Constituency Agents in the British Conservative Party*, mimeo, 1977.

TABLE 21

PERSONNEL EMPLOYED BY THE MAJOR POLITICAL PARTIES, 1963–1979

	Conservative			Labour			Liberal		
	1963	1974	1978/9	1963	1974	1978/9	1963	1974	1978/9
National level (Of whom: Re-	97	95	87	40	50	N.A.	15	16	17
search)	25	31	38	12	19	19	4	N.A.	N.A.
Regional level	60	41	N.A.	38	38	N.A.	10	6	N.A.
Constitu- ency level	520	390	350	208	120	77	64	16	N.A.
Total	677	526	N.A.	286	208	N.A.	89	38	N.A.

N.A.: Not available.
SOURCE: Rose, *Politics in England*; Rose, *The Problem of Party Government*. Also, private information.

constituencies. The electoral system is the same as the one used in British parliamentary elections, the first past the post system. The vexing question of whether a Euro-M.P. will also be able to sit as an M.P. in the British House of Commons (the so-called "dual mandate") has been left to the respective parties to decide. Labour has insisted on the single mandate; the Conservatives leave it to the constituencies to decide whether they are prepared to nominate a sitting M.P. as a Euro-candidate.

The selection process in both these parties differs somewhat from what we have described above.

Conservative Selection Methods. The Conservative party decided to contest the elections as a European party. Prospective candidates applied to party headquarters where a vice-chairman selected a list of some 200, although this did not preclude newcomers from applying to the constituency bodies. The candidates on the official list were asked which constituencies they wished to be considered for. They could list more than one choice, so they had to be rationed to no more than fifteen choices. The scene then moved to the Euroconstituencies themselves. In each constituency a council was established composed of six representatives for each parliamentary constituency in the Euroconstituency. London Central, for instance, comprises ten parliamentary constituencies. The council thus numbers sixty, and in turn has set up a selection committee composed of two members from each of the ten parliamentary constituencies. This committee eliminated forty of its sixty would-be candidates on the basis of their records and biographies and then, by a series of interviews, reduced the remainder to a list of six. Further interviews reduced this list to three. These appeared before a final selection conference consisting of twenty-five representatives from each of the ten constituencies.

Labour Selection Methods. The Labour party is deeply divided over the EEC, the left-dominated NEC being positively hostile to it. In each Euroconstituency, any would-be candidate must be nominated by a branch or affiliated oganization of one of the constituency Labour parties within the Euroconstituency. This follows Labour practice for parliamentary elections. Each constituency party received about eight nominations. Its selection conference then reduced the list to a maximum of three and sent the names of the Euro-Selection Organization, which consisted of twenty delegates from each local party. This was the body that interviewed candidates to make the final selection. The effect of this decentralized system was to permit the final selection of candidates who might either favor or oppose the EEC, according to the taste of the selection organization. Thus, in the Northeast London constituency, seventeen persons were nominated, and the five selected from this number all oppose the EEC. On the other hand, Earnest Wistrich, a leader of the movement that campaigned to bring Britain into the EEC has been selected in another Euroconstituency.

Changes in the Party Structures

In the period since the end of World War II the structure of both major parties has been marked by declines in membership, tightness of revenues, and relatively low levels of political activism.

Decline of Membership. The most striking change has been the decline in membership since the mid-1950s. In 1953 the Labour party claimed 6,096,000 members, of whom 5,057,000 were trade union affiliated members and 1,005,000 were individual members (34,000 were members of affiliated socialist societies). The figure for trade union membership is arbitrary, since it reflects the number of affiliation fees a union cares to pay to the party; as already noted, this may be higher or lower than the actual figures. Furthermore, although the law permits the non-Labour unionist to opt out of paying the political levy, many neglect to do so—possibly as many as 2,000,000—so that many trade union members are nominal members only.[30] A study made for 1964 showed that only 31 percent of trade unionists favored the unions' having close ties with the party. Unfortunately the study did not discriminate between trade unionists in unions affiliated to the Labour party and those in unions that are not. Third, the trade union membership overlaps with the individual membership, so there is some double counting. In the normal way it is sensible to regard only individual members as true members of the party. The figure of just over one million for 1953 is likely to be near the truth. At that time the minimum affiliation was based on 240 members, but since 1962 constituency parties must pay affiliation fees on at least 1,000 members, though few parties have anything like that figure. The party's official statistics for 1978 report 6,061,000 trade union affiliated members, but only 633,000 individual members. The last is greatly overstated, as explained above, and the Houghton Committee Report on Party Finance estimated that the average membership of a branch party was 500.[31] In that case, multiplying the figure by 623 (the number of branch parties), the membership in 1974 was a mere 311,500. Nor is this all: From the 1976 Annual Conference Report figures it appears that in 1975 more than half the individual membership was concentrated in a mere 100 local parties, which had an average membership of 1,691. In that case (working from Houghton's figures), the remaining 523 constituency parties must have only 142,324 members among them. This signifies that the average membership of these 523 constituencies was a mere 272!

The Conservative party is still far healthier, but it too has suffered a considerable decline in membership. It publishes no figures, but its claim to 2,805,832 members in 1953 is generally regarded as safe, if a little high, as it came in the wake of a membership drive. But according to the highly reliable statistics of the Houghton report,[32] the average membership of a constituency association in 1974 was 2,400.

---

[30] Martin Harrison, *Trade Unions and the Labour Party* (London: Allen and Unwin, 1960), p. 36. This figure relates, however, to the changeover from contracting in to contracting out in 1946–1947. How many are nominal members today is impossible to say. See also Butler and Stokes, *Political Change in Britain*, 1st ed., p. 169.

[31] *Report of the Committee* (Chairman, Lord Houghton) *on Financial Aid to Poltical Parties*, paragraph 5.11 (London: HMSO. cmd. 6601, 1976).

[32] Ibid., paragraph 5.10.

That figure, multiplied by the 623 constituencies, gives a round total of 1,500,000, which again is generally considered a fairly safe estimate. As in the Labour party, the Conservative party's youth movement is in decline: In the mid-1950s this was the largest youth movement in Britain. Current figures are unavailable, but no such boast could be—or is—made today.

There are no firm figures for the Liberal party in the earlier period, but from the Houghton report we can deduce that the membership in 1974 could not have been higher than 185,000. It is probably very much less.

Financial Decline? Parties require income, partly to maintain their national organization, partly to campaign in elections. The first, obviously, is a steady overhead, the second requires extraordinary one-shot efforts. Elections cost relatively little in Britain since a substantial proportion of the cost is borne by the state. At 1978 prices, the public items may be costed at approximately:

	£ million
Registration of voters (annually)	11
Free postal delivery of the candidates' election addresses to each voter	5
Administration of the poll	10
Free TV time for party political broadcasts	10
Total	36

The parties themselves must pay for two major items of election expenses. The first is their national publicity campaigns. In February 1974 the Conservatives spent £295,000, and in October 1974, £600,000; Labour spent, respectively, £430,000 and £600,000. (In 1979 prices these figures must be somewhat more than doubled.) Most went on advertising, broadcasting costs, and private polling. The law imposes no restriction on such expenditure, but does restrict the amount the local parties may spend on electioneering inside the statutory three-week campaign period. Most of the money goes on printing, stationery, and the hire of rooms. The statutory maximum was increased on July 30, 1978, and stands thus; for a county constituency, £1,750 plus 2p per elector, and for a town constituency £1,750 plus 1½p per elector. Broadly these sums would amount to £3,000 in the average county, and £2,750 in the average town constituency. In the past, parties have spent below these limits: In October 1974 the average Conservative candidate spent 79 percent, Labour 72 percent, and the Liberals 45 percent.

The sources of party income have not materially altered since 1945. Constituencies are expected to finance themselves, and in the Conservative case they make a substantial contribution to headquarters funds (one-third of the total), whereas constituency Labour party affiliation fees to headquarters are exiguous. Two-thirds of Conservative party headquarters income are donations from private companies, mostly small, but a few substantial. About one-third of this sum goes to the party indirectly through a "front" organization known as British United Industrialists, which is in effect a fundraising organization. In 1977–1978, the top nine contributors to the party contributed only £30,000–22,000 apiece, totaling some £200,000. The remaining £1 million came from some 800 firms, so that their average donation was only £1,250. By contrast, 89 percent of the Labour party's central income in 1977 came from trade union affiliation fees. The total political levy raised by the unions amounts to far more than the sum paid in annually to Labour party headquarters. Some of it goes to assist the regional agencies of the party, and much goes to the constituency Labour parties. Some is held in reserve and paid to the central headquarters ad hoc to finance its election campaign. The gross income from the entire political levy stood at nearly £3.35 million in 1977, whereas the sum paid in affiliation fees to Labour party headquarters was only £1,429,000. The sums raised by the top nine unions contrast formidably with the exiguous sums donated to the Conservatives by private enterprises. Thus, the TGWU raised £580,709 from its political levy, and the National Union of Public Employees, £486,036. The dues paid by trade unionists into their respective unions' political funds vary; in 1977 the lowest was 20p a year, the highest 80p. In 1980 the minimum is to rise to 32p a member, so that if this is multiplied by the six million or so affiliated members, the sum paid to Labour headquarters will rise from its present £1.27 million to no less than £1.85 million in 1980.[33] Table 22 shows the top Labour and top Conservative donors in 1977.

In 1974, however, runaway inflation and the financial depredations of the two general elections strained the parties' resources, and in this climate the new (Labour) government made available a small grant-in-aid to the parliamentary parties to assist their research activity. The grant is a maximum of £150,000 for any one party and is calculated on the formula of £500 for each parliamentary seat plus £1 for every 200 votes received. The Labour party, however, desired to subsidize the extraparliamentary organization also, and accordingly

---

[33] *Economist*, November 11, 1978, pp. 24–25.

TABLE 22

Top Labour and Top Conservative Donors, 1977

Top Labour Donors, 1977		Top Conservative Donors, 1977	
Union	Amount (£)	Company	Amount (£)
NUPE	387,968	Soc. of Metal	
TGWU	269,304	Mechanics	4,757
AUEW (Engineers)	265,983	Glaxo	25,000
GMWU	255,048	GKN	25,000
USDAW	114,669	THF	25,000
NUR	93,000	Brit. and Common-	
EETPU	73,733	wealth	23,545
Post Office Workers	66,687	Beechams	20,000
Construction, Allied		Cons. Gold	20,000
Trades	55,614	Rank Organization	20,000
APEX	47,642	RHM	20,000
ASTMS	45,382	Trafalgar House	20,000
COHSE	36,818	Inchcape	16,188
Iron and Steel Trades	35,842	Tate & Lyle	15,650
AUEW (Technical)	27,591	CT Bowring	15,545
Boilermakers	23,972	Fisons	15,000
AUEW (Foundry)	22,464	Taylor Woodrow	15,000
Tailors, Garment		Willis Faber	15,000
Workers	19,925	Lucas Inds.	13,000
Footwear and Allied	17,572	Littlewoods	10,570
SOGAT	16,852	Hambros	10,150
Dyers and Bleachers	14,305	Baring Bros.	10,050
Furniture and Timber	12,706	Bond Worth	10,000
ASLEF	13,303	Bowater	10,000
National Graphical	10,870	Cadbury Sch.	10,000
Bakers	10,455	Euroferries	10,000
Fire Brigades	10,201	Hill Samuel	10,000
Seamen	6,858	Kleinwort Benson	10,000
Colliery Overmen	6,004	S. Pearson	10,000
		Sun Life	10,000
		Tarmac	10,000

NOTE: Returns from National Union of Mineworkers unavailable.

ABBREVIATIONS: APEX, Association of Professional, Executive, Clerical and Computer Staff; ASLEF, Associated Society of Locomotive Engineers and Firemen; ASTMS, Association of Scientific, Technical and Managerial Staffs; AUEW, Amalgamated Union of Engineering Workers; COHSE, Confederation of Health Service Employees; EETPU, Electrical, Electronic, Telecommunications and Plumbing Union; GMWU, General and Municipal Workers' Union; NUPE, National Union of Public Employees; NUR, National Union of Railwaymen; SOGAT, Society of Graphical and Allied Trades; TGWU, Transport and General Workers' Union; USDAW, Union of Shop, Distributive and Allied Workers.

SOURCE: Labour Research Department and Conservative Research Department.

TABLE 23

LABOUR INCOME 1957, 1974, AND 1978

(pounds)

	1957, at 1957 Prices	1957, at 1975 Prices	1974, at 1975 Prices	1978,[a] at 1978 Prices	1978,[a] at 1975 Prices
Central income	235,000	634,000	1,200,000	1,750,000	1,200,000
Constituency income	450,000	1,215,000	1,750,000	1,850,000	1,250,000
Total income	685,000	1,849,500	2,950,000	3,600,000	2,450,000

[a] Estimated.

SOURCE: For 1957, Harrison, p. 99. For 1978, the estimate of the party treasurer, *Tribune*, January 12, 1979.

in 1974 the government established a Committee on Financial Aid to Political Parties under the chairmanship of Lord Houghton, a former chairman of the parliamentary Labour party. This committee reported in 1976[34] in favor of state subsidy, with a dissenting minority of two journalists, one SNP member, and one Conservative member. Although the Labour party (though not some trade unions) and the Liberal party (albeit not the Scottish liberals), approved the report, the recommendation was rejected by the SNP, the Communist party, and above all the Conservatives, and no action was taken.

The premises on which the proposal rested were first that "parties were the mainsprings of all the processes of democracy,"[35] and second, a near-panic view that the parties did not have enough money to carry out this essential political function and because of inflation would have still less in the future.

The committee's estimates of national and local income for 1974 suggest why the Conservatives rejected the recommendation whereas the Labour party enthusiastically endorsed it. And a comparison of these figures with an estimate of Labour income in 1957, as shown in Table 23, will throw light on whether or not it is true, as Houghton claimed, that the Labour party, at any rate, was in a financial crisis.

The Labour party was certainly poorer than the Conservative party, which had more than double the income of the Labour party.

[34] Houghton, Report of the Committee on Financial Aid to Political Parties.
[35] Ibid., p. 53.

TABLE 24

Estimated Income of Political Parties, 1974 (at 1975 Prices)
(pounds)

Party	Central Income	Constituencies Income	Total Income
Conservative	1,790,000	4,500,000	6,290,000
Labour	1,200,000	1,750,000	2,950,000
Liberal[a]	113,000	750,000	863,000

[a] The Liberal figures are lower than they ought to be; it is now clear that special funds held at headquarters were not included in the total. Pinto-Duschinsky's estimates in The *Economist*, November 11, 1978, for the average incomes of the two major parties in 1975–1977, do not significantly vary from the estimates above.
Source: Houghton, Report of the Committee on Financial Aid to Political Parties, p. 41.

But a glance at Table 24 shows that the discrepancy in headquarters income was not very large at all. The difference between the two parties lies in the much higher constituency income of the Conservative party; it was two-and-one-half times larger than Labour's. This reflects the smaller size and the general atrophy of the Labour grass-roots organization. The Houghton recommendation was, we may surmise, rejected by the Conservatives and adopted by Labour because the Conservatives have thriving local associations and Labour wished for public funds to make good its failure at the grass roots. That much was virtually admitted by the party treasurer (Norman Atkinson), a left-winger, in January 1979.[36]

Is the Labour party in financial crisis, then? Are its funds significantly less than in the past? Is it likely they will be significantly less in the future? Table 23 compares Labour income in 1957 with income today, calculated in 1975 prices, along with an estimate for 1978. Thus, in 1978 the party was somewhat better off than it was in 1957. The improvement is much more marked in respect of central income than constituency income. By 1974 central income was double that of 1957 in real purchasing power, and the improvement was maintained. It reflects the unions' decision to raise their affiliation fees. Note, however, the continued dereliction of the constituency parties. Between 1957 and 1974 they managed to increase their real income by about 30 percent; then it fell back, in real terms, to the 1957 figure.

[36] Norman Atkinson, "Should the Labour Party Go for State Aid?" *Tribune*, January 12, 1979.

In the future Labour's central income will grow because of the unions' decision to raise affiliation fees in 1980. The outlook for the constituency parties remains bleak.

For all that, the general conclusion would have to be that the parties have larger incomes than in 1957. It does not follow, however, that they have no financial problems. Though they can support a general election as well or even better at these financial levels than in the past, the year 1979 witnessed a spate of novel popular soundings. On March 1, 1979 referendums were held in Wales and in Scotland on the question of whether the respective electorates wished to have a local assembly. In addition, on June 7, 1979, the parties contested the eighty-one Euroconstituencies. Taking into account the general election and the local government elections, they were faced with as many as six election campaigns in all.

Low Level of Activism. Only a small proportion of the public pursues any political activity apart from voting. Only one in five helped on recruiting drives and fund raising, only 15 percent was elected to party office and a mere 3 percent took part in an election campaign.[37]

The weakness of the constituency Labour parties as contrasted with the Conservative associations, already attested to by their numbers and their poverty, is confirmed yet again by survey material. Conservative supporters were somewhat more likely to vote than their Labour counterparts, they were twice as active in fund raising, in their likelihood of serving as officers, and in their speaking publicly; and they were nearly twice as active in campaigning.[38]

"Lateral" Tensions in the Parties: Tendencies and Factions

Where only two major parties incorporate four-fifths (and often, many more) of the voting population, it is to be expected that a wide spectrum of opinion is to be found in either. The Conservative parliamentary party is best described as a party of "tendencies," where a *"tendency"* signifies a "cluster of attitudes . . . about a broad range of problems" and where the adherents "vary from issue to issue . . . and . . . are not self-consciously organized in support of a single policy and do not expect . . . to continue as a group supporting the tendency for a long period of time."[39] By contrast, the Labour party

---

[37] Robert Worcester, "The Hidden Activists," in Richard Rose, *Studies in British Politics* (London: Macmillan, 1976), pp. 198–203.

[38] Ibid.

[39] Rose, *Studies in British Politics*, p. 314.

inside and outside Parliament is a party of factions, where a *"faction"* means an organized, enduring group that takes a common stand on a range of issues.

Among the Conservatives some attitudes are, for all that, organized into groups. The Bow Group, founded in 1951, is largely a research organization with its main centers in London, Birmingham, and Manchester. It publishes a monthly, *Crossbow*. The Bow Group began as a distinctly reformist group on the center-left of the party. Today it is center-right; it is a full-blooded proponent of monetarism and an equally vigorous opponent of proportional representation.

The Bow Group's position on the left of the party has been partly filled by two other organizations, PEST (Pressure for Economic and Social Toryism, 1963–1975) and the Tory Reform Group, which has replaced it. The Bow Group had forty-six M.P.s as members in the 1974 Parliament, while PEST had forty-one. These groups are mostly university based.

In contrast, the Monday Club comprises some 10,000 members in thirty local branches. This is a toughminded group. It is, for instance, hostile to non-white immigration and shows sympathy toward Rhodesia and South Africa. It was established in 1961 to counter the Bow Group. It had sixteen M.P.s in the February 1974 Parliament and fourteen in the 1975–1978 Parliament. On the whole, all these groups play to empty houses. Conservative M.P.s are not very interested in ideologies; their aim is power. The most significant cleavage inside the Conservative parliamentary party has been the cleavage between the group that gathered around Margaret Thatcher, and the supporters (like Peter Walker) of the deposed leader, Edward Heath. Significantly, neither Heath nor Walker served in Thatcher's shadow cabinet. They stood for a consensus policy: power-sharing in Ulster, devolution for Scotland, economic interventionism, and an incomes policy. By contrast Margaret Thatcher's team threatened a tougher attitude toward terrorists in Ulster, opposed Scottish devolution, and instead of incomes policy put its faith in rigorous monetarism. It seemed to be falling back on a traditional Conservative role as the "English" party—implicitly casting the Labour party as the party of the ethnic minorities, which among other things, it certainly is. In opposition the parliamentary party rallied around Thatcher, if only because an election was imminent. But the strains in the party were evident in a recent vote in November 1978, on which the shadow cabinet recommended that the party abstain in a Commons vote on the renewal of sanctions against Rhodesia. Half the party defied the recommendation, voting to lift sanctions. Paradoxically, this was the right-wing group, the same group that replaced Heath with Thatcher.[40]

The smashing Conservative victory of 1979 temporarily eased these strains. For one thing, a parliamentary party rallies naturally to a leader who has led it out of defeat into resounding success. For another—with one marked and poignant exception—Margaret Thatcher, the new Prime Minister, selected a cabinet broadly representative of the entire parliamentary party. The great exception was Edward Heath himself; no offer was made to him, and he sits on the backbenches.

In contrast, the Labour party has always been a party of organized factions: Left-wing socialists, some of them quasi-Marxists, line up against the center and the right of the parliamentary party. Such a self-division has existed ever since the 1920s, when the left was represented by, among others, the Independent Labour party. In the postwar period, 1946 saw the founding in the parliamentary party of the Keep Left Group, numbering some twenty M.P.s. Its successor was a loosely knit faction clustering around the personality of Aneuran Bevan after his resignation from the cabinet in 1951. During the period 1955–1959, the combined "lefts" in Parliament had anywhere from fifty to ninety members, depending on the issues.[41] When Bevan returned to join the leadership in 1957, Ian Mikardo, founder of the Keep Left Group, persevered on his leftist course, taking over in 1958 a group that had been founded in 1944 and that called itself Victory for Socialism. Mikardo tried to extend its influence into the extraparliamentary party by founding fourteen local branches, an Annual Conference, and an Executive Committee. This is counter to the party constitution, and the NEC suppressed them. In 1964 the group broke up, and in 1966 the Tribune Group emerged as the chief left-wing faction. Its name comes from a neo-Marxist weekly that had been founded in 1937 by Sir Stafford Cripps and George Strauss. This paper, which still publishes, gives the group an informal but effective focus. In the late 1960s there were about forty Tribunite M.P.s. In the 1970–1974 Parliament they had increased to sixty-nine, and in the 1975–1978 Parliament they claimed seventy-seven M.P.s. This was one-third of the parliamentary backbenchers.

Following the party's defeat in 1970, this faction and its non-

---

[40] Cf. Trevor Russell, *The Tory Party, its Policies, Divisions and its Future* (London: Penguin, 1978). Russell writes as a former Labour activist and is currently a new member of the Tory Reform Group. The hero is Edward Heath, and from Russell's highly polemical standpoint he exaggerates the difference between the two tendencies.

[41] Hugh Bayard Berrington, *Backbench Opinion in the House of Commons, 1945–1955* (Oxford: Pergamon, 1973).

Tribunite supporters in the party—among whom the minister for energy, Tony Benn, must be reckoned the most influential—attained an unprecedented grip on the party organization. It was able to do so because of the changed political complexion of the party's Annual Conference (the body that votes the party program and elects the National Executive Committee).

This change in the political climate of the conference was brought about in turn by the leftward shift of the big battalions, the larger trade unions. The giant TGWU, with one million votes (roughly one-sixth of the conference total) had started to move to the left in 1956 when Frank Cousins became its general secretary, but this viewpoint was pressed with greater constancy after Jack Jones became general secretary in 1968. In that year also, the Amalgamated Union of Engineers, with some 800,000 votes, elected Hugh Scanlon, another left-winger, as its secretary. Furthermore, some other traditionally left-wing unions, like the National Union of Public Employees (whose leftist general secretary, Alan Fisher, was also elected in 1968), expanded in this period from 150,000 to 400,000. At the same time some previously right-wing and politically torpid unions, like the large (650,000 votes) General and Municipal Workers Union, which elected the lively and energetic David Basnett as its secretary in 1972, moved from the right to the center and became an altogether less predictable support for the center and right of the parliamentary party. Finally a general revulsion against the tepidity and the sterility of the Wilson government policies, 1966–1970, generated a propulsion toward more full-blooded socialism.

One effect was to swing the NEC to the far left. The radicalized unions replaced retiring trade union representatives on the NEC with leftist successors. Similarly, they voted leftists onto the women's section of the NEC. In 1964 there was one leftist trade unionist on the NEC, and there were eleven right-wingers. By 1974 the proportion had shifted to four left-wingers to eight right-wingers. In 1964 there was one left-wing women's representative to four right-wingers; by 1974 that proportion was exactly reversed. Taking the entire NEC together, in 1964 there were eight-left-wingers and twenty right-wingers; in 1974 there were fifteen left-wingers and only fourteen right-wingers. This leftward shift has continued; after the conference elections of 1978 the NEC was composed of eighteen left-wingers and eleven right-wingers.

The leftward shift of the conference and the NEC led to the adoption of socialist programs, such as *Labour's Programme 1973* (which became the foundation for the party manifesto of 1974) and

TABLE 25

How the Labour Party's NEC Moved to the Left, 1964–1978

Sector (total representatives)	1964		1974		1978	
	Left	Right	Left	Right	Left	Right
Constituency parties (7)	6	1	6	1	7	0
Women's section (5)	1	4	4	1	4	1
Trade union section (12)	1	11	4	8	3	9
Treasurer (1)	0	1	0	1	1	0
Socialist associations (1)	0	1	0	1	1	0
Young Socialist (1)	0	0	1	0	1	0
Leader (1)	0	1	0	1	0	1
Deputy leader (1)	0	1	0	1	1	0
Subtotal	8	20	15	14	18	11
Total	28		29		29	

the still more radical *Labour's Programme 1976*. Until 1968 the center and right of the parliamentary party could safely rely on support from the trade union votes. Now that group feels threatened, for instance, by the movement to permit constituency Labour parties to disown their incumbent M.P.s, which it thinks will lead these parties to replace them with left-wingers. It is also concerned with entryism (the insinuation of far-left elements in these small local parties), particularly by the Militant Group. The Militant Group claims no individual membership, having instead readership groups clustered around the *Militant*, a paper founded in 1964. Overtly Marxist and at variance with almost every point of the official party program since 1970, this faction has dominated the Labour Party Young Socialists. In 1972 it scored a signal success when the party decided to coopt a representative of the Young Socialists onto the NEC. The center and right were also alarmed when the party recently appointed Andy Bevan, a known Trotskyist, as the chairman of the Young Socialists. They were further alarmed at the NEC's endorsement of Jimmy Reid, a recent defector from the Communist party, as parliamentary candidate for a Scottish constituency.

In reaction, the moderates formed a parliamentary faction called the Manifesto Group. In 1974 it claimed some ninety members as opposed to the Tribune Group's seventy-seven. The Manifesto Group also has a grass-roots organization called the Campaign for Labour Victory. Founded in 1977, it argues that the root causes of leftist successes are the general decline of party membership, the apathy of the constituency parties, and the ramshackle central organization of the party. Its remedy for the decline of membership is to encourage recruitment. To cure the apathy problem the group proposes that the local constituency parties should cease to be bodies of delegates and become general membership bodies instead. The group, as a method of reducing left-wing influence, also proposes that parliamentary candidates should be selected by the entire membership and not by the executive committees and general management committees as at present. It considers the conference to be dominated by the trade unions' block votes, and seeks instead a larger voice for the constituency representatives. It holds the NEC in contempt, finding it too short on organization and too long on policy. The "Campaign's" ideology is in the revisionist social-democratic tradition of the early 1960s: practical policies to establish social justice, not "narrow ideological class-politics."[42]

At the beginning of 1979, an election year, the left had, apparently, established a commanding position in the extraparliamentary party. It had a two-to-one majority on the NEC. The larger unions had almost without exception rebuffed the Prime Minister's efforts to get the conference to accept his government's policy of a restriction of wage increases to 5 percent. They were supported in this by perhaps one-third of the parliamentary party also. And we have already seen how the NEC issued a stream of policy documents that contested on nearly every major point those policies the government was trying to pursue.

We have seen that the left-wing NEC did not get its way over the contents of the 1979 party manifesto. In the ensuing election, the party's share of the national vote fell to its lowest level since its historic catastrophe in 1931 and within six weeks a civil war had begun. Over the opposition of the former Prime Minister the NEC passed a resolution, stating that in future the NEC should draw up and have the final say on the party manifesto. Such authority would, of course, require a change in the party's constitution. Over the strenuous opposition of James Callaghan, the party conference carried a resolution to this effect in October 1979.

This was not the only act of the NEC. In addition, it waived the rule under which a proposal voted on at the conference may not be redebated for another three years. This move reopened two explosively controversial matters that had been voted down in the 1978

---

[42] *Times*, October 1, 1977.

conference. These proposals were (1) that the party leader should no longer be elected solely by the parliamentary party in the Commons but by either the Annual Conference or a special college; and (2) that there should be no automatic presumption that a sitting M.P. should be renominated as the candidate at the next election but that instead he should automatically compete with other nominations for the candidature within two or three years of his original election. These last points are taken up in the following section.

Vertical Tensions: Grass-Roots Militants vs. the Parliamentary Parties

Just as the Conservative party is a party of tendencies and the Labour party is a party of factions, so there is at present little tension between the Conservative constituency associations and the parliamentary leadership, while this is a perennial theme of Labour's internal politics. In 1969 the Greater London Young Conservatives published a pamphlet, *Set the Party Free*, which advocated that the chief officers of the Central Office should in the future be appointed by the National Union (the mass-membership organization) rather than by the leader; that the debates at the conference should be less stage-managed; and that the parliamentary party itself (rather than the leader) should appoint the party whips and elect the shadow cabinet (as indeed is the practice in the parliamentary Labour party). The suggestions were duly considered by a special party committee in 1970, but no action was taken and there has been no attempt to revive the argument.

In the Labour party, by contrast, the intermittent tension between grass-roots militancy and the parliamentary party reemerged strongly after 1976. Many hold that the NEC is unrepresentative. Unfortunately, the source of its unrepresentativeness differs according to the critic.

The women's section of five NEC seats is frequently a target. The section was created in 1918 when the election of women to public office was very daring. (Women did not receive the vote until that same year, and even then they had to be over thirty years of age to vote!) In 1968 the Labour party's Simpson Committee on party structure[43] recommended that the women's sector be abolished and its five seats divided, three to the unions and two to the constituency parties. The Transport Workers and the Engineers, both under left-wing influence at the time, even suggested that all five seats should

---

[43] *Report of the Committee of Inquiry into party organization*, 1968.

go to the constituency parties, because, one must suppose, the constituency parties were also predominantly left-wing at that time. On the other hand, inside the NEC the right-wing Miners and the General and Municipal Workers opposed the change, presumably for the same sort of ideological reason.[44] Abolition of the women's section is also urged in a Fabian tract of 1977, but this time as part of a wider reconstruction of the NEC.[45] The author would like the trade union panel to be reduced from twelve to nine seats, the constituency party panel reduced from seven to five seats, and the women's section abolished altogether. Instead, there should be one woman, as ex officio representative of the Conference of Labour Women, three representatives of the parliamentary Labour party, and eleven members elected at regional conferences. This new NEC would total thirty-five members instead of the present twenty-nine. The union block vote would be abolished; instead, voting cards would be issued to each individual member of the union's delegation.

The conference has not discussed these proposals, but significantly, before the 1977 conference met the General and Municipal Workers Union was also reportedly dissatisfied with the NEC's make-up, though in the opposite sense. This union, too, questioned the representation of women as such, but it also thought that the unions, far from having too much say on the NEC with their twelve seats, had too little in view of the fact that they put up almost all the cash.[46] In any event the union did not move its motion at that conference or subsequent ones. (Many other unions were reportedly anxious to initiate yet another inquiry into party organization as a whole.)

Since 1976 two resolutions have been introduced and debated in conference that would have powerfully strengthened the often tenuous and sometimes nonexistent hold of the conference over the parliamentary party. The first related to the way the party leader is elected and the second to the custom of readopting sitting M.P.s for their constituencies.

There is no such constitutional office as leader of the Labour party. There is the elected leader of the parliamentary party, who by custom has always been regarded as the leader of the entire party. Yet, as must be very clear by now, the NEC might more justly claim this title and indeed vociferously rivals the authority of the parliamentary leader. Constituency party delegates at the conference opened

[44] Minkin, *The Labour Party Conference*, pp. 256–57.
[45] D. Hayter, *The Labour Party: Crisis and Prospects* (Fabian Tract 451, 1977).
[46] *Guardian*, June 6, 1977.

this question in 1976, demanding that the NEC set up a committee to "define the office of Leader of the Labour Party," to "report within one year on the procedures for leadership elections," and to be "especially charged to consider appropriate means of *widening* the *electorate* involved in the choice of the Leader."[47] The proponents claimed a concern for party democracy, but underlying this concern lies the belief that if the conference or some kind of electoral college elected the leader, this could only increase the chances that he would be well to the left of the past and present leaders.[48]

When in 1977 the appointed committee duly reported to the conference, it put up three choices. Either the party could maintain its current practice, or the conference as a whole might elect the leader (much as it does the party treasurer), or an electoral college might choose the leader. This electoral college would consist of the parliamentary party, all endorsed parliamentary candidates, every constituency Labour party (each with one vote), and 500 representatives of the affiliated organizations divided according to the size of their memberships and having at least one vote apiece.

The committee sought the views of party organizations and received 11 replies from affiliated organizations and another 125 from constituency parties, as well as from the parliamentary Labour party as such. The parliamentary party put up five separate arguments for retaining the status quo, not one of which it must be said is intellectually convincing.[49] Of the eleven affiliated organizations that replied, nine favored the status quo. One preferred the vote to go to the conference. Among the 125 constituency parties, 45 preferred the status quo (nine of whom attached some conditions, however). Twenty chose voting by the conference in some shape or form. The remaining replies split: 11 favored the proposed electoral college, 15 wanted the choice to be confined to the constituency parties, another 18 wanted it to be opened to the entire individual membership.[50] When this report was debated in 1978, the conference voted to retain the status quo.

The second matter—the readoption of sitting M.P.s, also debated at the 1978 conference—was much more controversial.

We have already seen that a few individual constituency parties

---

[47] *Labour Party Annual Conference Report*, 1976, p. 212.

[48] For an eloquent plea for widening the election, see Ken Coates, *Democracy in the Labour Party* (Nottingham: Spokesman, 1977). It also offers convincing testimony to the *sous-entendre* stated in the text.

[49] See, for instance, Roy Gregory, "Choosing the Labour Party Leader," *The Times*, July 13, 1977. Cf. also Coates, *Democracy in the Labour Party*.

[50] *Labour Party Annual Conference Report*, 1977, pp. 380–81.

have become dominated by left-wing elements and that in some cases these have challenged the sitting M.P.'s right to be adopted as a candidate for the next general election. A sitting M.P. has no legal right to expect this, of course. To the contrary, the local party has both the moral and the legal right to refuse to readopt him and to select somebody else. It has been customary, however, that sitting M.P.s should be automatically readopted for the next election until they expressed a wish to retire, unless the local party had some serious grievance, such as an M.P.'s neglect of his constituents. The challenges we reported earlier, however, were ideological cases of left-wing general management committees out of tune with M.P.s whom they regarded as altogether too moderate. Altering these one by one would be far too slow a process to bring about a radical shift in the political complexion of the parliamentary party. On the other hand, if the custom were set aside for a new rule that sitting M.P.s must automatically seek renomination along with other prospective candidates, the way would be open for a nationwide challenge.

A left-wing Labour faction calling itself the Campaign for Labour Democracy (founded in 1973) seems to have been responsible for orchestrating sixty-seven resolutions from constituency Labour parties at the 1976 Labour conference. They requested a change in the party's constitution; specifically,

> the sitting Member of Parliament shall automatically be placed in the short list drawn up by his or her *constituency organization for selection conference* unless he or she wishes to withdraw from consideration, the selection conference to be held not later than forty-two months after the date of the last election. The General (Management) Committee may at any time intimate by resolution its desire that a specially convened conference take place in order that its candidate or MP may face re-selection.[51]

The NEC had the conference remit this resolution on the promise that at the next conference it would put down amendments to the constitution that would "provide automatic re-selection *in the way and in the sense* that the sponsors of those 60-odd resolutions want."[52]

This undertaking enormously agitated the M.P.s. Joseph Ashton, M.P., proclaimed that it would lead to the disintegration of the parliamentary party. If an M.P. was told he would not be reselected, why, he asked, should that M.P. continue to take the party whip? Again;

---

[51] Ibid., p. 324.
[52] Ibid.

in order to qualify for the redundancy payment (equivalent to a quarter-year's salary), a sitting M.P. must fight and lose an election. He would not qualify if he tamely withdrew after being refused re-selection by his local party. Hence, predicted Ashton, he would fight the constituency as an independent Labour candidate, split the Labour vote, and possibly lose Labour the seat.[53] The plausibility or im-plausibility of these predictions was irrelevant compared to the ideo-logical implications of the move and to the intention (and the very real possibility) of subordinating the parliamentary party to the con-stituency activists. It is essential to note the exact wording of the resolution quoted above; the italicized phrase made it quite clear that the power to disown the sitting M.P. was not to reside in the general membership of the local party, let alone in the party voters, but in the tiny and often unrepresentative general management committees. This point was made brutally clear at the 1977 conference, by Shonfield, a moving spirit in the campaign and the prospective candidate for Kensington. The resolution, he stated, was "about the way we control our M.P.s"; the left-wing Mikardo, leader of the Tribune Group and a member of the NEC, declared for his part that Labour party democ-racy was more than a counting of heads: "It is the democracy of the committed, of the ones that really do the work."[54] And in televised interviews the proponents tenaciously resisted the suggestion that the selection should be extended beyond the general management com-mittees: *they* were active. They *were* in some special sense the party.

The implications of this view are vividly illustrated by an un-usually caustic leading article in *The Guardian*.

> There are 60,000 voters in Kensington. The number of people likely to be involved in the re-selection process in Kensing-ton is unlikely to exceed 100. So that "we" in Mr. Shonfield's formulation . . . still leaves the vast majority of us out. The "we" who would control the MP would amount perhaps to 0.2% of the electors. . . . If the Campaign for Labour Democ-racy was really interested in representative democracy rather than in selective democracy of a particularly narrow kind, it would link these demands with a campaign to open up the selection process to a much wider party constituency. Its failure to do so gives the whole game away.[55]

At the 1978 conference, the NEC broke its promise. Put forward was a compromise: the general management committee of a local

---

[53] *Guardian*, March 3, 1978.
[54] *Guardian*, October 7, 1977.
[55] *Guardian*, October 7, 1977.

party would have the opportunity to decide whether or not it wished to adopt its sitting member as the prospective candidate, and if it did, that would be the end of the matter. Only if it decided to the contrary would a selection conference be set up, and in this the sitting M.P. would automatically be considered. Furthermore, in order to limit entryism, those entitled to attend and vote must have been members of that party for at least twelve months and must have attended at least one meeting of the general management committee in the previous year. The proponents of the original resolution insisted on it. "It would if carried, make M.P.s more accountable to the party and therefore increase the chances of the policies decided upon by conference being carried out in Parliament."[56] The matter hung in the balance, since it was known that the giant Transport Workers' delegation was thinking of supporting the original scheme and the almost equally large Engineers' delegation had been mandated to vote for it. When the matter was put to the vote, however, the original proposal was rejected by 3,066,000 votes to 2,672,000.[57] The next day it was discovered that Hugh Scanlon, leading the Engineers' delegation, had somehow failed to throw his union's block vote for that proposal. That vote was 800,000 strong, and had it been cast, the original proposal would have carried. Furious attempts to take the vote over again were ruled out of order by the conference chairman. The narrowness of the voting meant that the matter could not fail to be raised again.

The three-year rule would ordinarily have precluded immediate resumption of the debate, but the mood of the party after its shattering 1979 defeat was not ordinary. In July 1979, therefore, the NEC ruled to waive the three-year rule and so ensured that both the automatic reselection of M.P.s and the method of electing the party leader would be discussed by the party conference in September 1979. At the same time a dispute arose over the matter of party organization. David Basnett of the General and Municipal Workers once again pressed his previous demand for an inquiry, but the NEC retorted that this was unnecessary because its own organization committee was already studying the question. It seems that this interchange concealed a sharp divergence between the intentions of the two factions. The NEC suspected the General and Municipal Workers of wanting to strengthen trade union representation in the conference and in the NEC; for its part the union believed that the organization committee wished to allow a card vote for each 250 individual members as com-

---

[56] *Times*, October 4, 1978.
[57] *Times*, October 4, 1978.

TABLE 26

LENGTH OF PARTY MANIFESTOES, 1922–1979

(number of pages)

Years	Conservative	Labour	Liberal
1922–1935	4.5	3.75	4.5
1945–1959	11	6.5	4.5
1964–1974	19.5	18.5	10
1979	13.5	15	12

pared with the present figure of 1,000—that, in short, the voting strength of the constituency parties should be quadrupled. At the 1979 Annual Conference, the delegates finally agreed to the automatic reselection of M.P.s, and at the same time an inquiry into party organization was authorized also.

Manifesto and Mandate: the Degradation of the Democratic Dogma

Each party fights the election on a manifesto. This document justifies the party record in government or opposition as the case may be and lists what it proposes to do in the event of winning. It is important therefore as the list of commitments which the party espouses, which indicates to the candidates what they must *not* promise, and which the party expects to be judged on at the next election. Since 1945, and indeed from a much earlier period, the manifestoes have become longer, more specific, and, over recent years at least, unrepresentative.

Length. F.W.S. Craig has each document printed in a volume with a standard page format.[58] Hence, the number of pages of each document can be taken as a comparable unit of measurement.

Specificity. The number of specific commitments in the manifestoes rose in the Conservative case from a mere 3 in 1900 to 17 in 1924, to 87 in October 1974 and 74 in 1979. Labour made no less than 12 specific commitments at its very birth in 1900, but this number rose to 72 in the October 1974 manifesto, and in the 1979 manifesto soared to 133.

---

[58] F.W.S. Craig, *British General Election Manifestoes 1900–1974* (London: Macmillan, 1976).

Unrepresentativeness. The commitments made in the manifestoes are unrepresentative of many party identifiers and even more unrepresentative of the voters at large. On balance, Conservative manifestoes correspond to their supporters' preferences much better than do the Labour manifestoes. Rose[59] has demonstrated this for the Labour and Conservative manifestoes of 1970. On only one of eighteen major comparable issues did the two parties agree; in short the manifestoes represented antipodal policies. Where survey data permit comparison between the Conservative manifesto and Conservative voter preferences, twelve policies were supported by a majority of the voters. In two more cases they were supported by a plurality of the voters. Only in one case (the introduction of local commercial radio) did a majority of Conservative voters oppose. This manifesto was, therefore, in fairly close correspondence with party voters' views.

Not so with the Labour manifesto. On no less than seven issues, including vital items such as the proposal to extend trade union privileges, to increase public expenditure and cut no taxes, and to extend more welfare benefits, the majority of Labour voters opposed their party's manifesto. On only four items did a majority of them support it. For the election of February 1974, Table 27 strikingly shows the extent of opposition to some of Labour's key policies.

By implication the table also shows how unpopular nationally were many of Labour's policies: indeed all but the Common Market commitment and the proposal to increase pensions, which was a valence issue between both main parties, were rejected by substantial margins, over a period for most of which Labour was the governing party. Thus, those favoring tax cuts *rose* from 52 percent in 1963 to 65 percent in 1970, while those favoring increased spending on the social services fell from 41 percent to 27 percent, yet the Labour government continued to pursue its high taxation, high expenditure policies. Again, on nationalization, those demanding no further nationalization plus those demanding denationalization, combined, totaled 58 percent in 1963 and persisted at something like this level, reaching 69 percent in 1970, yet Labour nationalized the steel industry during this period.[60]

Although a similar exercise can be carried out for the 1979 election, the range of comparable issues is smaller than in the previous examples. Out of nine questions on which the two major parties took opposite sides (either explicitly in their manifestoes or implicitly in other ways) each party attracted a majority of its own supporters for

---

[59] Rose, *Problem of Party Government*, pp. 308–309.

[60] Butler and Stokes, *Political Change in Britain*, 2nd ed., pp. 459, 461.

TABLE 27

ELECTORAL SUPPORT FOR KEY LABOUR POLICIES, 1974

Policy	All	Labour	Conservative
Renegotiate terms of entry to Common Market	60	76	46
More nationalization	20	37	7
Nationalize North Sea oil and gas	41	58	28
Nationalize land	27	44	13
No restriction on supplementary benefit to strikers	41	60	26
Abolish Industrial Relations Act	39	55	23
Repeal Housing Finance Act	32	48	16
Raise pensions	94	97	91
Abolish Phase 3 controls on incomes	38	58	19

SOURCE: David Butler and Dennis Kavanagh, *The British General Election of February 1974* (London: Macmillan, 1974).

its own views on five. These were: whether to regulate trade union actions by stricter laws (Conservative) or by voluntary cooperation (Labour); whether to stop social security payments to strikers (not a specific Conservative pledge but widely believed to be their intention) or to leave things as they were (Labour); whether to put trade unionists on the directing boards of private companies (Labour); whether to levy a wealth tax (Labour); and whether to retain the existing powers of the House of Lords (Conservative) or drastically curtail them (Labour). On one of these nine questions, Conservative policy was accepted by only a minority of its supporters. That question was whether the National Enterprise Board should help finance private industry; the Conservative manifesto said no; the Labour manifesto pledged support. On three questions, only a minority of Labour supporters favored Labour policy. The Conservative proposal to ban secondary picketing by strikers was supported by 83.4 percent of Labour voters and opposed by only 16.6 percent. The Conservative proposal to allow the Commons a free vote on whether to restore the death penalty was supported by 87.6 percent of Labour voters and opposed by only 12.4 percent. And, finally, the Conservative proposal to initiate mass sales of council houses to sitting tenants was endorsed by 69 percent of Labour supporters, with only 31 percent opposed. On the whole, Conservative policies obtained wider popular support than did Labour policies, as shown in Table 28.

Manifestoes and the doctrine of the mandate. The discrepancy between a party's manifesto commitments and the popularity of such commitments even among its own voters makes no difference to the view, held to some extent by the Conservatives but very firmly by the Labour party, that, if elected, it is not only the party's right but its duty to carry out the manifesto to the letter. Not to do so in either party gravely embarrasses the party leaders, provoking as it does cries of treachery from the party's militants and charges of deceit from its opponents. Conversely, to have carried out all the manifesto commitments, especially if it has been done in double quick time, is the proudest boast party leaders such as Wilson and Heath could make.

A prime example is supplied by the *Labour Weekly* of November 14th, 1978. As a prelude to the coming election, it published a supplement to demonstrate its faithfulness in carrying out the 1974 manifesto. It listed sixty-eight commitments and claimed that it had carried out no less than forty-three in their entirety, with action in hand on another nine. This left fourteen commitments on which nothing had been done. The party blamed its failure to act on such important items as the introduction of a wealth tax, the nationalization of ship-repairing facilities, and the nationalization of ports on its minority status in Parliament. The same excuse applies of course for such controversial measures as the return of hived-off (that is, public property sold off to the public) assets of nationalized industries, the ending of National Health Service prescription charges, and the withdrawal of tax relief from private and fee-paying schools. The publication of this document at such a time is a striking confirmation of the importance that Labour attaches to honoring manifesto commitments.

Such a claim is justified by the doctrine of the mandate, which might run thus: The elector goes into the election with a clear choice between a variety of programs; he votes for one of these; a popular majority for any one of these programs carries the party that has put it forward into office; the party therefore has the duty to carry it out; and because the party has received a majority it also has the right to carry it out.

These assumptions are entirely fallacious. Very few electors ever read through an entire manifesto. Where voters have been presented with selected excerpts of five or even two policies propounded in the rival manifestoes, not more than three-fifths of Labour voters (in a 1950 study) or not more than one-third of them (in a 1955 study) approved of them. Even if each elector did read every line of every manifesto, it is wholly implausible that each would agree with every

TABLE 28

Popular Support for Labour/Conservative Policies, General Election, 1979

Majority Support	Pro	Con	No Majority Support	Pro	Con
Conservative Policies:					
Selling more council houses to tenants	80	20			
Stopping social security payments to families of strikers	60	40			
Cutting top income tax rate for people with large incomes	57	43			
Banning secondary picketing, i.e. picketing a company not directly involved in a strike	91	9			
Putting up VAT (sales tax) to reduce income tax	51	49			
Free vote on death penalty in House of Commons	90	10			
Labour Policies:					
			Reduce powers of House of Lords	43	57
			Introduce wealth tax	49	51
Government to give subsidies to industry, to create jobs	79	21			
			Giving trade union seats on boards of major companies	45	55

Sources: Gallup, BBC/University of Essex Election Study, 1979.

item on one manifesto and disagree with every item in all the others. Even if, most improbably, this were the case, it would only confer a majority mandate on the winning party if it won more than 50 percent of the popular vote, and the last time this occurred was in 1935. Clearly the larger, longer, and more detailed the manifestoes, the less meaningful the electoral choice between the parties and the more nebulous the claim that either party has a mandate to execute its manifesto. Election campaigns are fought and won on images, plus two or three highly salient issues that may not be "position" issues at all, but valence issues.[61]

Furthermore, voter-rationality in even these limited matters has not been assisted by a further development; to wit, the change in campaigning between 1945 and the present day.

Campaigning

Since 1945 the general election campaign has greatly altered. The broadening of party-political broadcasting and the subsequent advent of television has centralized the parties' propaganda effort; by the same token it has led to the decline of major speechmaking tours by the leading politicians (George Brown's eighty-nine election meetings in 1970 was probably the last tour of this kind that will be seen) and has led to the atrophy of public meetings in the constituency campaigns also. Second, more and more interest has focused on the party leaders and enhanced the gladiatorial nature of the election. This has probably eroded voter-rationality. In the 1970 election, for instance, 70 percent of the leaders' speeches were rhetorical attacks on their opponents' records rather than an exposition of their own views. Third, the central contest, fought out on the television screens, is no longer a confrontation on an agreed set of issues; it has become a confrontation to select the issue on which the voter will decide. For instance, Heath wanted to make, "who governs?" the issue to be decided at the February 1974 election, but his opponent, Harold Wilson, skillfully obfuscated this question (on which an overwhelming majority of the electorate supported Heath) by raising the counter-issue of the soaring cost of living and the general domestic record of the Conservative government. Wilson was able to impose his view of what the election was about and so to win a (qualified) victory. This development owes much to the advent of opinion polls. Since these regularly poll the public on the questions, "What are the most important issues?" and "Which party, in your opinion, is best able to handle it?", each party knows the issues on which it has stronger support than its rivals. And it little matters that on, say, nationalization, the public strongly disapproves of the Labour party if, at the same time (as is the case), it thinks this is a very unimportant issue compared with prices and unemployment. Furthermore, each party commissions private opinion polls that finetune the guidance given

---

[61] Salient position issues have changed over time, of course.

by the public ones. The effect of such tactics on the campaign is to remove its focus; the parties lunge past one another.

The recent enlargement of the media's discretion on how to handle the campaign has further randomized the campaign. Television interviewers have their own set of questions to ask, to which the politician can but respond, and these questions by no means necessarily accord with a party's own sense of priorities or, for that matter, with what any impartial and informed observer would regard as national priorities. On the contrary, attention is diverted into eliciting off-the-cuff reactions to the events of the day. The final point is that, unlike 1945, when only sound broadcasting existed and its impact was confined, the national campaign in any significant sense is nowadays an artifact of the media: the media rearrange the speeches, the manifold countrywide activities into a pattern, and thus campaign strategy is becoming less and less what the respective parties planned it to be.

One final point follows from this. At the most, the media manage to raise only a few of the issues mentioned in the party manifestoes; their own sense of priorities coupled with those of the contending party managers decides which. But the manifestoes, as we have said, nowadays contain from 70 to over 130 specific commitments. The voter who votes for a party on the strength of what he reads or hears or sees in the campaign is committed not just to the two or three items that may (assuming he is a rational voter) have convinced him; he is committed to the fine print also.

Fiddling the Economy: Economic Bribery of the Electorate

Domestic questions have come increasingly to dominate the election campaigns. At the same time it has been amply demonstrated that there is a marked correlation between the popularity of a government as measured by the opinion polls and the fluctuations in a number of economic indicators, among which unemployment and the balance of payments are the most significant.[62] It is a matter of proven fact that governments try to manipulate the economy to improve material conditions in time for the next election, and the failure of Heath in February 1974 may in part be ascribed to failure to have done so because of the unexpected timing of that election.

> October 1974 saw, once again, an election in which the incumbent government had manipulated the economy for its own short term electoral advantage. It is no accident that in

---

[62] Butler and Stokes, *Political Change in Britain*, 2nd ed., pp. 388–402.

every election for twenty years, apart from the unprecedented one of February 1974, real wages have advanced faster than prices over the months before polling day. In 1959 Mr. Wilson had castigated the Conservatives' practice of preceding elections with give-away budgets as 'sunshine elections.' But Labour's record in 1966 and 1970 was not much better; the 1966 campaign in no way prepared public opinion for the savage deflationary measures four months later. Wages and prices were both rising dangerously at the time of the 1970 election. In the autumn of 1974, despite ministerial remarks about there being 'no room for any increase in living standards,' the government was still acting so as to increase real incomes and public expenditure. Price increases were temporarily held back by controls, by subsidies to nationalized industries, by a cut in value-added tax in the summer budget, and by food subsidies. At the same time incomes were boosted by a big rise in pensions, and by threshold payments under Stage Three of the Conservatives' incomes policy. In this way in the three months *before* the election, inflation was cut to an annual rate of 8 percent. But in the *next* three months it accelerated to an annual rate of 20 percent. . . .[63]

Callaghan's defeat in May 1979 almost certainly owed a great deal to his being pitched out of office by the sudden "no confidence" vote of March 28, making it impossible for him to continue in power until the autumn. The country was still smarting from the hard winter (in some areas it was still snowing even on election day, May 3!) and embittered by the wave of winter strikes that had made the freezing temperatures so much harder to endure. The government's efforts to hold wages down to 5 percent had shattered against the determined opposition of the trade unions. The social contract of 1974 was dead, and the so-called Concordat between government and the unions had been too hastily patched together to have either meaning or credibility. Because of strikes among the government's computer staff Britain's balance of payments for the first three months of the year had not been published. When finally made public the figures showed that the country was sliding into recession, having run up a record £1.3 billion deficit in the first quarter.

The Unpopularity of the Two Main Parties

Unfortunately it is not possible to construct a time series on the popularity of the main parties or the party system as such. The best

[63] Butler and Kavanagh, *The British General Election of October 1974*, pp. 14–15.

we can manage in this respect is on the question of whether the public perceived a difference between the two main parties. Respondents who perceive no difference or little difference may be regarded as feeling that whatever the party in power, the outcome for them personally was the same—disappointing. This is indeed the correct way to interpret the response.[64] There can be no doubt therefore about the waning popularity of the parties. Between 1955 and 1970, Gallup found 74 percent of the respondents saying that they perceived a significant difference; in 1979, only 55 percent said so.

Whatever might have been the populrity of the two-party system in the 1950s, there is no gainsaying its substantial unpopularity today. The Houghton Committee[65] mounted a survey in 1976 that found 86 percent of the respondents agreeing "strongly" (55 percent) or a "little" (31 percent) that political parties were "essential to our form of national government"; this is unsurprising, since this form of government was created by the political parties as a suitable ambiance in which they could operate. Moreover, a further 77 percent agreed, strongly or a little, that the political parties "kept government on its toes by criticizing," and a smaller but substantial proportion, 65 percent, agreed that the political parties were "the only way to present the public's view."

These findings are unremarkable in view of the exposure parties receive in the media in the execution of their manifest functions of raising policy matters and criticizing the government. But against these bland responses must be set the widespread opinion that the parties "oppose each other for the sake of it" (66 percent, of which 35 percent "agreed strongly." Only 12 percent disagreed strongly).[66] A private poll conducted by ORC for the National Campaign for Electoral Reform found higher proportions: 77 percent agreed that "one political party automatically opposes what another party says or does"; 19 percent of the respondents denied this assumption. Whereas only 32 percent of the respondents favored "uncompromising majority governments," 47 percent favored "minority governments pursuing consensus politics," and no less than 52 percent favored an "all-party coalition." In September 1974, just before the election, an ORC poll found that only 19 percent of the public expressed great confidence

---

[64] Crewe, Svarlik, and Alt, "Partisan De-Alignment in Britain, 1964–1974," pp. 156–58.

[65] *Report of the Committee on Financial Aid to Political Parties*, pp. 232–33.

[66] *A Survey of Public Attitudes to Electoral Reform* (private distribution, April 1977).

TABLE 29

THE PUBLIC'S ESTIMATE OF POLITICIANS, 1944–1979

Category	1944	1972	1978	1979
For themselves	36	38	46	48
For their party	22	22	24	24
For their country	36	28	19	18
Don't know	7	13	11	11

SOURCE: Gallup Polls.

in M.P.s compared with 71 percent having great confidence in the police, 67 percent in doctors, and 60 percent in the armed forces.[67]

The Gallup poll for August 1979 revealed a remarkable fall in the public's esteem for politicians. Respondents were asked a question previously put first in 1944, then in 1972. The question was, "Do you think that British politicians are mainly out for themselves, for their party, or do the best for their country?" The answers are shown in Table 29.

The *Sun*, in January 1977, commissioned Marplan to carry out a survey asking the sample, "How capable are any of Britain's political parties of solving the economic and political problems facing Britain?" 26 percent replied "not at all capable," and another 37 percent said "not very capable." Only 6 percent replied that the parties were "very capable of solving these difficulties."[68] Some figures from the BBC/Gallup Election Day Survey 1979 suggest a similar conclusion. Of the respondents 16 percent "did not find the election campaign very interesting" and 48 percent did not think that the campaign had generally given the people the facts about the problems facing the country. When asked "How much will the election help to solve the major problems facing the country," only 21 percent replied "a great deal," 44 percent replied "a little," and as many as 36 percent replied "not at all."

Another indicator suggestive of increasing public disillusion with the parties is the index of public "approval of the Government's record to date," for all British governments have been formed by one of the two main parties. Gallup polls have asked this question frequently since 1946, and since the beginning of 1961 they have asked it every

---

[67] Butler and Kavanagh, *The British General Election of October 1974*, p. 16, fn. 1.
[68] *Sun, the Public View*, 1977.

TABLE 30

AVERAGE PROPORTION OF PUBLIC "APPROVING GOVERNMENT'S RECORD TO DATE"

(percent)

Time Span	Party in Office	Percentage of Approval
1946–September 1951 (5 years)	Labour	39.4
October 1951–October 1964 (13 years)	Conservative	44.9
November 1964–July 1970 (6 years)	Labour	34.1
August 1970–March 1974 (4 years)	Conservative	34.2
April 1974–December 1978 (5 years)	Labour	33.6
Average		37.2

SOURCE: Gallup Polls.

month except election months. The first point to notice is that over the whole period 1946–1978 an average of only 37.2 percent of the respondents registered approval. This apparently low index of satisfaction is somewhat misleading because a considerable proportion responded, "don't know." (In the period 1974–1978 these proportions fluctuated between 25 percent and 14 percent.) The average of 37.2 percent signifies broadly that up to about half the population disapproves of the government's policies. The decline of governmental popularity is clearly attested.

The approval rate registered higher than 50 percent in only four months of the year 1961, in two months of the year from November 1964 to November 1965, and in only three months of the year 1966 and never reached that level at all over the remainder of the period 1966–1978. Even if we lower our sights and note the number of months the proportion exceeded 40 percent, the figure is disappointing. In only three years, 1961, 1964 (to October), and 1978, did the rate exceed 40 percent for as long as nine months. In contrast the rate never reached that level at all in the years 1968, 1969, 1973, 1975, and 1976. Indeed, for 71 percent of the period 1961–1978, approval for the government's record was below 40 percent.

Furthermore as Figure 2 illustrates, the responses follow a distinct pattern over time. In the entire period 1946–1966, the approval rate never once fell below an annual average of 35 percent, but since 1966 it has only twice exceeded that average (barely, in April–December 1974, and once again, in 1978). Whichever party was in office, the general level of approval remained depressed.

FIGURE 2

APPROVAL OF GOVERNMENT'S RECORD, ANNUAL AVERAGES, 1946-1978

(percent)

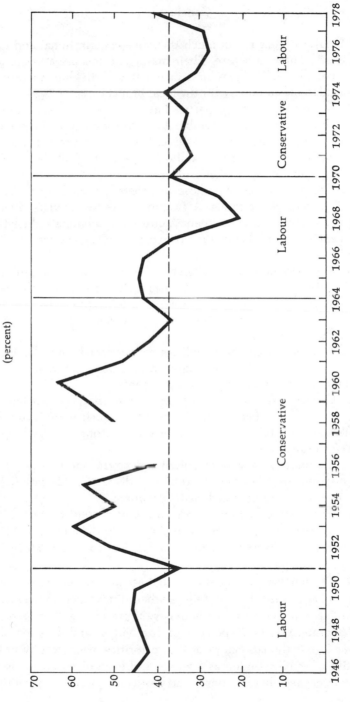

SOURCE: Gallup Polls.

133

Conclusions

1. The major parties retain much the same constitutional and organizational structures as before. Their major features are a hegemony in policy making for the parliamentary party, little bureaucratization, and considerable autonomy for the local branches.

2. Since 1945 the three parties have suffered a substantial loss of membership. Conservative membership represents only 11 percent of all conservative voters and 3.65 percent of the electorate. Labour individual membership represents only 2.7 percent of all labour voters and 0.75 percent of the total electorate.

3. The activists among these members are unlikely to be more than 15 percent of the totals. A fraction of these activists, averaging about 100 persons per constituency, effectively nominate the M.P.s in 75 percent of the parliamentary constituencies. They are the "selectorate."

4. The parliamentary leadership frames policy consistent with party conference views. The Conservative party's parliamentary leadership has a good deal of latitude in interpreting those views, but the Labour parliamentary party requires the support of three or four of the largest affiliated trade union delegations.

5. A selection of these policies is packaged into the electoral manifesto, which has become longer, more specific, and since at least 1970 more uncompromising to its opponents.

6. Conservative manifestoes are somewhat inconsistent with party voters' views; Labour manifestoes are much more inconsistent; and elements of both parties' manifestoes are opposed by majorities in the electorate.

7. Campaigns have been conducted so as not to subject these rival programs to a detailed and reasoned discussion, despite (perhaps because of) far more extended media coverage.

8. The party called on to form the government by virtue of the number of seats it has obtained in the election claims, via the mandate theory, a right and recognizes a duty to carry out all its manifesto commitments.

9. The party government does its best to carry out these commitments and apologizes for any failure when it next meets the electorate. In short, a number of party activists, representing 0.15 percent of the electorate, selects 75 percent of the M.P.s, and an even smaller number formulate national priorities, priorities often grossly unrepresentative of public opinion as a whole and even of party opinion as a whole. If elected these activists carry out such policies, pleading the

democratic right and duty to do so by virtue of their electoral victory, which, since 1935, has always proceeded from less than 50 percent of the popular vote cast.

10. Politicians have become increasingly unpopular since 1944, and parties as such have been increasingly unpopular since at least 1966.

4

The Parties and Other Institutions

Glendower: I can call spirits from the vasty deep. . . .
Hotspur: Why, so can I, or so can any man; But will they come
when you do call for them?

Henry IV, Pt. I
Act III, Scene I

The extraparliamentary party organizations do not control any political or social institutions of any consequence. Insofar as any degree of political control is exerted over these at all, it is by the leadership of the parliamentary party and only when that party is in office. Even then their authority must be distinguished from their effective power, which is weak and becoming weaker. British political parties never effected large-scale penetration of other social or public institutions and did not try to. The attempt would have run contrary to the political and economic philosophy of the nineteenth-century Liberal and Conservative parties, while the Labour party, unlike many of its European counterparts, never aspired to be a communitarian class party. The autonomy of social and public institutions from the political parties, rooted in the last century and very great in 1945 is, if anything, even greater today.

The Parties and Ancillary Organizations

All three major parties, Labour, Conservative, and Liberal, contain ancillary organizations for women, for youth, and for university students. All are numerically in decline from the high point of 1953. Furthermore, if the numbers of youth incorporated in any party—

136

for example, the 5,000–10,000 or so Young Socialists—are compared with the numbers of youth included in sports clubs, youth clubs, and organizations like the Boy Scouts, they are insignificant. A similar situation occurs if the numbers of Labour women or Conservative women are compared with the numbers found in nonpolitical organizations like the Womens' Institutes. Likewise the university clubs are a fraction of the student population. This is not to deny that the ancillary organizations of women and university students are not of considerable importance in the respective party organizations. They are very important indeed, though the same cannot be said for the Young Socialists and the Young Liberals, both of which have consistently embarrassed the respective parties rather than assisted them. The point here is, simply, that these ancillary organizations are not mass organizations of the youth, the women, or the university students of the country. Numerically they are an insignificant fraction of these.

The Parties and the Mass Media

Economics is important in understanding the press. Newspapers are comparatively very cheap in Britain and can attain huge circulations (around four million or more) because they derive vast revenues from advertisements. Hence a spiral economy: the larger the circulation the greater the amount of advertising and hence the cheaper the paper and hence the greater the circulation—and, of course, vice versa. At the same time it costs an enormous sum to launch a new newspaper.

The daily press unquestionably favors the Conservatives today, the Sunday press overwhelmingly so. Since 1945 there have been three major developments in this connection. The first is the absence of a party press. The only surviving party newspaper today is the Communist *Morning Star*, financially viable only through donations from its readership. In the 1930s the Labour party newspaper was the *Daily Herald*. It had a very large circulation, but after 1945 it lost readers. It was taken over by the International Press Company in 1962, folded, and was relaunched as The *Sun* in 1964, still retaining a party connection. In 1969 it was bought by the Australian magnate Robert Murdoch, but without political preconditions. Today it is the largest-circulation daily with a pronounced right-wing tendency. The Cooperative party's own *Reynold's News* (a Sunday newspaper) collapsed in 1967.

The political balance of the press has become more right-wing

TABLE 31

READING OF DAILY NEWSPAPERS, 1977

Affiliation	Newspaper	Circula-tion (millions)	Propor-tion of Circula-tion	Reader-ship (millions)	Propor-tion of Reader-ship
Pro-Labour	Daily Mirror	3.9		12.0	
Total		3.9	28	12.0	28
Independent	Times	0.3		1.0	
	Guardian	0.3		1.0	
	Financial Times	0.2		0.7	
Total		0.8	6	2.7	6
Pro-Conservative	Sun	3.8		12.2	
	Daily Express	2.4		6.8	
	Daily Mail	1.9		5.4	
	Daily Telegraph	1.3		3.2	
Total		9.4	67	27.6	67

SOURCE: Social Trends, HMSO, Government Statistical Service, no. 9, 1979.

since 1945. The Royal Commission on the Press gives the "affiliations" of the dailies as follows: in 1945, Conservative, 52 percent of circulation; Labour, 35 percent; and Liberal and independent, 13 percent.[1] In 1970 the balance had become 55 percent Conservative, 44 percent Labour, and 5 percent Liberal and independent. The change was due largely to the collapse of the Liberal News-Chronicle in that period. Today the balance is far more favorable to the Conservatives, since the Sun newspaper, with its 4 million circulation, must be added to the Conservative side and subtracted from Labour, which derives support only from the high-circulation Daily Mirror and, contingently, from the elite-circulation Guardian. It will be seen from Table 31 that the pro-Conservative sector of the daily press had, in 1977, reached 67 percent, and the Labour sector only 28 percent.

The pro-Conservative bias is similar among the national Sunday newspapers. As Table 32 shows, these can attain enormous circulations. Here the pro-Conservative percentage of total circulation is 68 percent and of total readership 66 percent, as compared with the pro-Labour figures of 21 percent and 23 percent respectively.

[1] Royal Commission on the Press, 1977 (Cmnd., 6810).

TABLE 32

READING OF SUNDAY NEWSPAPERS, 1977

Affiliation	Newspaper	Circula-tion (millions)	Propor-tion of Circula-tion	Reader-ship (millions)	Propor-tion of Reader-ship
Pro-Labour	Sunday Mirror	3.9		12.6	
Total		3.9	21	12.6	23
Independent	Sunday Times	1.4		3.8	
	Observer	0.7		2.3	
Total		2.1	11	6.1	11
Pro-Conservative	News of the World	5.0		13.5	
	Sunday People	3.9		11.5	
	Sunday Express	3.2		8.7	
	Sunday Telegraph	0.8		2.5	
Total		12.9	68	36.2	66

SOURCE: *Social Trends*, HMSO, Government Statistical Service, no. 9, 1979.

Not unnaturally the Labour party and the TUC charged persistent right-wing bias against them, but after careful analysis of the content and reporting in the national press (in contrast to leading articles) the Royal Commission did not find this bias a strong one. In a National Executive Committee document entitled *The People and the Media*, the Labour party proposed to strengthen the circulation of the weaker newspapers by pooling and subsequently redistributing all advertising revenues. The commission not only demonstrated the administrative impracticality of this scheme, but showed that it would actually enfeeble the very papers it was designed to assist. It found that the effects of variants on this scheme put forward by the TUC and private individuals would likewise be counterproductive. The Labour party and the TUC also demanded a launch fund to help start up new publications, but the commission found the cost likely to be prohibitive. For all that the two strongly Labour-committed commissioners submitted a minority report reiterating their claims, and public subsidization of the press remains Labour party policy.

This trend is only partly countered by a third development: that these newspapers are all *independently* Conservative, Labour, and so on, as the case may be; the *Daily Express*, the *Daily Mail*, the *Sun*, for instance, all have a highly idiosyncratic view of politics, which is not necessarily at all the same as the official party line. Also, all such papers have taken to inviting columns from political opponents, something rarely if ever done in the 1940s and 1950s.

Radio and Television Broadcasting. Sound and vision broadcasting is provided and/or supervised by two public corporations, the British Broadcasting Corporation (BBC) and the Independent Broadcasting Authority (IBA).[2] The BBC's revenue comes from license fees paid by the public, the IBA's from advertising revenue. The charters of both corporations, provide for their independence from the government, and equally prohibit partisanship. Parties or other organizations may not buy time for advertisements from the IBA to advance a political cause.

The content and style of political broadcasting has enormously altered since 1945. The media nowadays enjoy almost unfettered autonomy, subject only to the fairness norm, in their handling of political issues between and during elections.

In the immediate postwar period, the parties perceived radio broadcasting (the only medium until the early 1950s) as a threat to the supremacy of Parliament and subjected it to a variety of restrictions.

The "Fourteen-day rule" was devised by the BBC itself in 1944. It precluded broadcast discussion of any topic about to be debated in Parliament in the next fourteen days as well as any legislation currently before it. In 1945 this private rule became a formal *aide-mémoire* between the BBC, the government, and the opposition. When the BBC repented and tried to abrogate it in 1953, the party leaders refused and in 1955, the Postmaster General framed it as an official directive to the BBC, and it was upheld in the Commons by 271 votes to 126. But the victory was Pyrrhic, for in December 1956 the Prime Minister suspended the rule for six months, and after 1957 it was suspended indefinitely.

There were restrictions on broadcasts other than "party political broadcasts." These broadcasts were a novel feature of the 1945 election. They were arranged by a committee representing the three main political parties together with the BBC. This system, expanded to include the ITV, continued unchanged until 1959. In the 1945 election these broadcasts took place at 9 p.m. after the main news, each broadcast lasting twenty to thirty minutes. They were allocated on the basis of the number of candidates fielded by the respective parties,

---

[2] Formerly the ITV (Independent Television Authority).

so the Labour and Conservative parties had ten apiece, while the Liberals had four, and the Commonwealth and Communist parties one each. A somewhat similar arrangement still exists, although the length of the broadcasts has been reduced to ten minutes. Apart from these broadcasts, however, the BBC and, after 1954, the ITV[3] were completely forbidden to report the course of the election. In 1954 the stations were precluded from expressing their own opinions on current affairs. The Independent Television Act of 1954 stipulated that all political broadcasts except the official party broadcasts had to be properly "balanced."

All these restrictions have gradually been lifted. The break-through year was 1959. By then the television audience was far larger than that for sound radio. By 1970 the average radio audience was 450,000, whereas the least popular television program reaches 8.5 million.

In the 1959 election, for the first time, the BBC and ITV reported fully on the election news and broadcast special election programs outside the political parties' official broadcasts. Thenceforward such programs mushroomed, while the official party ones shrank. In the 1964 election, for instance, there were special magazine programs such as *Election Forum* and extensive campaign analysis in *Gallery*; in 1970 there were programs such as *Election Forum* and *Panorama*. A law case determined that candidates might legally make individual appearances on television. By as early as 1966, the parties' control over their "spokesman" had become vestigial, and "balance" had come to mean balance within a set of individual broadcasts, not within each individual one.

Finally coverage became more and more extensive, while the endurance of the viewing and listening public dramatically waned. In 1970 a survey found that 47 percent thought too much time had been devoted to the election. In February 1974 this figure had risen to 67 percent.[4]

At the time of writing, then, apart from respecting the principle of balance, these media are now completely free as to how they report the campaigns. This has had significant consequences. First, it has permitted them to portray party activities in ways that may run quite contrary to what the parties themselves wanted. Not the parties but television has come to define and shape the national campaign. Next, the style of electioneering has changed: Speeches are timed so as to

---

[3] Now renamed IBA.

[4] This account is based on the excellent book by C. Seymour-Ure, *The Political Impact of Mass Media* (London: Constable, 1974); see chapter 7.

get into the news broadcasts; the venue of speeches has changed—
for instance, the parties now usually hold a daily press conference
at their headquarters. Finally the focus bears increasingly on the party
leaders. In 1964 television and radio quoted sixty-one politicians; in
1966 they quoted fifty-six; but in 1970 they quoted only forty-four.
And the principal focus was on the party leaders, giving the campaign an increasingly "presidential" character.[5]

The Parties and the Interest Groups

British political parties (apart from the Cooperative party) have
always been politically and functionally distinct from interest groups
with the unique but vital exception of the trade union-Labour party
link, and even this is best seen as an interpenetration of two functionally distinct and independent organizations. The major interest
groups are still as distinct and independent of parties as ever, and
the interest group system as such aims to influence the same political
targets, through tactics similar to those they used in 1958.[6]

What has greatly altered is the distribution of power among
these groups. It began in the 1960s. The main changes have been a
marked growth in promotional groups,[7] and among the producer
groups a sharp decline in the power of manufacturer's groups, notably
the Confederation of British Industries (CBI), relative to the financial
interests—in other words "the City"—and above all to the trade
unions.

The Growth of Promotional Groups. Since the 1960s there has occurred an upsurge of protest movements and new promotional groups.
Many of these groups have attained success. The protest movements

---

[5] The randomizing of the campaign by the media's newfound latitude; the routini-
zation of the party political broadcasts; the general surfeiting of the audience—
all these pose a challenge to the problem of making the election campaign a
rational discussion of policy alternatives such as is assumed to occur. At the
same time, the experience of the 1970 and February 1974 elections suggests that
for the first time the campaign is proving decisive to the election outcome. This
is possibly bound up with the decline in strong partisanship that we have already
noted. In contrast, the electorate's disillusion with the parties is reflected in their
declining interest in political broadcasting. There is a need therefore to provide
coverage that sticks to the issues, ensuring that they are thrashed out methodi-
cally, rationally, and fairly, and yet manages to attract and activate the public.
Suggestions as to how this might be done are to be found in Jay G. Blumler,
Michael Gurevitch, and Julian Ives, *The Challenge of Election Broadcasting*
(Leeds: University Press, 1978).

[6] Samuel E. Finer, *Anonymous Empire*, 1st ed. (London: Pall Mall, 1958).

[7] R. Kimber and J. J. Richardson, *Pressure Groups in Britain* (London: Dent, 1974).

142

are typified by the once powerful Campaign for Nuclear Disarmament, which served as a model for later protests over Vietnam, Biafra, and South Africa. The most prominent promotional groups are concerned with welfare-state or environmental issues. The welfare type is typified by such groups as Shelter, the Child Poverty Action Group, and the Abortion Law Reform Association after its regeneration in 1963. Environmental groups that cared to register with the Civic Trust (an umbrella organization) grew from 200 in 1957 to more than 1,000 in 1973.[8] Many have been surprisingly successful, either in getting a serious hearing (for example, Friends of the Earth, the Child Poverty Action Group, Shelter) or even in achieving their legislative objectives, (the Abortion Law Reform Association).

The Changed Power-Balance among the Producer Groups. There is no easy way of quantifying the relative political power of organized groupings, and therefore what follows is impressionistic. In *Anonymous Empire*[9] (both in its first edition of 1958 and again, as late as the second edition of 1966), this author saw the industrial employers' and labor groups standing in a rough political and economic balance. That is no longer so. Organized labor has moved to a position of preeminence checked by little but the powers of organized finance as represented in the City of London, while the power of organized industry seems to have suffered a sharp and net decline since the early 1960s.

Organizationally. Both industry and labor have strengthened themselves. In 1965 the three peak industrialist organizations—the Federation of British Industry, (FBI) the National Association of British Manufacturers, and the British Employers' Confederation—amalgamated to form the Confederation of British Industry. Meanwhile trade union membership affiliated to the TUC expanded from 8,020,000 in 1951 to 11,515,000 in 1976; in terms of the total work force that represents an increase from 40 percent in 1951 to over 46 percent in 1975. In 1951 some 6.25 million members were to be found in the larger unions (those with more than 100,000 members apiece); in 1975 there were some 9 million members in such unions.

Economically. The power of industrial organizations seems to have decreased, that of the City to have increased, and that of the trade unions to have increased still more. The first is directly related to the increasingly poor performance of British industry after its surge in the late 1950s and early 1960s, and this in turn is related to its

---

[8] Ibid. pp. 11–13.

[9] Finer, *Anonymous Empire.*

increasing reliance on state subsidies. In 1964–1965 government assistance to private industry totaled only £80 million a year. By 1969–1970 the figure had risen to £872 million. Despite the Conservative government's initial decision to cut this back, the figure was still at £748 million in 1974–1975. In real terms this represents something on the order of a fivefold increase over the decade.

In contrast, the City, that loose nexus of financial institutions which has no centralized organization to direct it, rebuilt London's central financial position after it had been destroyed during the war years, and increased overseas earnings more than fivefold over the last decade. The current estimate of the City's net earnings from overseas is some £2,500 million.

Labour has greatly improved its economic bargaining position. The more capital-intensive an industry, the greater the proportionate damage to profits that a strike can inflict. From the seaman's strike of 1966 to the miners' strike of 1974, the union was in practically every case the clear winner, and this further encouraged militancy.[10]

Politically. The FBI and its larger and more comprehensive successor has never been the dominating institution that socialist writers have seen in it. "The CBI has little consistent direct influence over the politics pursued by government"[11]; admittedly it is able to influence considerably a particular piece of legislation, as for example, the 1975 Industry Act. But it cannot impose sanctions on its members. More important, it cannot easily impose a sanction on government apart from campaigning against policies it dislikes, since to refuse to cooperate in administering a particular policy is increasingly unlikely as industry becomes a supplicant for funds. In short: "neither the CBI nor individual manufacturing firms have a direct sanction equivalent to the political strike or the City's ability to move vast amounts of capital. . . ."[12]

A Commission of Inquiry into the workings of the City, currently being conducted by Sir Harold Wilson, will certainly make the relationship between the Bank of England, the City, and the governments of the day clear, but it is indubitable that politically the City wields an immense political influence; the simple proof is that successive Labour governments have had to come to terms with it. This is not because of Labour's respect for the invisible earnings it generates,

---

[10] For a further elaboration see S. E. Finer, "The Political Power of Organized Labour," *Government and Opposition* (Autumn 1973).

[11] Wynn Grant and David Marsh, *The CBI* (London: Hodder and Stoughton, 1977), pp. 212–13.

[12] Ibid.

although that consideration is not to be set aside. The City is perhaps the world's greatest center of finance and credit: the Stock Exchange quotes more securities than any other, and the Baltic Exchange is the world center for chartering ships and planes. The City contains the world's largest concentration of foreign banks (some 200), the largest gold market, the largest international insurance market, and some of the largest of the international commodity markets. The City contains the institutions—the money managers, who invest and reinvest the immense insurance and pension funds—that handle resources from practically every earning member of the population. Although not formally organized, the City is very much a collectivity. For instance, when a business is floated, a bank (or consortium) arranges for the raising of capital, then the sum is underwritten by all manner of different City institutions; once flotation is completed the Stock Exchange arranges the quotation of the shares. Merchant banks, clearing banks, discount houses, and insurance companies are all involved in financing international trade. The functional interdependence of the institutions is underpinned by an extensive crisscrossing pattern of interlocking multiple directorships. If these immense strengths are the necessary condition for the City's powerful political clout, the sufficient condition is supplied by the essential function of finance and credit in the regulation and management of the internal price level, the international value of the pound sterling, and the consequent handling of the country's vast but ever-precarious external account on which its prosperity, even its viability, depends. This role has been heightened by the recent cult of monetarism as the only safe counterinflationary strategy. In the end, so the current conventional wisdom goes, monetary and balance-of-payments imperatives must prevail, even if this means halting or even reversing the traditional high spending policies of a Labour government. Its expenditure cutbacks of 1976–1978 were a replay of those of 1966–1968.

City-political party relationships are a mirror-image of the trade union-political party relationship. The Conservative party has extensive personal links with City figures, almost none with leading trade unionists; Labour knows few leading City figures, but has intimate personal links with trade unions. The City is more influential than usual when the Conservatives are in power; the unions are more influential when Labour is in power. Each has a privileged access to one particular party, not to the other. When the Conservatives are in power, they must respect the potential trade union veto of their policies or suffer anew the confrontation of 1974, while Labour must respect the potential veto power of the City institutions.

145

The question remains, how far are the unions the captive of the Labour party, or the reverse? One view might be that the Labour party has succeeded, where the Liberals and Conservatives have failed, in capturing all leadership positions in the unions and so colonizing them with its supporters; but an opposite view might hold that through their overwhelming preponderance in the Labour party's Annual Conference and its NEC, as well as by their massive subventions to the party and their sponsoring of some 40 percent of its M.P.s (currently 48 percent) the leaders of the largest unions have subordinated a political movement to their own purposes.

Neither view would be correct. The union leadership and the party leadership continue to move on a parallel course, but today their structures and functions, their social composition, and their ideology are more differentiated than in the period 1945–1951. The Labour party's object is to win elections; the trade unions' is to defend their own economic interests; and these aims do not necessarily coincide at all. Until about 1960 the trade union-affiliated membership of the party was remarkable for throwing its weight behind the parliamentary leadership and in particular the party leader. After the electoral defeat of 1959, the party saw the unions as cloth cap and an electoral liability, and it sought to broaden its popular appeal. At the same time the new planning and consultative mechanisms created by the Conservatives after 1962 (notably the National Economic Development Council [NEDC]) attracted the union leadership into direct consultation and negotiation with the government as such, not with parliamentary parties. In the words of George Woodcock, then the general secretary of the TUC, the unions had "moved out of Trafalgar Square and into Whitehall."

As these functional divergences became apparent, they were reflected in a structural differentiation. In the 1920s and 1930s many localities had set up joint trade union and Labour party councils. These were now officially discouraged. Again in the early 1960s the Labour party ruled that trade union delegates to the Annual Conference must be individual members of the Labour party. Next this ruling was extended to trade union delegates on constituency Labour party general management committees. And, as we have seen, the National Council of Labour, which formally unites the three wings of the movement—the party, the unions and the cooperative movement—has been allowed to decay.

Yet another gap appeared: During the thirty-year period after 1945 a divergence arose between the social background of the unions and their leadership and that of the parliamentary party. We have already noted the decline in the proportion of former manual workers in the parliamentary party and a concurrent rise in its proportion of professionals. This trend was even more marked in the social composition of the cabinet. Until the advent of Wilson in 1964, the tradition was to share cabinet posts fairly evenly between former manual working class ministers and the rest. In the 1970 Wilson cabinet only one member was a former manual worker. Callaghan (himself an ex-trade unionist) only partly restored the balance, appointing seven former working class and thirteen middle class ministers.

At the membership level another striking change becomes apparent. To explain it, it is essential to grasp the distinction between the trade union movement as a whole (insofar as most unions in Britain are affiliated to the TUC), the trade unions that are affiliated to the Labour party, and the trade unionists within these affiliated unions who pay the political levy and are therefore members of the Labour party. The TUC is *not* affiliated to the Labour party. It is true that it is composed of delegations from trade unions that are, for the most part, affiliated to the Labour party, but many are not. Among the largest are the two white-collar unions, the National Union of Teachers and the National and Local Government Officers Association. The TUC elects a council composed of the general secretaries of leading unions, it appoints a secretariat including an economic section, and it elects a general secretary. The congress meets annually in September to review the work and progress of the last year, and discusses an enormous range of matters, many of which are of purely domestic concern to the movement and have no political bearing. Furthermore the TUC is represented on a very large array of advisory boards, about 120 in all. Through these it cooperates in the administration of public policies all the time, irrespective of the complexion of government. It can readily be seen that the views of the TUC as a whole may differ to some extent at any rate in some matters, from the views of the unions affiliated to the Labour party and even more markedly from the views of the affiliated Labour party membership in such unions.

The change in membership to be noticed, then, is that between the social composition of the TUC membership and that of the affiliated unions. Whereas in 1975 the white-collar workers represented some 30 percent of TUC membership, they represented at most only 10 percent of the Labour-affiliated membership. Thus the white-collar element is less well represented in Labour party policy making than it is on the TUC. The same trend is reflected in the fact that by 1976 almost equal numbers of the trade union membership

TABLE 33

TRADE UNION MEMBERSHIP, LABOUR PARTY-AFFILIATED, 1976

Number of Unions	*Number of Members*
Total, affiliated to TUC 115	11,515,920
Total, affiliated to Labour Party 58	5,800,069

were not affiliated to the Labour party as were affiliated. It is no wonder at all that in October 1974 the polls found 66 percent of trade unionists disapproving of trade union affiliation with the Labour party, nor that in the election of that month only 55 percent of trade unionists voted for the Labour party. The performance was even worse in 1979. The percentage of trade unionists voting for Labour declined to 51 percent, while the percentage voting Conservative rose from 23 percent (1974) to 33 percent.

Nevertheless, the party and the union leadership have by and large stayed together, except for the dour conflict of 1968–1969, when the Wilson government sought to discipline wildcat strikes on the lines laid down in its white paper, "In Place of Strife." This partnership persists because the union leadership is not necessarily representative of the political views of its rank and file, except in narrowly industrial matters relating to wages, conditions of employment, and legal regulation of their activities. This is a result of the sometimes wildly undemocratic procedures for electing general secretaries and/or executive committees in the unions, the dominance of militants in such elections, and the considerable latitude officers may enjoy in certain unions.[13] It has already been shown how a number of unions elected very left-wing executives and leaders between 1967 and 1969 and how these deserted the leadership of the parliamentary party to form a broad left alliance with constituency party militants and the more left-wing Tribunite membership of the parliamentary party. This alliance foundered in 1975, when its main architects, Scanlon (AEUW) and Jones (TGWU), found themselves faced with the responsibility for making or breaking the Labour government's incomes policy. Scanlon and Jones supported it; their erstwhile Tribunite

---

[13] Unions differ signally among themselves on each of these matters. See Steven Milligan, *The New Barons* (London: Temple Smith, 1976), especially part two, "Inside Today's Unions."

allies, who did not, found themselves reviled as being more royalist than the king.

Whereas the functional and social divergence between unions and Labour leadership is of long standing and continues to envolve, the identity of their viewpoints (or otherwise) is adventitious. The parliamentary party and unions are much more differentiated from one another than in the past. It is misleading to speak of permeation or control of the unions, or of union domination of the party. This is strikingly borne out by the history of their relationship since the 1968–1969 estrangement. The two sides collaborated in opposition to the Conservative Industrial Relations Bill of 1971 but not until 1972 did the organ that had concerted that opposition, the Liaison Committee (established in 1972) begin to elaborate a broader common policy. Significantly this body brings together the party and the TUC, and we must emphasize the TUC—the representative body of unions as a whole, not just those affiliated to the Labour party or even the affiliated trade union members. Since the trade union members dominate the party conference and the NEC, why were not those the forums in which policy was made? After all, that was the original intention of the party constitution. The Liaison Committee underlines the self-standing and independent nature of the TUC, while the subsequent conduct of the two sides bears every mark of the bargaining one would expect between two independent negotiators.[14]

Year by year the two sides established a set of quid pro quos. In 1973 they produced an agenda for legislation entitled *Economic Policy and the Cost of Living*. This formed the basis for the Social Contract formula on which Labour came to power in 1974. The unions would in effect exercise a voluntary pay restraint in return for a list of trade union oriented measures that the parliamentary leadership promised to promote. A second document entitled *The Development of the Social Contract* (June 1975) acknowledged implicitly that the unions had failed to deliver and that wage inflation was rampant and mounting. Shortly afterward, the government let it be known that it would reverse its pledge against statutory wage restraint. In this crisis the TUC drew up its own wage restraint policy and for the next two years managed to police it. The unions' patience ran out in 1978, when the Prime Minister publicly told the TUC that the wage norm must be 5 percent. At this point the differentiation between the two sides became as unchallengeably clear as it was in 1968–1969, or for that matter as it was under the Conservatives in 1975–1978. In the TUC conference of September 1978, the largest unions made

---

[14] Hatfield, *The House the Left Built.*

it absolutely clear that wage restraint was over and they would pursue a policy of entirely free collective bargaining. At the ensuing Labour party conference in October, the Prime Minister hinted that he would rather resign than abandon the 5 percent norm. Despite this and the expected announcement of a general election, the conference defeated the pay policy by an overwhelming majority. When a wave of strikes overwhelmed the country in January and February 1979, it became clear that the Labour government could no more control the trade union movement in the matter of incomes policy than the Conservative government in the winter of 1973–1974. The two sides did indeed meet again to produce a joint document, the so-called Concordat. This document does not contain a hint of interference with free collective bargaining. It is also significant as an indication that for all their fundamental disagreement on wages, strikes, and picketing, the unions still publicly backed the Labour party as its party in the forthcoming election and that the Labour party, for electoral reasons, had made the best bargain open to it in the face of union recalcitrance.

To summarize: Nowadays more policy is floated outside the parties by private promotional groups than in the immediate postwar period; the major economic organizations work directly through civil servants and ministers rather than through the party, at least in the first instance; the trade unions now occupy the center of the stage, along with that nebulous informal network known as the City, while the power of the industrialists' organizations has declined vis-à-vis the parties along with the decline in profitability and increasing dependence on state aid. Taken by and large, the hold of parties as such upon all these groups may be said to have decreased significantly in the last thirty years.

Parties and the Central Bureaucracy

The parties as parties do not control the permanent civil services; on the contrary, there has been a continuous effort since 1855 to immunize these permanent officials from any kind of political interference except that of their masters, the ministers of the Crown. Until 1964 this effort succeeded.

Neither the extraparliamentary party organizations nor the parliamentary parties themselves have any say whatsoever in the appointment or dismissal of civil servants. Civil servants are recruited by the independent Civil Service Commission on a merit and career basis, by a system of open competitive examinations and/or interviews.

Higher civil servants are not permitted to engage in party activities, nor may they stand as parliamentary candidates unless they resign from the service. (This ban is partly relaxed for an intermediate range of civil servants and entirely relaxed for those whose function is routine.) In practice there is almost no interchange between the civil service and Parliament, unlike many European countries, such as France and West Germany, where a high proportion of legislators are former civil servants.

Not only do the parliamentary parties and the extraparliamentary organizations have no influence at all over the personnel and tenure of the civil service, they have no direct authority over their activities, either. The constitutional position is clear: The officials in each department are answerable only to the minister, who in turn is answerable to Parliament. He is a channel—and a wall. He assumes a vicarious responsibility for all acts of omission and commission by his civil servants. Thus the members of the parliamentary party can influence the policy of the civil service only to the degree that they can influence the minister and, in turn, the degree to which he can control his senior officials. There are select committees of the House that can cross-question civil servants on matters of administrative practice and detail, as opposed to policy and one of these, the Public Accounts Committee, can and does effectively control faulty or wasteful administration. The others duly report to the House of Commons, but usually without effect.

There are thus three critical links in the long chain of party control over the bureaucracy: The extraparliamentary party-M.P. link; the M.P.-minister link; and the minister-senior civil service link. Central to such control is the doctrine of the individual responsibility of a minister for the administration of his department; the minister is the link between Parliament and the executive. He is public, they are faceless and voiceless; he is responsible for policy, they are there to follow his directions. If the Commons wants to know what the civil servants are up to, it must ask him to explain. If his civil servants want the Commons to know what they are up to, he is their mouthpiece.

This situation largely corresponded to reality when the convention first emerged. When Lord Palmerston was foreign secretary, 130 years ago, he had one senior adviser and a number of clerks, and he personally wrote every dispatch that went off, usually without consultation. It was therefore broadly true that he was responsible for policy, and so it was appropriate and effective for the House, if it did not like what he was doing, to censure him; if censured he would feel bound to resign his post.

Since then Big Government has arrived. In Palmerston's day there were 39,147 civil servants and 14 cabinet ministers—one for each 2,796 officials. In 1978 there were 737,984 civil servants and 24 cabinet ministers—one for each 30,749 civil servants. In Palmerston's day the state spent about 9 percent of the GNP. In 1977–1978 it was spending (directly or by making transfer payments among the various sectors of the public) some £60,000 million, some 45 percent of the GNP.

This vast increase in the magnitude of a minister's task suggests that his scrutiny of departmental activities must perforce be very perfunctory, but it has been weakened by two other developments. Most ministers have little time to familiarize themselves with their department before they are moved to another one. In 1945–1951, the average tenure of a minister in one department was two years; in 1951–1964 it was 2.33 years; in 1964–1970, a mere 1.75 years. Further, many government operations must nowadays be arranged over a long time—witness the building of the Concorde, the selection and construction of nuclear energy plants, or the elaboration of a state pension and superannuation scheme. Furthermore, as these same examples suggest, many governmental activities are complicated and technical.

Consequently the old minister-civil servant dichotomy no longer exists. Left to themselves, ministers could not take decisions on the entire range of their department's affairs even if they wanted to. In practice they do not; to the limited extent that they do, they depend on the advice of their senior civil servants. Yet as long as the convention of individual ministerial responsibility exists, and the minister is presumed to be the only begetter of the policies he expounds, it is not constitutionally possible to pin blame on his officers.

This state of affairs nowadays causes widespread and intense frustration, and the civil service has come under continuous criticism in the press, among the political parties, and among backbench M.P.s. These criticisms take two main forms, which can and sometimes do overlap. The first is politically neutral, the second partisan. The politically neutral approach seeks to control the civil service by a variety of devices including the courts, the ombudsman (known in Britain as the parliamentary commissioner), and Parliament. It implicitly reaffirms the eighteenth-century distinction between legislature and executive and the accountability of the executive to the legislature. The partisan line of attack variously affirms that the senior civil servants are unequipped, by training, background, or prejudice, to act as the neutral servants of a reforming or progressive government.

Such views are advanced chiefly by certain members of the Labour party, inside and outside Parliament. The consequences of all such criticisms taken together have been a modest politicization of the higher reaches of the civil service; proposals to strengthen a minister's power over his senior officers; and proposals to strengthen the powers of the House of Commons or the members of the governing parliamentary party over ministers and their civil servants alike.

Politicization of the Civil Service. In order to overcome the alleged conservatism of senior civil servants, various individuals and organs in the Labour party have urged that the ministers be empowered to appoint special political advisers or form a politically partisan *cabinet de ministre*. When Wilson formed a Labour cabinet in 1964 he appointed two special advisers, but in 1974 he went much farther, setting up a special policy unit in the Prime Minister's private office. The object was "to provide a team with a strong political commitment to advise on, propose and pursue, policies to further the Government's political goals."[15] In 1979 the team numbered six, and was credited with having produced studies on unemployment, Ireland, the EEC, Civil Service pay, and Devolution. Its head, Dr. Bernard Donoghue, rewrote the government's Green Paper (an advisory document) on Education in 1977 and on the uses of North Sea oil revenue in 1978.[16]

In addition Wilson authorized cabinet ministers to appoint their own special advisers, though he limited these to two for each department. Thirteen ministers used the opportunity and the number of advisers, including those in the policy unit, was thirty-eight. This compares with 850 top-rank civil servants (those with the status of under-secretary or above), and their compensation was small—in 1978 it was reckoned at only £188,476.[17]

The special adviser is still a very controversial position, especially where pay and status are concerned. Many think it wrong that committed political partisans should be appointed at all, but far worse if they are given permanent status and put on the public payroll like other civil servants. Their legal status is that of "temporary" civil servants; they were originally appointed on five-year contracts

---

[15] Harold Wilson, *The Government of Britain* (London: Weidenfeld, 1978).

[16] *Times*, June 13, 1978. For a description of the way the unit works see Joe Haines, *The Politics of Power* (London: Hodder and Stoughton, 1977), chapters 2 and 3. This book contains an account of the unit's attitude to civil service pay and how, according to the author, the civil service contrived to defeat its proposals.

[17] *Times*, June 13, 1978.

only, and there has never been any doubt about the ability of a new Prime Minister to fire such persons. The controversies have instead concerned their numbers and status. In June 1974, halfway between one election and the one to come, Prime Minister Wilson tried to get legal authority for the advisers to stand as parliamentary candidates. This privilege is denied to permanent civil servants, as we have noted, and Wilson's attempt to acquire it for the temporaries failed. In 1978, apparently at the request of the Prime Minister, the Civil Service Commission drafted a scheme that envisaged a corps of perhaps 100 special advisers forming a special new category of public officers with a career structure, but automatically terminated if their government suffered an electoral defeat.[18] In May 1978, the Prime Minister himself was troubled because, under their five-year contracts, some advisers including the head of his policy unit, would have to retire by March 1979.[19] Wilson was relieved of this particular embarrassment by a Civil Service Commissioner's ruling that it was legal to appoint such advisers for any indeterminate period short of the number of years required for a civil servant to acquire superannuation rights.

The value of these political advisers is also controversial. The permanent civil servants no longer seem to be troubled by such advisers, save in one or two cases, perhaps, such as the Department of Energy. The policy advisers themselves, of course, put up a strong case for their indispensability,[20] and one of them is credited with drafting sections of a Labour party-NEC policy document that recommends that ministers should be permitted

> to appoint a private office of their own choosing containing as many special advisers from outside Whitehall as they need; and to make greater use of junior ministers and special advisers who should be allowed to sit on interdepartmental Cabinet Committees. . . .[21]

On the other hand Lord Rothschild, a former head of the Cabinet Policy Review Staff, acidly commented on them that they combined "the functions of lesser politicians with the salaries of higher civil servants."[22]

---

[18] *Times*, June 13, 1978.

[19] *Times*, May 31, 1978.

[20] Roger Darlington, "Why there should be more advisers in Whitehall," *Times*, July 18, 1978. Darlington was a special adviser, 1974–1978.

[21] *Times*, June 13, 1978. Additionally, the House of Commons Executive Committee, in its Eleventh Reform, also recommended the institutionalization of the special adviser.

[22] Ibid.

There was some doubt how an incoming Conservative government would react to these (mostly Labour-inspired) innovations. On balance, Conservatives seemed hostile to any politicization of the civil service. All doubt was resolved after the May 1979 election. Margaret Thatcher's government allowed both the special policy unit and the ministerial political advisers to lapse.

Ministerial Control over Senior Departmental Appointments. In present practice, authority to appoint, dismiss, or change a permanent secretary lies with the head of the civil service. In practice all such decisions are taken with the concurrence of the Prime Minister; hence when a minister wants to change his permanent secretary he may do so, but only with the agreement of the Prime Minister. The matter goes farther, however, for he cannot change a more junior official unless his permanent secretary agrees.

This matter came up before the Expenditure Committee of the House of Commons during its examination of the civil service, and it unanimously recommended that while the permanent secretary should only be removable by the procedure outlined above, there should be a change in respect to the junior officials. "We believe," they said, "that contrary to the present official position, Ministers should be able to *require* Permanent Secretaries to make changes of this sort. . . ."[23] To this the Labour government gave a frosty answer: it was up to the Prime Minister and not his ministerial colleagues to decide on senior Whitehall appointments and on "machinery of government questions" after "consultation as appropriate with his colleagues and the Head of the Civil Service."[24]

Departmental Watchdog Committees. On both sides of the House backbench M.P.s have clearly become more and more frustrated over the years at their apparent inability to penetrate the veil of ministerial secrecy and find out what really goes on inside the department. The most obvious device for doing this is a select committee of the House, which, conventionally, produces a unanimous report representing the opinion of the House as a legislature in contradistinction to the executive. In 1956 the House established a select committee on nationalized industries, and in the late 1960s a number of similar, specialized committees were set up. These have at best been all bark and no bite. For one thing they are too few and too unsystematic to conduct a

---

[23] *Eleventh Report from the Expenditure Committee: The Civil Service* (HC 1 July 1977), vol. 1, para. 145–46.
[24] *Guardian*, March 16, 1978.

current review of all administrative responsibilities. They are empowered to appoint part-time staff for special purposes, but they have done so sparingly and under certain restrictions. They have a prima facie power to send for persons, papers, and records, but for a variety of legal and procedural reasons, this turns out to be highly restricted in practice. And when they have reported, the government does not necessarily make time for a debate: In 1971–1977, eighty-three reports were published, only forty-four debates took place, and only eleven of these were pressed to a floor vote.[25]

The Expenditure Committee found this situation highly unsatisfactory and recommended the establishment of committees "specifically related to the Departments of State" that would be serviced by "adequate specialist staff."[26] The government rejected this recommendation. "Ministers," it said "are responsible to Parliament for policy, and any extension of the accountability of civil servants must recognize the overriding responsibility of the Departmental Minister for the work and efficiency of his Department." The proposed Committee system "would involve a fundamental change in our parliamentary system and in the relationship between the executive and Parliament."[27]

Only four months after the government had spoken, however, it was confronted with the findings of a select committee on the procedure of the House of Commons, which had been sitting for the last two years. Its report is the most comprehensive and innovative since the Third Report of the Select Committee of 1946.[28] It repeated the call for watchdog committees over the departments, specifically recommending that the committees be reorganized to provide the House with the means of "scrutinizing the activities of the public service on a continuing and systematic basis"; that the system should be based on subject areas and twelve new subject committees should be established; that they should be free to appoint whatever advisers they required; that they should regard any refusal by a department to give information—unless fully explained and justified to their satisfaction—as a serious matter that should be brought to the attention of the House; that they should have the power to order the attendance of a minister and the production of papers and records

[25] *1st Report from the Select Committee on Procedure,* Session 1977–78, (HC 588-1 1978) vol. 1.

[26] *11th Report from Expenditure Committee,* the Civil Service; (HC 1 July 1977, volume 1) para. 161.

[27] *The Guardian,* March 16, 1978.

[28] *1st Report from the Select. Comt. on Procd.,* Session 1977-78, pp. ccv–cxxvii.

by him, and that his failure to do so should be the subject of automatic debate in the House; and that special time should be allocated for debates on the committees' reports.[29]

Initially, the government declined even to find time to debate this report. The opposition, which subscribed to its main recommendations, forced it to do so in February 1979, but only on a "take note" motion—in other words a general debate not ending in a vote. Nevertheless it became clear that there was overwhelming support for the changes, not only from the opposition benches, but also from many Labour M.P.s, both on the right and the left of the parliamentary Labour party. This fact points to another, inner dimension of this debate. As it stands, the proposal would strengthen backbenchers, in other words, the House as such, against the executive. But this is not merely the same thing as strengthening *party* control of the executive: it is the exact opposite and this is precisely why the scheme was rejected so passionately by Michael Foot, the leader of the House and leftist deputy leader of the party. In his view, since the select committees conventionally arrive at unanimous or consensual reports, then the scheme would result in "consensus politics" which, as a self-confessed leftist, he rejected. In this Foot is not alone. The left-wing Labour members of the expenditure committee, in their review of the civil service, and the Labour party NEC both concur in this rejection of consensus politics. The scheme they propose is a variant on the procedure committees, designed to turn the select committees away from their traditional role into partisan committees.

The arrival of a Conservative government in May 1979 gave the Commons a new opportunity to debate the reform of committee structure. Under its guidance, the House voted overwhelmingly to establish the comprehensive network of watchdog committees recommended in the select committee report. Significantly, however, the government did not support two other of its key recommendations: that these committees should be given legal power to compel the attendance of ministers and the surrendering of official papers and documents; and that House of Commons time should be made automatically available for debating the reports. Consequently, neither has been adopted.

The New Patronage: Quangos. It is possible to politicize a bureaucracy without using ministerial patronage by moving career civil servants in and out of sensitive political offices, for example, in accord-

---

[29] *1st Report from the Select Committee on Procedure*, Session 1977–78, pp. ccv–cxxviii.

ance with the fit between their political outlooks and those of the minister. This is the way a German chancellor ensures the appropriate political outlook in his office. Similarly, it is possible to feather-bed the public service with dependents without giving it a marked political bias; the early federalist presidents of the United States did so.[30]

The latter course is apparently ruled out in Britain, since all appointments to the career grades of civil service must pass the appropriate merit tests administered by the civil service commissioners. Suppose, however, that side by side with the permanent career service there were another, parallel establishment, outside these rules. That is precisely what now exists. Side by side with the regular civil service departments has mushroomed a great cloud of organizations, the appointments to which are the personal gift of ministers. Some appointments are paid; others are entitled only to recover out-of-pocket expenses plus, perhaps, per diems; some are full-time and some are part-time. But in no case are the civil service recruitment rules observed. These bodies are known as *Quangos*, from the original name, "quasi-nongovernmental organizations." This is now taken to mean "quasi-national-governmental organizations." Whereas one hundred years or so ago, the radical John Bright described the British Foreign Office as a "gigantic system of outdoor relief for the aristocratic classes," the *Quangos* are a gigantic system of outdoor relief for party hacks—of both parties to be sure, but positively including one's own. In 1929 Lord Hewart wrote a famous polemic against civil servants entitled *The New Despotism*. What has arrived nowadays may be called "The New Nepotism."

As definitions of a *Quango* vary, it is not possible to say precisely how many there are. A survey of primary legislation, from August 1, 1945 to October 26, 1977, lists 370 bodies, of which 96 are advisory.[31] This total consists mostly of national bodies, however, whereas there are several hundred local or area bodies in existence as well. In 1976 the Civil Service Department published a directory of *Paid Public Appointments Made by Ministers*. It names 295 national and local bodies, but omits all those whose members are unpaid (even though they are often able to claim expenses). A third directory, entitled *Survey of Fringe Bodies*[32] lists only those bodies whose

---

[30] See S. E. Finer, "Patronage and the Public Service," *Public Administration* 30, 1952.

[31] P. Holland and M. Fallon, *The Quango Explosion* (London: Conservative Political Centre, 1978), p. 6.

[32] G. Bowen, *Survey of Fringe Bodies*, Civil Service Department, 1978.

staffs' salaries and conditions of service are subject to ministerial control. These number 171. Whichever definition is used, the bodies range from hived-off organizations like the University Grants Committee, or the boards of nationalized industries, to lowly ones such as the Dental Estimates Board or the China Clay Council.

The number of these bodies has increased sharply. It is reckoned, for instance, that 165 have been set up since 1964 by primary legislation alone—in other words, excluding further bodies set up under these acts by subordinate legislation. One report suggests that, taking local and area bodies as well as all the national ones into account, there may be as many as 800–900.[33]

We are not here concerned with the important question of the public accountability of such bodies. In this respect they strongly resemble what the President's Commission on Administrative Management of 1936 called the independent regulatory agencies, a "headless fourth branch of government."[34] The concern of this paper is with the growth of ministerial patronage. Parliamentary questions have elicited the picture that emerges in Table 34. Table 34 makes it clear that seventeen ministers dispose of 8,411 paid appointments and nearly 25,000 unpaid ones.

Although ministers clearly provide for their political supporters, they by no means exclusively appoint from this source. It is true that very large numbers of leading trade unionists are appointed to these bodies; for instance the thirty-nine members of the TUC General Council held 180 such appointments between them. At the same time, however, a large number of such appointments go to serving civil servants. For instance, of the ninety-one appointments in the gift of the Minister for Overseas Development, twenty-one are civil servants from the ministry. Appointments are made to political opponents as well as friends. For all that the friends have to be, and are, looked after. In 1969, for instance, the Labour party NEC brought pressure on ministers to this effect.

> In response to complaints about minor patronage appointments—to regional hospital boards, boards of prison visitors, Justiceships of the Peace and such like, there was a concerted effort to channel them to nominees of constituency Labour parties. A great many positions went to defeated Labour Councillors.[35]

---

[33] Holland and Fallon, *The Quango Explosion*, p. 6.

[34] The *President's Committee on Administrative Management Report* (Washington, D.C.: Government Printing Office, 1937), p. 39.

[35] Butler and Pinto-Duschinsky, *The General Election of 1970*, pp. 60–61.

TABLE 34
Salaried, Fee-Paid, and Unpaid Appointments in the Gift of Each Minister, 1978

Departments	Salaried	Fee-Paid	Unpaid	Cost
Agriculture	107	281	1037	£143,000
Defense	26	644	1872	N.A.
Education	11	127	594	£185,000
Employment	76	2456	5661	£306,102
Environment	313	856	1102	£509,636
Energy	148	1	73	£911,000
Foreign/Commonwealth Office	20	12	313	£ 54,738
Home	54	117	2115	£310,000
Industry	78	14	403	£727,102
N. Ireland	30	61	148	£122,810
Prices & Consumer	26	49	989	£253,750
Scotland	.... 422		N.A.	£380,000
Social Services	140	1949	8700	N.A.
Trade	52	9	244	£345,264
Transport	206	—	289	£488,876
Wales	69	57	412	£175,158

N.A.: not available.

NOTE: This table excludes a small number of appointments made by other ministers such as the Lord President of the Council, the Chancellors of the Exchequer and the Duchy of Lancaster, and the Minister for the Civil Service. The Prime Minister does not directly appoint but advises the Queen on appointments to twenty bodies involving sixty-six members at a cost in 1976 of £756,000.

SOURCE: Holland and Fallon, *The Quango Explosion*; derived from answers to parliamentary questions, June 28, 29, 1978.

Some ministers make such appointments to reinforce the party ideology in a particular body or service as much as to reward their supporters. In 1977, for instance, the secretary of the Department of Health and Social Security was reported to have removed thirty-two of the ninety previous chairmen of the Area Health Authorities and replaced them with partisan appointments.[36] Another minister has openly stated that such agencies "have a responsibility towards government policy, and I think that one makes sure that they react to that properly, by appointing appropriate people."[37] A few politically sensitive organizations, like the Arbitration and Conciliation Service, have deliberately been saturated with trade unionist and labour-inclining members. But on the whole, the appointments are made

[36] *Sunday Telegraph*, July 3, 1977.
[37] Holland and Fallon, *The Quango Explosion*.

haphazardly by secret processes, often reliant on personal recommendations, from what has well been described as "stolid phalanxes of union and industry representatives topped up with favourite academics and 'safe' pressure group activists with the odd Peer to leed the respectability of past achievement. . . ."[38]

The significance of the development of the *Quangos* is not, then, that it has given political direction to an important part of the public service, but that it provides party leaders with a new means to reward the party faithful or to provide a fat retirement cushion for those who have served it well in the past.

Conclusions

1. The extraparliamentary parties have never been communitarian; they neither incorporate nor control any numerical significant categorical groups—such as youth, women, university students—in British society.

2. At no level do parties control the media, which have become increasingly independent of them since 1945.

3. Private promotional pressure groups float more policy outside the parties than they used to, and the major economic organizations increasingly operate on civil servants and ministers in the first instance rather than on the parliamentary and extraparliamentary parties.

4. At all levels the parties' command of trade unions and industrial-financial organizations has markedly weakened since 1945.

5. Neither the extraparliamentary nor the parliamentary parties direct or even control the central civil service, and the limited introduction of special ministerial advisers was a reaction to parties' consciousness of their reduced capacity to do so. In the *Quangos*, ministerial patronage has strengthened party leaders' hold on supporters but has not given pronounced party-direction to these bodies.

---

[38] Holland and Fallon, *The Quango Explosion.*

GENERAL CONCLUSIONS TO PART ONE

1. At the parliamentary-governmental level the party system is recognizably as it was in 1945: There is a party duopoly of seats and a party monopoly of executive government, the latter enjoying, via the doctrine of parliamentary sovereignty, unfettered legislative, administrative, and financial authority.

2. The party duopoly is wholly the product of the electoral system, which is one of disproportional representation.

3. At the level of the electorate, the two major parties form an ever-diminishing and insignificant fraction of the public. They are supported by fewer and fewer voters. At the same time they frame policies that are more ambitious than before, more mutually exclusive than before, though often remote from public demands, and less capable of being executed than before.

4. The two major parties and the two-party system are more mistrusted, more unpopular, and more condemned than a decade ago, and probably more than in 1945.

PART TWO
The Appraisal

5

The Effectiveness of the Party
System

I believe that without party, Parliamentary Government is impossible.

BENJAMIN DISRAELI

Before assessing the effectiveness of the British party system it is well to restate its major characteristics. It is a two-party system of the classic mold, certainly, but it is a *British* system, with distinctive idiosyncratic features.

The Two-Party System, British Style

At the parliamentary level the two-party nature of the system has never been in doubt since 1945. Even at the electoral level the two major parties took four-fifths of the national vote in 1979. These two major parties are adversary and sharply opposed, more so since 1970 than before.

The two major parties alternate in office. This alternation is decided by the outcome of a system of disproportional representation that is highly susceptible to minute changes of net voting preferences, so that a mere 1 percent net swing from one party to the other can produce a gap of some twenty seats or more between them.

The parliamentary-constitutional arrangements are on a winner-take-all basis. Not only does the victorious party install its leaders in office, but the opposition is excluded from all effective participation in governmental policy formation.

The discipline of the parliamentary party ensures to its leaders, in their new roles as ministers of the Crown, uninterrupted and unchallengeable control of the House of Commons. The House of Commons is in turn the supreme policy-making organ of the United Kingdom. It can be checked only temporarily by the House of Lords, and it is subject to no constitutional constraint by the Crown or the Judiciary.

The authority of the government that results from this system is not subject to the constraints of any written constitution nor to any necessity, conventional or legal, to submit its proposals to popular verdict by way of referendum. In short, Parliament is sovereign. This is so important that it is desirable to quote once again the famous passage by W. Blackstone, and especially to note its concluding sentences:

> The power and jurisdiction of parliament, says Sir Edward Coke, is so transcendent and absolute that it cannot be confined either for causes or persons, within any bounds. And of this high court, he adds, it may be truly said, 'si antiquitatem spectes est vetustissima; si dignitatem, est honoratissima; si jurisdictionem est capacissima.' It hath sovereign and uncontroulable authority in the making, confirming, enlarging, restraining, abrogating, repealing, reviving, and expounding of laws, concerning matters of all possible denominations, ecclesiastical or temporal, civil, military, maritime, or criminal: this being the place where the absoloute despotic power, which must in all governments reside somewhere, is intrusted by the constitution of these kingdoms. All mischiefs and grievances operations and remedies that transcend the ordinary course of the laws, are within the reach of this extraordinary tribunal. It can regulate or new-model the succession to the crown; as was done in the reign of Henry VIII, and William III. It can alter the established religion of the land; as was done in a variety of instances, in the reigns of king Henry VIII, and his three children. It can change and create afresh even the constitution of the kingdom and of parliaments themselves; as was done by the act of union, and the several statutes for triennial and septennial elections. It can, in short, do every thing that is not naturally impossible; and therefore some have not scrupled to call it's power, by a figure rather too bold, the omnipotence of parliament. True it is, that what the parliament doth, no authority upon earth can undo. So that it is a matter most essential to the liberties of this kingdom, that such members be delegated to this important trust, as are most eminent for their probity, their fortitude, and their knowledge; for it was a known apophthegm of the great lord treasurer Burleigh that England could 'never be ruined but

by a parliament'; and as Sir Matthew Hale observes, this being the highest and greatest court, over which none other can have jurisdiction in the kingdom, if by any means a misgovernment should any way fall upon it, the subjects of this kingdom are left without all manner of remedy.[1]

The Party System as the Prime Mover

The goal of the British political party is to win elections. This can be expanded to say that its goal is to empower its leaders to form the government, by nominating parliamentary candidates, and campaigning for their election.

In the literature these three activities are frequently called functions, and since they are self-acknowledged intentional activities, they are called manifest functions. In performing them the parties must also do other things that affect society. Since these are not intentional, they are called latent functions, meaning (in effect) unintended good consequences of party activities.

There is considerable subjectivism built into the term function, so a list of such functions is bound to be idiosyncratic. The items in a list will not be logically necessary to the concept of a party system, and the classification adopted in one list is likely to cut across the classification used in another.

One way to proceed is to search the literature for all mentions of functions and bring these together in a checklist. This has been done by Anthony King in his article, "Political Parties in Western Democracies: Some Sceptical Reflections."[2] That article will be the basis for this appraisal.

King lists six party functions: structuring of the vote; integration; mobilization; leadership recruitment; organization of government; and policy formation. These six functions, however, subsume certain other activities or 'unintended good consequences' that appear to be central. They are, communication, representation, participation, and legitimation.

Forming an Executive Government. With one or two exceptions, in the war cabinets of World War I and World War II, British governments are exclusively formed from parliamentarians—in other words from M.P.s and Peers—and such governments are exclusively gen-

---

[1] W. Blackstone, *Commentaries on the Law of England* (London: 1825) vol. I, Book I, chapter II, pp. 160–61. Emphasis added.

[2] Anthony King, "Political Parties in Western Democracies: Some Sceptical Reflections," *Polity*, vol. II, no. 2 (Winter 1969), pp. 111–41.

erated by interparty competition at the electoral and/or parliamentary level. The party system has ensured the alternation of single party governments ever since 1945, as already noted. This function then is fulfilled by the party system, exclusively and completely.

Recruiting Political Leaders. There are precious few independent candidates, and even fewer have ever been elected. M.P.s are therefore *party* M.P.s, and governments are drawn exclusively from the parliamentary parties. In few countries is the political leadership at any or all levels so exclusively a matter of party. At rare intervals a handful of important individuals like Ernest Bevin, Lord Woolton, or Frank Cousins have been brought into government from the outside. Then they have either been given a peerage to enable them to sit in the House of Lords or, if their post required that they answer to the Commons, some safe constituency has been found for them. The incumbent M.P. has been persuaded to resign in return for some other honorable post, and the outsider has been incorporated into the party system. This should be compared with, for example, the French situation, where significant proportions of the cabinet are often non-partisan experts brought in from the civil service, where one President, Georges Pompidou, was brought in from merchant banking, and the present prime minister, Raymond Barre, is a nonparty economist. And of course it contrasts even more sharply with American practice, where almost all secretaries of state are brought in from outside the party organization. By contrast, if an individual aspires to political leadership in Britain, he must attach himself, usually from an early age, to a political party.

Structuring the Vote. There is a weak sense and a strong sense to the term "structuring the vote." In the weak sense, it may merely signify the parties' ability to persuade voters to respond to their respective labels by coming out and voting for them. By this definition, the party system is clearly failing. As we have seen the electoral turnout declined from more than 80 percent during the 1950s and early 1960s to a bit more than 70 percent after that. The two-party system has failed even more signally than the system as a whole insofar as the two parties' share declined from nearly 80 percent of the total electorate to 68 percent in 1966 and to 61.3 percent in May 1979.

In the stronger sense, "structuring the vote" refers to the parties' ability to persuade the public to adopt particular points of view.[3] This requires us to compare the party's policies with that of its supporters.

---

[3] King, "Political Parties in Western Democracies."

Two sets of data each suggest in different ways that the parties' capacity to persuade voters to adopt particular opinions is not high.

To begin with, Rose[4] has shown that the policy preferences of M.P.s and voters differ substantially. Whereas the two major parliamentary parties opposed one another on ten out of fifteen issues, the electorate divided on only three out of eighteen issues. The index of interparty difference (calculated by the difference between the affirmative answers to a question) was 46 percent among the M.P.s but only 17 percent among voters.

It follows from the above that policy preferences of M.P.s differ from those of their electors. On seven issues Rose found that the *voters* (both Labour and Conservative) tended to show the highest agreement—the average difference between them on the seven issues was only 16 percent. The next greatest degree of accord was among Conservative M.P.s and Conservative voters—the average difference between them was 27 percent. The average difference between Labour M.P.s and their voters, however, was 38 percent.

We cannot from these data conclude absolutely that party leaderships are unable to persuade the voters to adopt the view they propound. It could be that voters vote for parties for other reasons than approval of their policies, and, indeed, there is much evidence to suggest that they do indeed vote for images rather than issues.[5] It could also be that party leaders make no effort to persuade voters to adopt their policies, but this is simply not so. Only if we first assumed that voters vote for candidates because they propound particular policies, and also that parties make an effort to get voters to adopt these views, could we even begin to prove with finality whether party leaderships are unable to persuade voters to adopt these views.

Fortunately, another piece of evidence leads to a more conclusive answer.

It is not that the electorate is ignorant of party stands. On a number of issues there is a clear understanding of the line each party takes. The 'structure' uniting these perceptions is illustrated by the relationship between the positions which their supporters thought their parties were taking on the issues of nationalization and nuclear weapons. There was fairly high consensus that the Conservatives stood for keeping the Bomb and Labour for extending public ownership. [Table 35] shows how closely the two perceptions were re-

---

4 Rose, *Politics in England Today*, pp. 287–88.
5 See, for instance, Butler and Stokes, *Political Change in Britain*, chapter 16 and the literature cited there.

TABLE 35

PARTY STANDS ON NATIONALIZATION AND NUCLEAR WEAPONS AS
PERCEIVED BY LABOUR AND CONSERVATIVE VOTERS, 1964

(percent)

		Most Likely to Extend Nationalization	
		Own Party	Other Party
Most Likely to Keep	Other Party	76	5
Nuclear Weapons	Own Party	24	95
Total		100	100

lated in 1964. Indeed any standard correlation calculated from the frequencies underlying the table would have a value approaching +0.7 percent.

Nothing like this coherent structure is, however, found when we examine the attitudes that partisan voters expressed towards these same two issues. [Table 36] gives a very much weaker correlation between these attitudes.

By most standard measures it would be a little more than +0.1 percent. Plainly the degree to which voters pattern their beliefs on those of their parties, even on key issues, is very modest.

Even party activists fail to conform. . . . [I]t is striking that the tie between attitudes on nationalization and nuclear weapons was no stronger among those minorities who subscribed to a party or did party work than among the bulk of

TABLE 36

ATTITUDES TOWARD NATIONALIZATION AND NUCLEAR WEAPONS HELD BY
LABOUR AND CONSERVATIVE SUPPORTERS, 1964

(percent)

		Nationalization Should Be Extended	
		Yes	No
Britain Should Give			
Up Nuclear	Yes	65	51
Weapons	No	35	49
Total		100	100

the electorate. There could be few more striking comments on the limited extent to which party orientations reach down into the mass public, or on the limited role which tightly clustered policy beliefs play in the motives for party work.[6]

We conclude then: in either the weak or the strong sense of the expression, the parties capacity to "structure the vote" is modest.

Defining the Political Issues. In this context[7] it is essential to bear in mind the distinction between the extraparliamentary party organization, the parliamentary party, and the party-supported government, since the performance of the issue-defining function varies accordingly. The party system then may define the political issues negatively, by suppressing or compressing raw demands, or positively by raising them and combining them into a package—the so-called aggregative role of the parties.

There are two possible measures for assessing the party system's capacity to raise issues: the range of issues and the degree to which other social groups also raise issues. As to the former, the British parties are most impressive if indeed they are not unique in the multiplicity of the items they identify for political action. One possible measure of the range of issues is the number of party policy documents and specialist policy committees. The Labour party's NEC report for 1977–1978 lists thirteen specialist subcommittees and eight study groups, as well as seven other policy-formulating groups or committees. It also lists nineteen new policy documents, ranging from "Argentina, Chile and Brazil" to "Local Authority Mortgage Lending" and "Transport Policy." The Conservative party operates on a similar scale. The parties seem not to overlook or ignore any significant problems. On the contrary, the major parties feel they must have an answer and a policy for anything that is even remotely in the public sphere of interest and, if anything, produce far too many policy documents. Such remorseless appetite for formulating policies on everything and anything is reminiscent of Jonathan Swift's "Meditation on a Broom-

---

[6] Ibid., pp. 314–16.

[7] Here we depart from King's treatment. King writes of the "policy-formation" function, distinguishing between its electoral and governmental aspects. On the latter he has no difficulty in showing that elements other than the party system help form policies. We prefer to distinguish policy *formation* from policy *formulation*, or more precisely, the definition of the political issues, to which King devotes only a perfunctory attention. Furthermore, King lists "the aggregation of interests" as a separate function, while we prefer to subsume it under the heading in the text.

stick": a party "sets up to be a universal Reformer and Corrector of Abuses, a Remover of Grievances" and "rakes into every Slut's corner of Nature, bringing hidden corruptions to the light and raises a mighty dust where there was none before."[8]

True, other sources exist; books are written, pamphlets printed and the media, particularly "investigative journalists" and television producers, also raise issues that become foci of controversy—civil rights in Ulster, the Thalidomide case. But it would be hard to think of a serious policy matter, as opposed to examples of specific abuses, that has been raised by the media independently of or ahead of the parties. A more weighty independent source of policy formulation is to be found in reports of royal commissions and other official inquiries. Public inquiries such as those into the trade unions, the press, or the future of broadcasting supply most important material to the policy debate. Yet in most cases a political party will already have given the matter thought and often will even have given evidence before the inquiry. Even more certainly, a party will take its own stand on the recommendations of such inquiries.

The same must be said about the issues raised by promotional groups such as those concerned with child poverty or one-parent families, with homelessness, or with the plight of the aged. Even if these are the first to raise an issue, the parties take their stands on it, incorporating it or otherwise into their priorities.

When the electors must make up their minds on how to vote, the influence of party formulation becomes pervasive. As Robertson has observed,[9] the voter is informed that social problems exist in four ways: his own experience, which is very narrow; the experts, here meaning almost exclusively the mass media, which offer only very selective and partisan aid; the opposition parties; and the government, which is a competitor. And so Robertson justly comments:

> The voter's position as a decision maker can be seen as very strange for his information about (a) what problems need solving and (b) which policy-set is best, comes from the policy-sets themselves. It is as though a civil servant was restricted when making a decision, to talking only to the exponents of rival policies and to having to accept their word that the situation was one he should be spending time on at all.[10]

---

[8] Jonathan Swift, "Meditation on a Broomstick" in *Gulliver's Travels and Selected Writings* (New York: Random House, 1946), p. 458.

[9] D. Robertson, *A Theory of Party Competition* (London: Wiley, 1976), pp. 12–13.

[10] Ibid.

The aggregation of interests. Since its formulation by Almond,[11] this term has become a catchword. Almond considers the political party to be "the specialized aggregation structure of modern societies."[12] "To aggregate" does not in itself mean anything more than to "gather together into one whole." Not all political parties do this. The nationalist parties in Britain, for instance, certainly gather a number of proposals into one whole, but their number and range are much more limited than those of the two major political parties, whose manifestoes contain from 70 to 130 specific political commitments. Certainly the Committee on Financial Aid to Political Parties believed in this "aggregating" role of parties; "the parties," it said, "provide the framework within which . . . the many demands and efforts of smaller groups in society can be aggregated and merged into a small number of workable alternative programmes."[13]

The major parties do unquestionably function in that way. They are much more programmatic than most parties in other western democracies, and furthermore, go to pains to make these programs explicit. To do this requires them to establish priorities and to bring them into some harmony. Hence certain interests are deprived of their full expectations. Party history is replete with examples of conflict between the party and its client—for example, trade unions and the Labour party in 1969, manufacturing industry and the Conservative government in 1963–1964, and the small storekeepers against the Conservative government in the dispute over the Resale Price Maintenance Bill of 1964.

Gate-Keeping. But just as parties compete with each other in naming items for political attention, so by their gate-keeping location can they also prevent issues from becoming public. One of the most striking examples is that of non-white immigration from the Commonwealth. From its beginning around 1948 until 1959, immigration went on without interruption, without restriction, and without discussion. Only when the 1959 election brought some new Conservative M.P.s into the Commons from West Midlands towns that contained many immigrants were questions raised in Parliament; and it was not until 1961 that the Conservative government introduced the first of many bills to control the inflow. Until then the two parties had tacitly agreed that there was no problem. Similarly with the EEC; although

---

[11] G. A. Almond and J. S. Coleman, *The Politics of the Developing Areas* (Princeton: Princeton University Press, 1960), p. 39.

[12] G. A. Almond and G. B. Powell, *Comparative Politics* (Boston: Little, Brown, 1966), p. 29.

[13] Report of the Committee on Financial Aid to Political Parties, p. 18.

the Treaty of Rome was signed by the six European countries in 1956, the only British party to raise it as an issue was the Liberal party. Because of the Liberal party's weakness, the question did not receive much of a hearing. The two major parties ignored it until the Conservative government raised it as a serious option after its return to power in 1960.

In short, the political parties not only perform the function of issue definition but they over-perform it. It can fairly be said that they engross practically every actual or potential issue simply by insisting that it is an issue. And just as their definition of what is an issue makes it one, so their refusal to name certain items makes them non-issues. The parties monopolize the national agenda.

Integration. Another unintended good consequence of the party system is that it "integrates [the private citizen] into the group";[14] that "individuals acquire psychological and social attachments to political parties, and through them to the wider public. . . ."[15] We can expand this to make it mean the function of bringing voters into the political community and getting them to work according to its rules.

In historical perspective the success of the British party system in bringing Britain's nascent manual worker class into the political community is as impressive as it is undeniable. Not merely was it incorporated into the Liberal-Conservative system in the late nineteenth and early twentieth centuries, but the process by which the emerging Labour party displaced the once dominant Liberals was both orderly and peaceful.[16] If one rereads the left-wing literature of the 1930s, the difference between its tone and today's is striking. It was a commonplace then that the capitalist ruling class (identified of course with the Conservative party) would resort to violence and fascism rather than accept socialism. Today 28 percent of the civilian work force is in the public sector, more than 50 percent of the national income is spent or transferred by the state, rates of direct tax were the highest in Europe (until the advent of the Conservative government of 1979), and the differential between the top and the bottom level of earnings is the lowest. This may not be socialism but it isn't anti-socialism either.

---

[14] King, "Political Parties in Western Democracies."

[15] S. Neumann (ed.), *Modern Political Parties* (Chicago: University of Chicago Press, 1956), p. 396.

[16] The remarkable success of the Conservative party in involving the manual workers in the political community is convincingly demonstrated by McKenzie and Silver, *Angels in Marble*.

If we turn to the present day, however, what would be appropriate measures of how well the party system performs this integration function? There seem to be at least three. The reciprocals of integration are apathy, alienation, or frustration.

Apathy. This can be quantified by the extent of persistent nonvoting, which is small. We have already referred to Crewe's finding that the proportion of electors who failed to vote in all the four elections of 1966–1974 was a mere 1 percent and the proportion who managed to vote only once is itself only 3 percent.

Frustration with or incomprehension of the system? The reciprocal of a measure of this would, presumably, indicate how much the system makes voters feel that they are participating in the process of government. The measures of satisfaction with the British system are very low in this regard. Thus, the Essex British Election Study team ran a time series on the question, "Over the years, how much do you feel that the government pays attention to what people think when it decides what to do?" In 1963, 50 percent of the respondents replied, "not much," but in 1969 that proportion had risen to 61 percent.[17] A 1969 Gallup poll found that 57 percent of the respondents felt "they had no influence on the country's future"; in 1973 that number had increased to 63 percent. The political parties received a good mark for their part in making the government pay attention to what people think: 50 percent thought they were effective in this respect in 1963, 48 percent in 1969. On the other hand, more people hardened their dislike for the parties: in 1963, 16 percent said "parties had no such effect"; in 1969, 26 percent. The reason is that the number of "don't knows" had declined in this period.[18] Responses about the importance of elections in making governments "pay attention to what the people think" show a similar pattern. The majority think that elections are effective in this respect: 72 percent said so in 1963 and exactly the same proportion in 1969, but as in the case of political parties' "effectiveness," the number affirming that elections did not have much effect rose from 9 percent in 1963 to 16 percent in 1969.[19] On the question of the responsiveness to public opinion, the proportions are significantly different. In 1963, 41 percent thought M.P.s paid a good deal or some attention to their electors when they decided what to do in Parliament, and in 1969, as many as 50 percent thought so. But those who thought that M.P.s were not so guided in their

---

[17] Butler and Stokes, *Political Change in Britain*, p. 467.

[18] Ibid.

[19] Ibid.

TABLE 37

ATTITUDES TOWARD THE SYSTEM OF GOVERNMENT
(percent)

Categories	1970	1977
It works extremely well and could not be improved	5	10
It could be improved in small ways, but mainly works well	43	24
It could be improved quite a lot	35	33
It needs a great deal of improvement	14	29
Don't know	4	4
Total	100	100

SOURCE: The 1970, *Royal Commission on the Constitution* (Kilbrandon, 1973) Vol. I. For 1977, ORC Poll, 1977, for the National Campaign for Electoral Reform (privately distributed).

considerations numbered 32 percent in 1963 and 36 percent in 1969.[20]

This increasing disesteem for key political institutions is matched by opinions about how well the political system is working. In 1970, 49 percent thought it was not working well, in 1977 no less than 62 percent thought so. Table 37 splits up the responses.

Yet public disapproval of the political system is not reflected in alienation or (save in Ulster) political violence. There have been no "long, hot summers," no *évènements*, no violent occupation of city centers as in Italy. It is true that pickets are used to keep away goods or other workers from entering a factory (a widespread practice in British industrial disputes), and they often use intimidation and violence. For purposes of estimating the legitimacy of the political system, what is significant about this violence is not that it occurs, but that it is overwhelmingly condemned by the general public. Polls taken during the strikes of January-February 1979, showed an overwhelming percentage of the respondents condemning such activity. Respondents overwhelmingly favored the legal banning of "secondary picketing" by nine to one.

The reason that the public thinks rather little of the political system but does not translate this into antisystem activity is that the people are overwhelmingly concerned with material matters. They want the system reformed, but they give this a very low priority. The poll that ORC conducted for the National Council for Electoral Reform in 1977 shows this clearly. The respondents were asked what were

[20] Ibid., p. 468.

the "most urgent tasks" for the government. The results indicated control of rising prices (55 percent); unemployment (32 percent); taxation (20 percent); the economy generally (18 percent). Only 2 percent mentioned constitutional reform and electoral reform, and only 3 percent mentioned the devolution of certain central tasks to elected assemblies in Wales and Scotland.

Alienation. Alienation could be indicated by the number of electors who refuse to vote because they reject the party system. Only 3 in 100 electors failed to vote or voted on only one occasion in the four elections ending October 1974. How many did so because they rejected the system? We should expect nonvoters of this kind to be very heavily engaged in politics. In fact, only 7 percent of this tiny fraction of nonvoters expressed a "great interest" in politics, and only one-third expressed "some interest": whereas more than three in every four said that they "only rarely" talked about politics. Again, when the persistent nonvoters were asked after the February 1974 election "which party would they have voted for?", only 8 percent said that "they would not have voted at all." Clearly, those who fail to vote do not abstain because they are alienated.

Further confirmation comes in the replies of the 3 percent non-voters to questions about the functioning of the political system. Only 18 percent (the equivalent of 0.5 percent of the total British electorate) said that Britain was badly governed compared with other countries. When asked whether M.P.s and local councillors paid "a great deal" or "some" attention to the public, 45 percent answered "a great deal" to only 38 percent who replied "little or none." We can accordingly infer that militant dissatisfaction with the political system is insignificant.[21]

Communication. "In spite of television, radio and the press, the party organizations will have an important part to play in informing the electorate about party politics . . ." says the Houghton Report on Financial Aid to Political Parties.[22] And it goes on,

> The local party organizations are a valuable means of keeping party representatives constantly aware of the views and concerns of their supporters. The role of parties in communication is thus a complex process: from the parties to their members and to the public; and from the public and party members to the parties and to party headquarters. . . ."

[21] Crewe, Fox, and Alt, "Non-Voting in British General Elections," pp. 69–71.
[22] Report of the Committee on Financial Aid to Political Parties.

In principle, *upward communication* can be achieved without political parties. Constituents can make their grievances known to their M.P. even if he is an independent. This kind of upward flow is a function of the representative system, not of parties as such. It is arguable, however, that the competitiveness of parties makes for better performance of this function where it concerns not individuals, but categories of citizens like the handicapped, old-age pensioners, or the unemployed. The individual M.P. can press individual remedies for individual cases, but only a party is capable of generating the collective policy necessary to redress the grievances of a category. It is widely agreed that the views of M.P.s when they return to Parliament from their constituencies after the weekend is a most important factor in shaping the views of the parliamentary party leadership.

The influence of such upward flows on the leadership is sometimes spotlighted in dramatic fashion. In 1964, for instance, the Conservative leadership was trying to enact a bill to illegalize the fixing of retail prices by manufacturers of a product—the Resale Price Maintenance Bill. The practice was much favored by small storekeepers, since it insulated them from competition, and small shopkeepers were and are notoriously sympathetic to the Conservatives. The bill provoked a serious revolt of backbench M.P.s, who were plainly worried as their constituents lobbied them and wrote letters of protest. The M.P.s found the spontaneity of these letters and meetings most impressive; the debates show that they were inured to the organized lobby that the bill's numerous antagonists were mounting.[23]

As to *downward communication*, the Houghton Committee stated that "some of our witnesses felt that the parties were failing in what might be expected of them in this field" and that "this evidence was supported by our survey of public opinion."[24] A study cited earlier quoted strong survey evidence showing that most of the public are able to identify the major policy stands of the respective parties. That evidence is borne out by, for instance, checking the replies respondents gave to questions asking them what they would expect to happen in a number of policy areas if *either* the Conservative *or* the Labour party were returned at the next election. In October 1978, for instance, Gallup questioned respondents about policies in ten areas, on the assumption that the Labour party would win the election. Three questions did not admit of any correct answer, but respondents returned

---

[23] *Times*, January 18, 1964, February 21, 1964. See also Finer, *Anonymous Empire*, pp. 69–72.

[24] Report of the Committee on Financial Aid to Political Parties, p. 18. This author, however, found no such reference in the survey.

accurate answers to all the remaining seven items. Eleven items were mentioned on the hypothesis that the Conservatives would win the next election. In this case two matters were problematic, but the respondents returned the correct answers in all nine of the other cases.

These policy items, it must be stressed, were salient issues: More or less control over individuals? More or less direct taxation? More or less trade union power? On these major issues, the party organizations seem to have communicated their message with success.

Representation. The Houghton Committee explicitly stated that representation is a "purpose and main task" of the parties:

> Political parties are essential because they carry out a number of vital *functions* in our political and parliamentary life which cannot be successfully undertaken in any other way. . . . *Parties are the agencies through which the electorate can express its collective will; . . . they are also the means whereby members of the general public are able to participate in formulation of policies.*[25]

In this context we ought to distinguish two senses of the term "representation." The first, weaker form, resembles "virtual representation," the second and stronger carries the implication that the party policies are policies that the members have helped to shape.

Edmund Burke defined virtual representation as being "that in which there is a communion of interests, and sympathy of feelings and desires, between those who act in the name of any description of people, and the people in whose name they act, although the trustees are not actually chosen by them."[26] There can be no doubt whatsoever that many people, indeed the great majority of the electorate, whether party members or not, adhere to a party because they feel that it somehow or other stands for their interests. What is more, they are very often right. A municipal garbage man would be well advised to vote Labour rather than Conservative, while a company director or property developer might be forgiven for supposing that his life would be better under the Conservatives.

In this sense then the parties certainly "represent" particular groups or interests in society to the greater or perhaps total exclusion of others. It is most important to note, however, what this implies about the very nature of parties and their relationship with the electorate. It implies that at a given moment, parties are going concerns;

---

[25] Ibid. Emphasis supplied by author.

[26] *The Works of the Rt. Hon. Edmund Burke,* "Letter to Sir Hercules Langrishe Bart M.P." (London: Rivington, 1808), vol. VI, p. 360.

parties and their policies are "there," and members of the public arrange themselves behind them. Parties are bands of leaders, and the public is a following. This is how Max Weber saw the political parties. "A relatively small number of men are primarily interested in political life and hence interested in sharing political power. They provide themselves with a following through free recruitment, present themselves or their protegés as candidates for election, collect the financial means, and go out for vote-grabbing."[27]

The opposite view sees the parties as republics, whose members collectively determine policies and make leaders adopt them. This involves the second and strong sense of representation, as an upward flow of decision making. But this study's findings on the locus of policy making in the Conservative and Labour parties lend little support to this view. Gathered together in the parties Annual Conferences, the rank and file acts as a constraint on the leadership—but with an extremely wide tolerance. Beyond that the parliamentary party is the principal locus of policy making for both major parties, the conferences acting as reactive and responsive organs. The Conservative party conference is highly malleable. The Labour party conference may be less so at times when two or three of the larger union delegations concert a policy that contradicts the platform, but its composition is arbitrary; the (decisive) block vote of powerful union delegations is manipulable and manipulated by accords between the union leaders and the platform; the parliamentary party is autonomous and, although it reports to the conference, its report cannot be voted on; and a Labour government can and often does act in sublime independence of conference resolutions. The worm's-eye view of the Labour party activist has been well captured by Ken Coates, who wants to have the leader selected by the extraparliamentary party precisely because he believes that it is the Prime Minister who makes policy and not the party.

> Any ordinary trade unionist who seeks a particular social or industrial reform is likely to recognize this dilemma. He goes to his branch and wins support for a motion advocating his suggested policy. There begins a long process of democratic argument. If all goes well for him, the motion in question is ultimately table at the union's Annual Conference. There it carries. Assuming his union leaders have been convinced by the arguments our rank-and-filer may now expect them to begin the work of carrying his proposals through

---

[27] "Politics as a Vocation," in H. H. Gerth and C. Wright Mills, *From Max Weber* (London: Routledge, 1964), p. 99.

the TUC and a Labour Party Conference. If that effort suc-
ceeds and the pressure is maintained, then we may in time
find the favoured policy included in an election manifesto.
If we campaign with enthusiasm we may win the subsequent
election. At this point, an enormous convergence of democratic effort has taken place, involving many hours of voluntary work and sacrifice. At this point, also, we discover
that there is a virtually complete and yawning discontinuity
in the process of reform: action upon our commitments may
be scotched by a hostile minister, or fudged in some totally
inexplicable parliamentary compromise, or simply set
aside. . . .[28]

The two senses of representation and the corresponding two visions
of the party can be amalgamated by conceiving of three levels—
the voters, the party activists plus the parliamentary party, and the
party government. The electorate is much more moderate than the
party activists and party M.P.s; there will be no difficulty at all in
demonstrating how often and with what great effect a party government will, after its initial taste of office, proceed to carry out policies
that either never appeared in its election manifesto or are in direct contradiction to it.

If the parties perform a representative function at all, then, it is
in a very unstraightforward way. There is no one-to-one relationship
between the views of the party voters, the party activists and M.P.s,
and the government. There may even be a direct contradiction between
the views of any of these two layers. Houghton's image of parties as
"agencies through which the electorate can express its collective will"[29]
is singularly inappropriate.

Participation. "The parties," says Houghton, "are also the means
whereby members of the general public are able to participate in the
formulation of policies."[30] This study has already presented evidence
to the contrary: the decline of voting, the fall in party membership,
the minute fraction of party members who select parliamentary candidates. Furthermore, although the parties do try to correct some of
these faults through recruitment drives and energetic electoral organization, neither party tries at all to extend the selection of candidates
to all constituency party members. The reverse is true; they jealously
restrict the "secret garden of British politics" to a narrow circle.

---

[28] Ken Coates, *Democracy in the Labour Party* (Nottingham: Spokesman Books,
1977), pp. 13–14.
[29] Report of the Committee on Financial Aid to Political Parties, p. 18.
[30] Ibid.

The Legitimation. Since parties are structures, organizations, they themselves can legitimate nothing, for only beliefs legitimate. What is *believed* about the constitutional role of the parties? No consistent or even explicit theory of political consent exists in authoritative form in Britain. Its people have no Declaration of Independence and written Constitution to guide them like the Americans, or a *Declaration of the Rights of Man and the Citizens* and a *Preamble* to the 1946 Constitution, as do the French. But they do have a historical tradition, and that tradition is both liberal and democratic. It is that the sovereign power —the Crown-in-Parliament—must be representative of and responsive to the wishes of the population, while being circumscribed by what Burke called the "rights of Englishmen"—the traditional common law rights of the citizenry. To acquire this character the sovereign power must be, in effect, elected at short intervals, the rationale being that the election will reflect popular opinion while the revocability of the parliamentary mandate will guarantee that the elected body will not wander too far from this opinion.

This is not meant to be a concise formulation of British constitutional theory and practice, merely a highly uncomplicated statement of its operative ideals for the purpose of demonstrating how the party system fits in. The parties are supposed to be channels of public opinion; broadly representative of their membership, which is open to all citizens; and competitive with others which equally communicate with the public and represent their own membership. Out of their competition, it is supposed, a legislature will emerge that is broadly representative of public opinion and bound never to stray too far from it, because party competition during the term of its life will ensure close attention to popular feeling.

In practice, governments are unpopular for most of their term of office irrespective of their party complexion, and the system is seen as unresponsive to popular preferences and in need of some kind of reform. Yet, never have the government's works and deeds been regarded as *illegitimate* (except from time to time by small sectional pockets of opinion). Government is still taken as in some sense or other the Voice of the People. Nowadays this Voice of the People is the Voice of the Party which commands a majority of seats in the Commons. Nothing illustrates this more strikingly than the elections of October 1951 and February 1974. In both elections, the largest party in the House, which consequently formed the executive government, was elected on *fewer* popular votes than its rival, yet its legitimate right to reform the government was never questioned.

Conclusion. From all that has gone before it may be concluded that the party system structures the vote, recruits the political leadership, forms and sustains the government of the country, and preempts and engrosses the function of determining which issues are political and which are not. By these standards the parties are the Pooh-Bahs, the Great Panjandrums, the prime movers of the entire political system. In the constitutional sphere, parties claim all the attributes of the Divinity except one: invisibility. But the parties do not exist in a power vacuum: The parties are *not alone*.

The Parties as Co-Agents

When King expounds his "sceptical reflections" on parties, he deflates their self-importance by showing that they are rarely the only institutions that perform the "functions" assigned to them by the conventional wisdom of political science.[31] And of course, he is quite right. When a British party accedes to office a miraculous transformation takes place: Its head becomes the government and is detached from its body.

The policy pursued by the respective parties may be represented as a certain fit between three elements, thus:

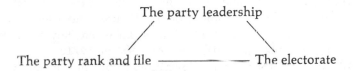

We know that this fit is a very loose one. Usually one element is out of kilter with at least one and often with both of the other elements. This misfit becomes pronounced, however, when one of the parties is in power because once the leadership becomes the executive government of the country, it is instantly plunged into contact with two new worlds. The first is the official world of policy advisers and executants: the world of the civil service, the armed forces, and the judiciary. The second is the world of pressure groups. When a party is in opposition, the electorate is an object of market research. The opposition party sees it as a passive container of certain attitudes and desires. When the party comes to power, the electorate materializes as a set of power centers, some minor, some, like the City or the trade unions, indomitable. As we have seen, the party system in no way incorporates

---

[31] King, "Political Parties in Western Democracies."

the permanent officers of the state, it incorporates no mass sector of society, and it incorporates no interest group. All it does is to sustain a group of leaders who are empowered in their new and constitutional capacity as ministers of the Crown to issue authoritative instructions.

Hence, these leaders are subjected to a new set of policy influences on the one hand and a new set of constraints on the other. As to the first, it is the task of the higher civil service and the heads of the public-sector industries to brood continually over the problems of the state and to frame agenda. The judiciary, likewise, is the authoritative body, after Parliament, for interpreting the laws in force. At the same time, a host of interest groups and promotional groups in society have their own sectional policies. A government sooner or later notices that it is one thing to legislate and quite another to give effect to a policy. A law may be passed, but when tested in court it may turn out to mean something quite different from what the government drafts-men intended; or it may prove administratively unworkable, like the ill-fated Land Commission established by the Wilson government of 1964–1970. Turning to the world of the private groups: Highly pro-gressive tax rates are imposed to hit the higher income groups and so relieve the poorer, but this means in practice that tax relief, like the off-setting of mortgage interest against tax, benefits the former much more than the latter. Finally, at the extreme of the spectrum of public reaction, a group may openly and officially declare its intention to end cooperation with the government or its executive agencies on certain matters, as for instance the trade unions did when they resolved not to register under the Industrial Relations Act of 1971.

All this is pretty old hat. Government does not act on a tabula rasa. Its lack of control over the bureaucracy increases, perhaps ex-ponentially, with the increased scope of government. Its reach exceeds its grasp, since the bigger Big Government becomes, the larger the number of officials required to manage it, and the less able are the politicians to manage them. At the same time, as the area of private interests invaded by government expands, so does the defensive reaction of the invaded.

Complications enter the simple triangular model outlined above even if we assume that the government is acting consistently with its parliamentary and extraparliamentary party. The complications be-come worse if the government acts inconsistently with them or even in opposition to them.

In the first event, five possible distortions can arise. First, the government may press on with the punctilious execution of unrepre-sentative policies. As we have seen, nationalization and increased social service expenditure are nowadays unpopular with Labour supporters and even more with the public at large. Second, the government may fail in executing a policy. For instance, although the government's income policy of 1977–1978 was intended to limit raises to 10 percent, they rose to some 15 percent. Third, a policy that is popular with the party rank and file may produce the reverse of the effects intended. For instance, to assist the homeless, successive Labour governments have passed acts that protect sitting tenants from eviction except under very restricted circumstances and in addition subject the level of rents to adjudication by rent tribunals. This has certainly protected the tenants, but it has made private rentals so unrewarding to landlords that the pool of private rental has shrunk, and the shortage of accommodation has been accentuated. Finally, in the special context of the *British* party system, two final complications may arise—and indeed, they have. One is the generation of a train of mutually cancelling policies. The alternation of antagonistic and increasingly polarized parties has led one party's government to reverse the legislation of the party it has just defeated. The number of policy areas in which this has occurred is far too long to cite here, but they include housing and housing finance policy, incomes policy, pensions policy, and pricing policy for the public sector.[32] The other is unidirectional legislation. Some policies, such as the progressive extensions of the franchise that have been irreversible, were the product of long and mature—perhaps overlong and overmature—deliberation. In these days, however, electoral policies can be introduced by the spin of the electoral die, not merely undeliberated but actually opposed by the bulk of the electorate. The nationalization of great industries is a case in point. The public generally opposes this; the mass of Labour supporters opposes it, though not by so large a margin; but it is an article of faith for the party rank and file and M.P.s. Once nationalized, a major industry cannot be denationalized. Governments can print the money to buy out an industry, but private consortia, which have to find the money from private pockets, cannot possibly raise the vast sums necessary to buy it back again. Thus an initially unpopular measure gets on to the statute book and then stays there.

In these many ways the fit between party leaders/government—rank and file—the electorate, a loose one from the outset, sometimes becomes distorted beyond any fit at all.

While such outcomes emerge even if a government is acting in accord with the sentiments of the party membership, a quite different

---

[32] For a longer list see S. E. Finer (ed.), *Adversary Politics and Electoral Reform* (London: Anthony Wigram, 1975), pp. 15–16.

misfit occurs when, shortly after election, a government proceeds to carry out policies not mentioned in its manifesto or in direct contradiction to its manifesto. Every successive government since 1964 has after one or two years in office made a massive U-turn on its central policies. The regularity with which they have done this has become something of a cynical joke. Certain theories have been invented to explain it. For instance, it is said that after the relatively irresponsible atmosphere of opposition, the new party leaders now-turned-government press on with their brand-new central measures until, after perhaps one or one-and-one-half years in office, they realize their limits and tack and veer accordingly. Others ascribe the retreat to the steady attrition of ministers by a civil service that is in its own way apolitical and centrist in direction. Yet others stress the political dimension: once in office, the government must heed the state of public opinion as a whole and not just party opinion if it is to win a future election.

Whatever the full explanation, it is a matter of history that after a short period in which the new government carries its main manifesto promises through Parliament, it retreats onto a more centrist position and that entails measures inconsistent with its promises and sometimes overtly opposed to rank-and-file feelings. The Labour party acceded to office in 1964 with commitments to develop a national economic plan, to increase public spending on the social services, and to defend the traditional right of unions to strike in the process of settling wages by free collective bargaining. The financial crisis of 1966 blew the first two policies to the winds, and in its In Place of Strife proposals of 1968–1969, the government tried to regulate unions and their right to strike. It ended its six years in office in disgrace with its rank and file and in open dispute with its allies in the trade unions. Heath's Conservative government, which succeeded it in 1970, had not positively committed itself to negotiate British entry into the EEC, yet it did so with great haste in its first year of office. Furthermore, it came in pledged to oppose a statutory policy on wages and salaries, to reduce government intervention in the economy, and to ensure the legal regulation of the trade unions. In its first two years of office it vigorously pursued all three policies and did indeed put its Industrial Relations Act on the statute book. But in early 1973, faced by high inflation as well as rising unemployment, it reversed itself on its two other major commitments: it expanded aid to failing industries, and it introduced statutory control of wage increases until this brought it into collision with the miners in late 1973 and led to the confrontation and then the general election of February 1974.

Meanwhile, the Labour party, in opposition, had committed itself against the statutory incomes policy and emphasized its intention to expand public spending and its determination to repeal the Industrial Relations Act. When it returned to power in 1974, it lost no time in doing all three. One result was a massive wage-induced inflation in 1975. It accordingly introduced a wages policy that was voluntary in name only. The economy continued to deteriorate until the financial crisis of 1976 induced the government finally to cut back public spending. Both these policies were bitterly contested by the rank and file, and in October 1978, the trade unions flatly rejected the incomes policy.

In all these matters, it is worth remarking, the governments of the day were supported by the mass of public opinion. They were not supported by *party* opinion.

Conclusions

1. The parties monopolize the formation of the executive government, the recruitment of political leadership, and the framing of the national agenda, and in the course of doing the last they satisfactorily perform the task of aggregating interests.

2. In performing these functions, however, they are exclusive rather than participatory, although they have successfully integrated sectors of the public into the political community and are effective channels of two-way communication.

3. They are only modestly successful in turning out the vote, are often unable to persuade their supporters to adopt their policies, and are frequently unrepresentative of their supporters' views, still less of the general public's.

4. In office (as the government) the leadership tends to become even more unrepresentative of members' views but often more representative of general opinion, as its perception of the national agenda is subjected to extraparty influences from the bureaucracy, the pressure groups, the media, and the general public.

5. Policy outcomes are in practice the result of the interaction among the party government, the party membership, the general public, and the agencies mentioned above.

6. There is an incongruence between the parties' maximal performance in the functions listed in the first paragraph above, and the consequences of its taking office. Observers, especially partisans, perceive the incongruence differently according to their assessment of

the respective weight of party as against extraparty influences and to the importance they attach to the performance of the parties' major functions, listed in the second and third paragraph above. These perceptions and normative judgments combine, differentially, to generate different views about the worthiness of the party system as it stands, and correspondingly different views about the ways to reform it.

6

Toward Reforming the Party System

Welcher recht hat, weiss ich nicht—
Doch es will mich schier Bedünken,
Dass der Rabbi und der Mönch,
Dass sie alle beide stinken. . . .

HEINRICH HEINE, *Disputation*

There is a general agreement that the party system performs maximally the three functions of forming the executive government, recruiting political leadership, and framing the national agenda. Some equate this with the establishment of strong, stable, durable governments with distinctive programs. Those for whom these are prime desiderata, resist change. Others, with similar value preferences, nevertheless, regard such governments as hamstrung by officials and pressure groups. This is the *impediment* hypothesis. Its proponents want to *strengthen party control* over them. Others draw the opposite conclusion: for them a party-government is too strong: it has unlimited legislative authority, it carries irreversible policies. This, the reverse of the impediment hypothesis, is the *dictatorship* hypothesis, and the remedy proposed is a system of *checks and balances*. Yet others, starting from the same presuppositions stress the self-cancelling consequences when one strong and politically motivated government is succeeded by another of the opposite political tendency. This is the *adversary politics hypothesis,* and the remedy proposed is to enfeeble the power of the legislature by dividing it against itself—not the external restraints of the dictatorship hypothesis, but internal restraints—and this would be achieved by reducing one party's chance of winning an all-out majority. The way to achieve this is by *electoral reform*.

189

There is a fourth line of criticism, not yet espoused by any significant body of opinion, and put forward here for the first time. It stresses the system's poor performance of the representative function, and sees the parties as self-appointed busybodies who have brazenly arrogated to themselves the right to say what shall or shall not be a political issue, and in consequence have forced unwelcome measures on a muzzled and sullen public. This is the *elitist hypothesis*. The remedy it proposes is not so much the referendum—which is one of the devices canvassed by, for example, proponents of the dictatorship hypothesis —but the *popular initiative*.

The Conventional Hypothesis: Defense of the Status Quo

Many people see great strength and value in the present two-party system and do not want to change it. They include most Labour candidates and M.P.s, and a majority of the Conservative ones also. As these are the beneficiaries of the present system, this is not surprising. Furthermore, they would be very odd partisans indeed if they did not believe that the best thing for the country was a perpetual diet of undiluted Conservatism or Labourism. One cannot refute an argument, however, merely by imputing it to the bigotry or the self interest of its proponents. The argument for the present system may be valid, notwithstanding, and indeed until only a few years ago was widely accepted. At the root lies the axiom that the purpose of elections is to produce a strong, stable, programmatically distinct government. If this means sacrificing representativeness, so be it. In practice, however, even if the origin of such a government is unrepresentative, in office it is highly sensitive to public opinion. And the argument suggests that the alternative is far worse—a multi-party system with coalition governments that are muddled, diffident, and short-lived.

Specifically, the advantages of the present two-party system are said to be:

1. The electoral system helps manufacture absolute majorities of one party in the House of Commons, and this produces a homogenous cabinet that is at one with its disciplined parliamentary supporters. Cabinets are therefore strong, stable, durable, and distinct. Their political homogeneity makes it easier for them to take decisions quickly, to act decisively, and to take unpopular decisions.

2. The programs of such governments are politically distinctive.

3. Consequently, at election time, electors are presented with clear-cut choices between alternative programs and teams of leaders.

4. Although the government then elected is unlikely to have received an absolute majority of votes cast, it does (usually at any rate) represent the "largest minority" in a system where all parties are minorities of some size or another. The voter knows that in voting for one party rather than another he is voting for a policy and a program. In a multi-party system he might and probably would find that the government he got was a coalition between his party and another, or even between two of the parties he did not vote for at all, so that the outcome would be undemocratic.

> The people's majority choice is being flouted. Decision is removed from the ballot box to small rooms where party leaders strike bargains and make compromises to keep the coalition alive. It means trading for places in the ministry in return for a block of votes, and it means exacting a price in terms of policy if the government is not to be torpedoed on a division in the House. The people's will and the people's need no longer tower in the government's thinking as the over riding point of reference.[1]

5. However narrow its basis in electoral votes, the government generated by the party will be both moderate and popularly responsive. It will be moderate because, as one of the two parties in a two-party race, it must always seek the middle ground where the votes lie thickest, and it will be popularly responsive because a net swing of 1 percent of its votes to its opponents will cause it to lose some ten to sixteen seats—in other words, its majority would be reduced by twenty to thirty-two seats.

6. When the time comes for a new election, the electorate knows whom to blame.[2]

In one way or another, all these propositions are countered, or at least heavily qualified, by one or other of the four schools of critics. For instance, the "impediment" school says that proposition (1) is only true formally, since the real decisions are taken by such bodies as the civil service, and again, that although proposition (5) is true, a government has no business to be more moderate than the rank and file of its membership, which mandated it to certain policies. Or again, the "adversary politics" school would distinguish between the stability and

---

[1] David Wood, in the *Times*, February 25, 1974; quoted in Rose, *The Problem of Party Government*, pp. 118–19.

[2] Among the most persuasive—and lengthy—encomiums of the two-party system is that of Sir Ian Gilmour in *The Body Politic* (London: Hutchinson, 1969), pp. 33–62. Subsequently he has recanted: see Sir Ian Gilmour, *Inside Right* (London: Quartet Books, 1978), pp. 222–27.

durability of a government over time and the stability and durability of a policy over time.

The question here, however, is what has undermined the traditional view that the two-party system has such strength and durability? Principally, three things. The first is the manifest underperformance of the representative function. In the eight elections up to and including 1970, the argument that the government represented the largest minority was plausible. In 1951 the Conservatives obtained 48 percent of the vote; in 1955, 49.7 percent; and in 1959, 49.3 percent. Labour obtained 48 percent in the 1945 election and 48.1 percent in 1966. These percentages of the votes cast are high, so high that in a number of countries with electoral systems of proportional representation—for example, in Scandinavia—they would be enough to guarantee a party an absolute majority of parliamentary seats. So it was reasonable to argue that figures of this magnitude were quite high enough to qualify for majoritarian status, even though technically short of it. As for the lesser percentages cast by winning parties, in 1950 and in 1964 the party's parliamentary majorities were also very slender, and both these elections were regarded as interims, to pave the way (as in fact they did) for a decisive shift at the ensuing election. But in 1970 the winning Conservatives only gained 46.4 percent of the vote, while some 10 percent of the voters who voted for "Others" were barely represented in the House. This might have passed as another interim malfunction, but it was followed in 1974 by what was widely regarded as a massive injustice: roughly one in four of the electors who had voted for "Others" received a derisory 6 percent of the seats in the Commons, and the Liberals, who cast almost one-fifth of the total votes, received only thirteen seats—a mere 2 percent. Clearly something was wrong. The May 1979 election did no more than mitigate the offense. On the surface it marked a return to Britain's classic two-partyism. Certainly it returned the Conservatives with a decisive majority over Labour and over all other parties in the House. But at the electoral level, the Conservatives had won only 43.9 of the total national vote, and the one-fifth of the electors who had voted for Liberals and other parties received only twenty-seven seats, that is only 4 percent of the House of Commons.

The second development to undermine the traditional defense of the system was that although the system was supposed to generate strong governments it often failed to do so. In 1950, 1951, 1964, and October 1970, the government's margin was very slender, and in February 1974 it was nonexistent. In short, in half the cases, the election failed to produce the outcome that was its principal justification. But the third and perhaps the principal factor undermining the old view was the combined effect of rapid alternations of government conjoined with their increasing polarization. The conventional wisdom affirms that cabinets are strong and durable—which is true—and that they therefore impart a consistent direction to a broad policy which has received general approval at an election. But this has become increasingly false, as can be shown by two observations. First, the Labour governments of 1964–1970, the Conservative government of 1970–1974, and the Labour governments since 1974 were all forced by internal and external events to make savage U-turns in the very policy on which they had been elected. Second, all these governments, even the majoritarian ones, 1966–1974, found that their power consisted of getting the Commons to accept their legislation but stopped short of getting determined sectional interests to obey it.

The conventional wisdom further affirms that as cabinets tire in office, so they are replaced by another team which, though its ideology or policies may be anathema to some, is at least endowed with fresh energy and imagination. Hence the conclusion that the alternating majoritarian party system endows the country with firm and stable government, generating changes that are incremental and evolutionary.

This verdict rested on an unstated, or perhaps understated, presupposition: that a successor government, though of different political complexion from its predecessor, would on the whole accept the legislation of that predecessor. Until the middle 1960s there was much support for this view. The Conservatives preserved the welfare legislation and most of the nationalization of the Clement Attlee government; the Labour party, in its turn, accepted in office much that it had found unpalatable or even immoral in opposition, such as commercial television and the restriction of non-white immigration. Indeed, Clement Attlee called the post-1951 Conservative denationalization of road transport and steel "a regrettable departure from precedent" and said that it had been the general practice of British politics "not to seek to reverse the major actions of the preceding government."[3]

In those lost days of Butskellism[4] and consensus, the alternation of the two major parties in office could well be defended as benign. But since then that presupposition has been eroded: the alternations have become more rapid, the party policies more sharply opposed, and the consequential reversals of policy have created such a climate of uncer-

---

[3] Gilmour, *Inside Right*, p. 210.

[4] Butskellism: Hugh Gaitskell was the Labour Chancellor of the Exchequer in 1951, R. A. ("Rab") Butler his Conservative successor. So similar were their policies that the phenomenon was described as "Butskellism."

tainty as to affect economic growth and disillusion the public. Whereas in the twenty years 1945–1964, there was one alternation of party complexion, in the last fifteen years there have been three. The parties have become more extreme. And the effect is that the incoming party cancels the bulk of its predecessor's work. Of the major legislation of the Heath government 1970–1974—the so-called "quiet revolution"—not a shred now remains except British adhesion to the EEC, and even that had to be put to a popular referendum.

To this partisans could respond, in the words of a Conservative delegate at the party's 1975 conference:

> There are those in our Party who for reasons of—is it justice or consensus or continuity or whatever—would seek to stampede us into changes. They are champions of proportional representation as we have heard, of the single transferable vote, as has been clearly explained to us, or similar esoteric devices. I agree with them. I agree that by these methods we should achieve their avowed aims. *We would achieve continuity; we would achieve consensus. But it would be the continuity of mediocrity and the consensus of the lowest common denominator. We live in troublesome times. We shall not overcome our difficulties nor shall we serve our country or our party by compromising these basic beliefs of all true Conservatives. Let us not be tempted to change our democratic system which has served us so well.*[5]

This view, if not the exact sentiments, was adopted by an overwhelming majority, and, changing the words "Labour" for "Conservative" throughout, the same speech would have won equal applause and acceptance at a Labour party conference. It is natural for partisans to believe that "there is nothing like leather." On the Labour left, however, there exists a view that *even in office, even after popular election,* leather is the one thing a Labour government cannot provide. This is the impediment hypothesis.

The Impediment Hypothesis: Toward "Doorknocker Democracy"

A coherent ideological program of reform has emerged in a section of the Left. Its intention is to create a great chain of accountability by which ministers will control their civil servants, and the party rank and file will control the ministers. In Britain it is the custom at election time for the party activists to bring voters to the polls by calling at

---

[5] Report, 92nd Conservative Conference, Blackpool, 1975, p. 68 (emphasis added).

their houses—"knocking at doors."[6] The doorknockers, then, are the party activists, and they are to be the beneficiaries of the reform: hence my expression "doorknocker democracy."

There is no single document in which this entire program is set forth, but it is possible to collate it from several sources. At its root lies a fierce ideology, whose nature is less misleadingly captured by giving it a label than by perusing the following passage:

> We regard the resolution of the struggle for power between the executive by which we basically mean the Cabinet and the bureaucracy, by which we mean those top civil servants who claim to be policy advisers, in favour of political power and authority and against bureaucratic power and authority, as a central need of our age. It is part of the struggle for democracy itself. As such it should be seen as one of a series of parallel struggles for the democratic control and extension of power in our society taking place between the elected House of Commons and the unelected House of Lords, the executive and the bureaucracy, Parliament and the executive, party political supporters and party representatives, shop stewards and combine committees on the one hand and trade union officials on the other, and finally workers and managers as against shareholders.[7]

The paragraph comes from a statement that was intended to form part of a Commons Select Committee Report by a group of eleven Labour M.P.s; it was drafted by Brian Sedgemore, M.P., a former civil servant.[8] It was defeated on a fifteen-to-ten vote and consequently appears in the proceedings of the committee as a discarded variant: for all that, it served, as perhaps it was meant to, as a manifesto of the doorknocker democracy school. The program can be set out as follows:

1. *A unicameral legislature:* The House of Lords to be abolished, and supreme authority to vest in the elected House of Commons.

2. *The strengthening of parties as such by* public subsidies to the parties and public arrangements not necessarily involving public subsidies, to assist in either the establishment and/or circulation of newspapers and periodicals.

3. *The constituency activists, in other words the general management committees of the constituency Labour parties, to control the*

---

[6] The actual expression, in fact, is "knocking-up," but as this has a very different connotation in the United States, I have changed my text.

[7] 11th Report from the Expenditure Committee (Civil Service) 1976–1977, p. lxxix.

[8] He was defeated and lost his seat in the 1979 election.

Parliamentary Labour party through the automatic reselection of M.P.s, the election of the party leader by either the Labour party conference or a special electoral college, and the drafting of the manifesto.

4. *The extraministerial M.P.s, in other words the backbenchers, to control the ministers through* watchdog select committees of the Commons and party control of these select committees. In addition, the patronage of the Prime Minister is to be eliminated; in particular, cabinet ministers are to be elected and allocated to their departments by the caucus of the parliamentary Labour party.

5. *Ministers' control over their civil servants through* personal political advisers and increased powers to move senior civil servants and remodel the top organization of the ministries.

The present status of these proposals is as follows:

At its 1978 conference the Labour party overwhelmingly approved a resolution calling for the abolition of the House of Lords. This does not yet commit the party to dispensing with a second chamber altogether, but this is the conclusion reached by a NEC statement, dated 1977 and subsequently reaffirmed.[9] Prime Minister Callaghan and the party NEC collided over this matter when drafting the 1979 election manifesto. The Prime Minister induced the NEC to accept a watered-down proposal, that is, "to abolish the delaying power and legislative veto of the House of Lords. . . ."[10] But, constitutionally, until the resolution of the 1978 conference is formally rescinded, abolition of the Lords remains part of the party program.

The subsidies to the parties and the assistance to the press would in principle benefit both major parties equally, but as the press is overwhelmingly pro-Conservative and the Labour constituency parties in a state of deliquescence, the proposals must differentially benefit the weaker, the Labour party.

The vote on the automatic reselection of M.P.s in the 1978 conference was very close and, but for the foolish mistake of the veteran leader of the Engineers' delegation, the vote would actually have carried. Under the party's constitution a matter may not be redebated for another three years. But the left-leaning NEC, furious at the party's defeat, voted in July 1979 to permit the matter to be debated once again at the ensuing party conference. It did so and carried this reform.

---

[9] *The Labour Party*, Statement by the National Executive Committee, (debated and approved by the 1977 Annual Conference): "The Machinery of Government and the House of Lords."

[10] *The Labour Way Is The Better Way* (Labour party election manifesto, 1979).

As to the proposal to vest election of the party leader in some body outside the parliamentary party, it is worth quoting the rationale expressed by Ken Coates, writing from the extreme left.

Today the Party as a whole has resolved upon a new kind of programme and it becomes impossible to avoid the question: how is it possible to go to the electors with an ambitious programme calling for the democratisation of the main power-centres in the economy and society, and yet to exempt from such a reform the structures of the Labour Party itself? As we preach the need for more and wider accountability throughout industry and the public services, can we rest content with the degree of accountability we have established in our own movement?

It becomes illogical for Labour activists to canvass vigorously for the widening of the industrial franchise, and yet to leave unquestioned all the rituals which have crystallised in the interaction between their own Party bureaucracy and the least desirable conventions of constitutional practice. These rituals affect what is done and what is not, and so they have a far greater importance than other such habits as the cultivation of archaic manners and exotic fancy dress, which foibles have regularly, from time to time, brought on adverse commentaries. A British Prime Minister presides over an enormous and quite unjustifiable pyramid of patronage, which has recently been the subject of sustained criticism. He disposes of considerable arbitrary powers, including the power to determine who shall serve in the Cabinet, and at what post they shall be put to work. Less and less do the Cabinets he appoints actually govern. Nowadays not only do they not receive budgets in time to change them, but they may well be deprived of other vital information when decisions are taken in their names and yet all the time they are alleged to be bound by a doctrine of so-called "collective responsibility" which prevents them from reporting adequately to their constituents when they need guidance or support on some contentious issue. In half a hundred ways, the power of prime ministers has increased, is increasing, and ought to be diminished.

Whatever is thought about the constitutional implications of change, the pressure for reform from the Labour Movement is mounting. In July 1972 more than forty MP's endorsed a pamphlet written by Frank Allaun, Ian Mikardo and Jim Sillars, entitled *Labour—Party or Puppet?* This was a radical statement of the case for accountability of Labour's representatives at all levels, and its most important proposal is that the leader—although an MP—should be the leader of the whole party and not merely the parliamentary party, and that he should therefore be elected by the whole Party at Conference. This would do more than anything else to close the gap between the Party and the Parliamentary Party, and to ensure that the parliamentary leadership attached due weight to the decisions of Party conference, and would go a long way towards removing what have at times been major causes of dissension, friction and disappointment within the party. It would give the members the feeling that, for the first time, they can exercise meaningful influence where it matters most. A leader chosen in this way, subject to the discipline of having to seek fresh support from those without whose efforts he would have no political existence, would be at pains to ensure that his parliamentary strategy in no way flagrantly offended the Party as a whole. His report to Conference would be much more meaningful than the present procedure under which he introduces a parliamentary report which Conference is not allowed to discuss.

The role of Deputy Leader would disappear. The deputy leadership was created twenty years ago to provide a seat on the NEC for Herbert Morrison because he could not win one in an election. We see no continuing justification for this artificial arrangement.[11]

In the aftermath of electoral defeat, the NEC decided (as also in the matter of candidate reselection) to permit the party to redebate the mode of electing the party leader in the 1979 conference. (The conference had rejected it in 1978.) But this time around, the issue went deeper. Ken Coates' views, quoted earlier, were now expanded and developed by Tony Benn, the former energy minister and a self-appointed spokesman of the left. He expressed them in a public lecture entitled "The Case for a Constitutional Premiership." Here, among other things, he condemned the British Prime Minister's extensive patronage. For Benn this was not only inherently undemocratic and hence unjust; it was also the means by which the Prime Minister bent the parliamentary party to his will. Not merely must this practice be abolished, but in particular the Prime Minister must lose his power to appoint ministers. Instead, Benn demanded "The election of Cabinet Ministers by Labour M.P.s. If all Cabinet members were elected by the Parliamentary Labour Party," he wrote, "and their appointments to Departments were put to Labour M.P.s for approval, there would be a real sharing of power that would greatly strengthen the role of

---

[11] Coates, *Democracy in the Labour Party*, pp. 14–15.

the government's supporters."[12] One is reminded of Lenin's remark that "the Bolsheviks would support the provisional government as the rope supports a hanged man."

Benn, who was supported by Eric Heffer, another prominent left-wing Labour M.P. and chairman of the NEC's organization committee, put these views to the parliamentary party on June 20, 1979, and they followed them up with still more, on July 11. They now demanded that the party caucus should become the final authority on parliamentary activity, that all party spokesmen should be elected, and that the parliamentary party's research staff should be integrated with the NEC bureaucracy. In all this they were strongly supported by members of the Tribune Group and just as roundly attacked by the members of the Manifesto Group, and there for the moment the matter rested.

At the 1979 conference, however, the proposal to elect the leader by an electoral college was defeated, but the more radical proposal—to vest the manifesto exclusively in the NEC—was (as mentioned earlier) carried. Such proposals would ensure backbench dominance of ministers. There is also another means of achieving this. It is the one put forward by Brian Sedgemore and other Labour members of the select committee of expenditure's subcommittee on the civil service. It appeared as the rejected minority submission in that subcommittee's printed report. This submission provides an ideologically motivated rationale for subjecting ministers in office to the permanent control of their parliamentary backbenchers, while giving these ministers, in their turn, increased power over their civil servants. In this radical outburst, the points to notice are first, the characterization of senior civil servants as class-prejudiced centrists, the charge that they rule their ministers rather than vice versa, the proposal to subject them to their ministers via personal political advisers, and the way in which the select committees, traditionally nonpartisan, are to be converted via different teams of specialist staffs for each party and by majority voting into organs of the party backbenchers. Note finally how this device is applauded as the way to avoid the consensual politics that many Labour M.P.s, and notably the deputy leader, Michael Foot, had inveighed against. To bring out these points, we have supplied the emphases.

> 1. Politicians exist to improve society by facilitating social change. That they are not very successful at this is in part due to the structure of power in our society which is undemocratic and hence unresponsive to changing needs and

---

[12] The lecture (from which these quotations are drawn) is summarized in *The Observer*, July 15, 1979.

circumstances. *Civil servants exist to serve elected politi-cians. That they do not do so well as they should is too well established to merit long and hard debate.* It is the experience of all of us whether as Members of Parliament with access to ministers and civil servants, as Parliamentary Private Secretaries, or as former ministers and civil servants.

2. From the point of view of politicians most of the prob-lems of the civil service stem from the fact that top civil servants misconceive their role in our society. They come to the civil service, as we show in a later chapter, with what Balliol men used to refer to as the unconscious realisation of effortless superiority—though judging by the evidence we received from Sir Douglas Allen their superiority is becoming less unconscious. The role that they have invented for them-selves is that of governing the country. They see them-selves, to the detriment of democracy as politicians writ large. And of course as politicians writ large they seek to govern the country according to their own narrow, well-defined interests, tastes, education and background, none of which fit them on the whole to govern a modern techno-logical, industrialized pluralist and urbanised society. *They can and do regulate Ministers to the second division* (appro-priately enough they call their own union the First Division) *through a variety of devices.* These include delay, which is a potent one when governments are in a minority situation or coming to the end of their political life: foreclosing options through official committees which parallel both cabinet sub-committees and a host of other ministerial committees; inter-preting minutes and policy decisions in ways not wholly intended; slanting statistics: giving Ministers insufficient time to take decisions; taking advantage of Cabinet splits and politically divided Ministerial teams; and even going behind Minister's backs to other ministries and other Ministers including the Prime Minister. In doing all these things they act in what they conceive to be the public good. Some would say they perceive that good in the interest of their own class: others that they see it in terms of the tenets and taboos of their caste. In doing all these things there is an esprit de corps which can be frighteningly intense as between Min-isters' Private Offices and as between Permanent Secre-taries. Fifteen years ago the complaint was often heard that civil servants in one Ministry regarded their colleagues in another Ministry as though they were representatives of foreign powers. Today the complaint is more that they are tempted to regard Ministers as representatives of foreign

powers wanting to pursue policies different and apart from their own. Morale is high and not unexpectedly growing as civil service power itself grows. But this is hardly the point. In doing all these things civil servants are frustrating democracy. They are arrogating to themselves power that properly belongs to the people and their representatives.

3. *It would be as wrong to accuse top civil servants of overt party political bias as it would be foolish not to recognise that Labour governments seeking to alter society in a socialist direction have more difficulty with civil servants* (who are seeking in conjunction with other establishment figures from the City, the Bank of England, industry, the established Church and the monarchy to maintain the status quo) *than do Conservative governments who wish to leave things roughly as they are.* By their very nature bureaucracies become conservative however radical their intake. *Conservative governments who come unstuck in the same manner as Labour governments are those who want to change society in a radical direction.* Seen in this light the nineteen seventies has been a good decade for the civil service and a bad decade for the politicians. For it is a matter of record and observation that civil servants obstructed the radical Selsdon-man policies of the last Conservative government as much as they have frustrated the more socialist policies of this Labour government. Sir Bryan Hopkin, the Chief Economic Adviser to the Treasury, commented on his impending retirement that the politicians had "messed up capitalism." It might be truer to say that he and others at the Treasury had messed up everything over the past twenty-five years.

4. We recognise that our nation is not very good at facing up to problems such as those we have outlined and develop further in this report but we believe that it is urgent that steps be taken to re-establish or possibly establish for the first time political power and authority in the land. This will necessitate more than fundamental changes in the recruitment, training and organization of the civil service even if these spheres are desperately needed. *It will call for a conscious effort to build up countervailing political power.* It will require a more open society, an end to Section 2 of the Official Secrets Act, and more public scrutiny of the process by which we are governed and the information upon which decisions are taken. *It will require that Ministers and the Cabinet be given weapons to take on the civil service. Whether through the appointment of powerful ministerial*

back-up teams or "cabinets," chosen by Ministers and in-
cluding Members of Parliament if Ministers so desired and
to whom civil servants at Deputy Secretary and Under Sec-
retary level would report and be accountable, or through
developing the role of political advisers, or through political
appointments of top civil servants at Under Secretary level
and above, or through other devices Ministers must inject
more party political clout into the upper echelons of the ad-
ministration. It will require that Parliament and back-bench
MP's be given weapons first to help the Cabinet in combating
the power of the bureaucracy and second to help check what
the executive itself is doing. The establishment of powerful
investigatory committees on a systematic basis covering the
work of each Department by the House of Commons is one
overdue weapon in this field. A more powerful and profes-
sional system of audit and efficiency answerable to Parlia-
ment is another long overdue weapon. The latter proposal
might be linked to the former.

5. Arising out of the work of our General sub-committee on
Public Expenditure *we see the need,* for example, to *set up
Select Committees on Economic Affairs* which should,
through statutory backing, be given a new and important
investigative and advisory role in economic affairs. *The new
Committee should have its own specialist staff. Indeed the
major political parties represented* on the Committee should
have *their own specialist advisers paid for through government funds.* These might work along the same lines as the
advisers to the Joint Economic Committee of Congress in the
United States.

6. We recognise that the changes which we propose would
alter the balance of power within the Constitution. But they
would steer a middle course between those who see Parliament merely as the servant of the executive and a place
where the only function of back-bench Members of Parliament is to get the government's business through; and those
who believe that we should move firmly in the direction of
the separation of powers and in the process take the purse
strings from the executive and give them back to Parliament.
*Indeed under our proposals it is clear that back-bench Mem-
bers of Parliament* would be *playing a dual role*—helping
the executive in its struggle with its own bureaucracy on the
one hand and challenging the executive on the other hand.
*The main effects of our proposals would be to place far
more power than at present in the hands of back-bench
Members of Parliament* in general and *in the hands of back-*

bench Members of Parliament of the majority party in particular. They would get round the objection voiced by the present Leader of the House, the Rt. Hon. Michael Foot MP, *that* if the emphasis in Parliament moved from the floor of the House and into a new and powerful committee structure then *we would get consensus government by all-party committees. Effectively our proposals would lead to the dispersal of power in Parliament and parties.* This we believe is the right way for democracy to develop and for the House of Commons to play a much more important role in the development of that democracy than at present.

7. We are conscious that in a country where democracy has gone to sleep there will be profound resistance—not least by the bureaucrats—to the necessary changes which we put forward in this Report but who better than a group of elected politicians to begin the process. We believe that our proposals will contribute to four major objectives:

(1) a more relevant and efficient civil service
(2) a bureaucracy which is properly accountable to the executive for which it works
(3) an executive which together with its bureaucracy is properly accountable to parliament; and
(4) an executive and a Parliament which accept the *reality of the party political struggle as being the essence of democracy in Britain today* [13]

The Dictatorship Hypothesis: Checks and Balances

Just as the socialist aims to transform society as radically and as quickly as possible by the political process, so by definition the Conservative aims to interpose to such change the maximum amount of deliberation, scrutiny, and delay. Such a person sees majority party, in charge of an omnicompetent House of Commons, as much too strong. The present form of government is, in fact, says Lord Hailsham, an "elective dictatorship." [14]

---

[13] *Select Committee on Expenditure*, Eleventh Report, 1976–1977 (The Civil Service) vol. I, pp. ixxix–lxxxiii.

[14] Lord Hailsham, *The Dilemma of Democracy* (London: Collins, 1978), chapter XX: "Elective Dictatorship." Lord Hailsham says that he has been taken to task for describing the British governmental system in these terms and that one critic describes it as "a contradiction in terms." In fact, the term is first used by Aristotle, *The Politics*, ed. E. Barker (Oxford: Clarendon Press, 1946), lines 1284b4-1285a9. "There is also a third (type of monarchy) . . . which goes by the name of dictatorship (*Aisumneteia*). This may be roughly described as an elective form of tyranny. . . ."

> I have been discussing our system of government on its merits. I have tried to show that it is breaking down. It accords unlimited power to a legislature normally dominated by a party, and within that party by the leadership. It is elected by a method which ensures that the majority can use its inherent advantages in such a way as to carry through legislation for which the electorate would never have given approval, and that the power of dissolution gives even such an administration a better than even chance of perpetuating its life.[15]

This view is widely held in Conservative and Conservative party quarters, and the remedy proposed is some form of checks and balances to confine this legislation. There is little doubt that many Conservatives would happily introduce some version of the American system with a written constitution by judicial review, a separation of powers between the executive and the legislature, and possibly some form of federalism. They recognize, however, that such a scheme is impracticable. Instead, three suggestions are commonly made: a reformed upper chamber, a bill of rights, and the referendum—either alone or in combination.

The second chamber. The NEC of the Labour party recommends the abolition of the House of Lords and the introduction of a unicameral system. Precisely the opposite is urged by the dictatorship school. Currently, the House of Lords cannot hold up money bills and can delay for only one year other bills passed by Commons. Nor can it use this power very often because of its "vice of origin." The life Peers, who acquire that status on the nomination of the incumbent Prime Minister, number only 295 in a House of 901 members.[16] The remainder, apart from some thirty-seven ex-officio members (Bishops and the Law Lords), are all *hereditary* Peers. The moral authority of this predominantly nominated or hereditary House is very weak—indeed, nonexistent compared with that of the elected House of Commons. Furthermore, the House of Lords is overwhelmingly Conservative. In February 1977, of the Peers in receipt of a party whip (a good half do not take a whip at all), the Conservative Peers numbered 262 to Labour's 105 and the Liberals 36. The political bias also discredits any attempt to play the role of impartial umpire. In consequence, the Lords does little to impede the legislation of a Conservative govern-

---

[15] Ibid.

[16] Figures for 1975–1976. The full complement of the House was 1,139, but 95 of these were Peers for whom no writs had been issued, and another 143 were Peers with leave of absence.

ment because it does not think it necessary and does little to oppose Labour legislation when this party has a strong majority in the Commons, partly because it hesitates to challenge a so-called mandate and partly because it fears that the consequence of such a challenge would be its abolition.

Virtually no Conservatives defend the present composition of the House, but a second chamber of some sort is in their opinion a necessity. Lord Home, who chaired a party committee on the matter put it thus:

"If the House of Lords were to be abolished and nothing put in its place it would be possible for a government with even a tiny majority to put through the most radical changes without fear of check or restraint and even to prolong its own life. . . . In such a situation we do not believe that the Conservative Party can do nothing."[17]

Lord Hailsham, however, makes a reformed second chamber a vital part of a coherent plan of constitutional reform. His view is that there is virtue in permitting a party to form the government, even though it is elected by less than an absolute majority of the votes cast, since this makes for vigorous executive and fiscal action. What is wrong is that it gives the party "unlimited powers of legislation," which he wishes to check.

> My preferred solution would be to have a second chamber proportionately elected side by side with the House of Commons, not entitled to settle the political colour of the executive government or to control finance, but entitled to have the other functions of the House of Lords and more than its existing power.[18]

This requires a change in its composition. Hailsham favors a house composed of entirely elected members, but elected by proportional representation, possibly by a regional list system. Lord Hume's committee suggested, instead, that one-third of the reformed second chamber be nominated and the remainder elected (again by proportional representation). Gilmour proposes a variant, in which a hereditary element would survive, though the bulk of the members would be elected by proportional representation. He also suggests that the house should be perpetual, like the U.S. Senate, one-third retiring every two years.[19]

---

[17] The House of Lords, *The Report of the Conservative Review Committee* (Conservative Central Office, 1978).

[18] Hailsham, *The Dilemma of Democracy*, pp. 129–30.

[19] Gilmour, *Inside Right*, p. 214.

This reform of the House of Lords has occupied very distinguished minds for the whole of this century and, apart from the shearing of their powers in 1911 and 1948, with no effect. The reason the Lords still exist in its present shape is because it is so difficult to alter it to fill the role prescribed for it. If it is elected on the same basis as the House of Commons, then it has equal moral authority and indeed, if it were elected on proportional representation it would have even more; in that event, strong powers conferred on it would certainly be used. Consequently, the Commons, unwilling to brook a rival, would concede it only the weakest of powers. Strong powers and weak moral basis make a tolerable base for continued existence. So do weak powers and a strong moral basis. Strong powers and a strong moral base challenge the supremacy of the Commons.

The bill of rights. A partly entrenched bill of rights is a component of Lord Hailsham's new constitutional settlement. There exists a widespread (and nonpartisan) demand for some legal formulation of citizens' rights, akin to (and quite easily based on) the formulation in the European Convention on Civil Rights to which Britain has adhered. The problem is the legal status of these rights. Ideally they should be unrepealable by Parliament. This is difficult (some say, impossible) in a system where Parliament is legally sovereign, since an act incorporating such rights could be repealed by any subsequent Parliament. Hence two variants of the notion. The first is to follow the Canadian precedent and pass an ordinary statute, a "Bill of Rights," which would specify the rights and instruct judges to give them preeminence when they were interpreting statutes and the actions of the administration. The second, favored by Lord Hailsham and others, would seek to entrench these rights by putting the "Bill of Rights" to a referendum. The implication is that if passed by a referendum, a subsequent Parliament would find it morally difficult to repeal the bill of rights unless it put that issue to a referendum, also.[20]

The referendum. "The people's veto" is what the great constitutional lawyer, Albert Venn Dicey (a convinced Conservative) called the referendum. From time to time—for example, during the great constitutional crises of 1909–1911 and again in 1930—the Conservative party contemplated the referendum as a great conservative braking force, only to turn aside. The idea is popular again, and a Conservative party committee has presented a report recommending the adoption

---

[20] Hailsham, *The Dilemma of Democracy.* For other references to a bill of rights see Peter Wallington and Jeremy McBride, *Civil Liberties and a Bill of Rights* (London: Cobden Trust, 1976) and Emlyn Hooson, *The Case for a Bill of Rights* (London: Liberal Publication Department, 1977).

of such a device, and so have others of right-wing inclination. One of the referendum's potential uses is to underwrite the importance of certain statutes, such as the proposed bill of rights. The Conservative party committee suggests that certain matters which it dubs "constitutional" should require a positive vote in a referendum before being changed by Parliament. The matters so denoted were bills affecting the unity of the United Kingdom, altering the prerogatives and status of the Crown, or altering the method of electing M.P.s, and, preeminently the "existence of a Second Chamber."

> Before any changes in these matters occurred the statute would provide for a referendum. While the sovereignty of Parliament makes it impossible to prevent such an Act being repealed by a bare majority and without a referendum, it would require an exceptional set of circumstances for a government to act so boldly without incurring a serious electoral liability especially if in time the Act came to acquire a constitutional standing approaching that of the Bill of Rights, 1689.[21]

Here at last is a suggestion that *directly* affects the party system. In the present context, it is one of a set of possible checks and balances on the power of the party controlling the House of Commons. But of course, the referendum is an appeal from Philip drunk to Philip sober, from the elected representatives of the people to the people themselves, and in this sense it is also an antielitist, or if one wishes, a *populist* measure.

The Adversary Politics Hypothesis: Toward Electoral Reform

The adversary system is a stand-up fight between two adversaries for the favor of the onlookers. In common-law courts the two parties to the cause make out their respective cases, cross-examine the opponents, and reexamine their own witnesses in accordance with strict rules of procedure, to persuade the judge or the jury to a verdict in their favor. Since 1945 especially, British public life has been conducted in a similar way, with two rival teams of politicians in open contention before an election, during an election, and also after the election in the form of continuous polemic across the floor of the Common where a powerless opposition confronts an all-powerful government, in the hope of winning itself a more favorable verdict at the next general election.

---

[21] *The Referendum and the Constitution* (Old Queen Street Paper, Conservative Research Department, September 12, 1978).

The adversary politics school contends that the alternation of governments, each of them enjoying such unbounded legislative power, creates grave discontinuity in policy, and that the root cause of both lies in the unrepresentative electoral system.[22]

Defects of the Present Adversary System. The present system ensures the alternation of increasingly polarized party opposites in power. This is wholly the result of the electoral system. It has five bad effects.

The party in office, in order to accommodate its extremist wing, is pulled away from the center attitude of the Commons as a whole and to a greater degree, from the central attitude of the electorate as a whole.

The ruling party has never been elected by a majority of the electorate since 1935. In 1974 it was elected by less than 40 percent of the votes cast. In 1979, it was elected by only 44 percent of the votes cast.

Since Conservative alternates with Labour, the right-of-center policies of the former alternate with the left-of-center policies of the latter, so that the discontinuity in national policies over time is exaggerated according to the distance between these two poles of policy.

Since backbenchers of the majority party will never be prepared to overturn their own government, amendments to the government's policy are rarely decided on the floor of the House. They are, rather, the result of compromises hammered out in private between government and its own backbenchers or, alternatively, between ministers and outside interests in Whitehall. The House, under majoritarian rule, becomes a rubber stamp.

The system generates uncertainty. The electoral system makes the outcome of future elections highly speculative, and this generates the expectation that policies may alter very drastically. This in itself generates uncertainty, but it is enhanced by the clients of one party dragging their feet over cooperation with the government of the day in the expectation that their own party may return to power and amend or repeal the acts these clients find distasteful; trade union defiance of the Industrial Relations Act, 1971, is a case in point.

The Advantage of Electoral Reform. The claim is that these defects would disappear, or become less obnoxious, if the current electoral

---

[22] This view was propounded first by the present author ("In Defense of Deadlock," *New Society*, September 5, 1974) and subsequently elaborated in *Adversary Politics and Electoral Reform* (London: Wigram, 1975). Subsequent statements of this view can be found in Joe Rosaly, *Parliament for the People* (London: Smith, 1976) or *The Report of the Hansard Society Commission on Electoral Reform* (London: Hansard Society, 1976).

system were replaced by a system of proportional representation: either the German additional member system with a high threshold, or the single transferable vote (STV) system as used in the Irish Republic.

As a consequence of this change, it is maintained that the following benefits would accrue.

To form a majority in the House, a party would require the votes of more than 50 percent of the electorate. Failing that, it would have to coalesce with another parliamentary party, and this too would imply that it had the support of at least 50 percent of the electorate.

Voters would be fairly represented.

There would be greater stability and continuity in governmental *policies*, since governments would not be elected, as they are nowadays, by tiny swings of between 1 percent and 3 percent of the electorate.

There would be greater moderation in policy since the extremes in either party would not be able to blackmail their moderate colleagues: Since the system would become multi-party, a party would usually have to form a coalition with some party or group of parties taking a central attitude.

Consequently, the alternations in government would not be absolute and abrupt, as at present, where they occur between two polarized parties eager to repeal the bulk of their opponent's legislation. On the contrary, the changes would be damped by the need for either of the two major parties to coalesce with some other party. In principle, this might be a particularist party like the SNP, but given the bell-shaped distribution of voter preferences shown in the opinion polls, it would most likely be a party of the center.

The contingent nature of a majority so formed would enable the Commons as such to regain many of its powers over finance, administration, and legislative amendment. The proof is to be seen in the history of Parliament once the government lost its majority, November 1976–March 1979.

Objection. The proponents of the present adversary system do, however, point to no less than five different ways in which (so they allege) coalition-type government is defective compared with single-party majoritarian government. First, "single-party governments are *strong*; coalitions are not." It is hard to refute this without some objective indicator of strength. Let us assume that it means either the ability to pass legislation through Parliament, and/or the ability to take unpopular decisions, and/or the ability to see that its legislation is obeyed. In not one single respect can it be argued a priori that single-party government is better than a coalition. A coalition, since it is based on a majority in the House, can pass its legislation just as easily as a single-party government and as a matter of fact, one of the complaints against the Dutch system was precisely that it reduced the power of parliament vis-à-vis the government.[23] Next, if "strong" means that single-party governments possess a superior ability to take unpopular decisions, there is again no a priori reason why this should be so and a good reason why the reverse should be true. A single-party government in Britain is elected by less than 50 percent of the electorate and is exquisitely dependent on quite tiny swings in popular opinion for its survival. The number of seats that change hands with a swing of merely one in a hundred varies between ten and sixteen, thus reducing a government's majority by twenty to thirty-two for each swing of 1 percent. The adversary parties are therefore unlikely to take unpopular measures unless these occur very early on in the lifetime of a Parliament. Not at the end, though: "For when the tide rises and the sharks are around, their voice has a timid and tremulous sound."[24] A coalition government, however, would have to be based on some 50 percent of the electorate, and usually would be based on more than that. Right from the start, therefore, it would possess a greater moral authority than the single-party majority government. Second, it would have far less to fear from swings. A 1 percent swing from it to the opposition would cause it to lose some 6 seats or so in a House of 635 seats, reducing its majority by 12, a far cry from the losses the single-party government would incur. Finally, "strong" may mean that a single-party government's legislation is more likely to be obeyed than a coalition's. It is hard to see why, since the coalition would have much wider electoral support than the single-party government. But in any case, neither the Labour nor the Conservative governments have had marked success in getting their more unpopular legislation obeyed: the Conservatives could not implement the Industrial Relations Act and the Labour Government had limited success in controlling inflationary wage demands. It would seem that coalition-type governments have distinct advantages over single-party governments in insisting on unpopular legislation: wider backing, and less timidity in the face of electoral swings against them.

Next it is argued, single-party governments are more stable than coalition governments. If "stable" means united over the lifetime of a Parliament, then this statement is likely to be true. There is more

---

[23] Hans Daalder, "Extreme Proportional Representation—The Dutch Experience," in S. E. Finer (ed.), *Adversary Politics and Electoral Reform*, 1975.
[24] *Alice in Wonderland*, chapter 10, "The Lobster Quadrille."

probability of a two- or three-party coalition breaking up in the course of a five-year term than of a single party splitting in two, especially under the plurality system, which makes splits of this kind so suicidal. But though single-party governments are likely to be more stable in the short term, this is a trivial sense of the word "stable," which could appeal only to the party bigot or placeman. For, if by stability we mean steering the same course over periods that are longer than the lifetime of single parliaments, then all the evidence shows that the proportional representation coalition governments of Europe have out-performed Britain in this respect.

Third, say some, this British system of just putting an "X" against the name of the preferred candidate is far more comprehensible than the complicated mathematical manipulations of the proportional representation systems, the transfers of preferences, the necessity to number the candidates in order of choice, and so forth. The only reply that is required is to point out the implication—that while the British are a nation of dolts, the Dutch and Belgians and Italians and Irish are all pocket Einsteins.

A fourth argument is that the proportional representation systems entail multi-member constituencies, and this breaks the intimate link between the member and his constituencies. One might make the debating point that Britain had plenty of multi-member constituencies before 1885, and they were only abandoned to serve what the Conservatives then thought was their self-interest;[25] but more to the point one might ask whether this link really is as intimate as has been suggested and also whether it might not be improved rather than impaired by multi-member constituencies. The answer to the first of these questions is "no" and to the second, "yes."[26]

One final argument remains: that in contrast to the present single-party adversary system, coalitions that derive from proportional representation are in Benn's words, "profoundly undemocratic." Now this argument should not be brushed aside, for this very point became the focus of a widespread debate in the Netherlands after the insurgence of the Democrats '66 party in the 1967 elections.[27]

But the counterarguments—in the British context at least—seem overwhelming. Benn's argument turns on the assertion that the formation of the coalition is carried out by parliamentary leaders over the

---

[25] Michael Steed, "The Evolution of the British Electoral System," in Finer, *Adversary Politics*.

[26] Ivor Crewe, "Electoral Reform and the Local M.P.," in Finer, *Adversary Politics*.

[27] Daalder, "The Dutch Experience," in Finer, *Adversary Politics*.

head (or behind the backs) of the electors, whereas the single-party majority represents the straight and undiluted preference of the voters. If the formation of a coalition in this way is profoundly undemocratic, though, what words can be found to express the character of our present system? Benn's argument would be valid if (but only if) a clear and absolute majority of the voters voted for one party. But in that case it would not need coalition partners. His implicit argument— that it is "profoundly democratic" that his (Labour) government should enjoy the total and undiluted exercise of power on the basis of a pitiful 39.3 percent of the total votes cast—has only to be stated for its inherent silliness to be seen.

Second, it does not follow that coalitions betwen parliamentary parties need be or are in fact removed from popular pressures and choices. It is not only possible for the parties to announce before the elections that they are prepared to coalesce with other parties: In many countries it is the practice. Even where this has not occurred—as in the British February 1974 election, where Thorpe finally turned down Heath's offer of a cooperative arrangement—Thorpe did not do this as a private whim. He had been profoundly influenced by the clamor that went up from the vocal leftists in his "party-in-the-country"; and in March 1977, Steel, Thorpe's successor, put the Lib-Lab pact to an extraordinary party conference. No party leader would enter a parliamentary coalition unless he was assured of support from his extra-parliamentary supporters.

The Elitist Hypothesis: Beyond the Party System

There is still one further variant of reform, more radical by far than any yet described. The elitist hypothesis derives its name from its presupposition: that the national agenda is framed by unrepresentative parties and put into effect in Parliament by M.P.s selected for the most part by tiny groups of party militants in the constituency parties. It sees politics as a closed shop for party politicians, and it desires to break this closed shop wide open. It recoils from what it sees as a closed choice of candidates and a closed choice of two lengthy, miscellaneous and above all dissociable packages of specific policies, made worse by the high likelihood that the elector's individual vote will make no difference at all to the end result of the election if he resides in a safe seat, as three-quarters of the electorate does, and that even if it did have an effect this would probably be cancelled by the mechanical effect of the electoral system in squeezing out third-party representation and/or by returning more seats to the party with the lesser number of votes than to a party with more. It resents not being able to state what issue is to be decided, and after that having no effective voice in the decision of that issue.

What this school proposes is compatible with all the suggestions of the adversary politics school—in other words, electoral reform and the preference for coalition politics to alternating uni-party politics, but it wants to endow the electorate with new channels of self-expression which can, where so desired, bypass the parties and rob them of their current monopoly of issue-definition.

Primary elections. The first (and lesser) reform propounded by the anti-elitists is, in fact, acceptable to a number of other critics: the opening up of candidate selection. This was recommended by Peter Paterson, in his book *The Selectorate*, which is subtitled, "The case for primary elections in Britain."[28] This recommendation has been reiterated recently by the *Report of the Hansard Society Commission on Electoral Reform.*[29] The right-wing Campaign for Labour Democracy wants to transform constituency Labour parties into membership parties and to entrust candidate selection to all the members.

Opening up the selection process implies some kind of primary election. Nobody has proposed "open primaries" on the American model, but it should be noticed that one variety of proportional representation would have a similar consequence. That is the Single Transferable Vote (STV) method favored with almost messianic fervor by the Proportional Representation Society. Under its system of preferences cast in multi-member constituencies, the elector is able to vote not only for the party he favors most, but for that one of the party's candidates he favors most, also.

What is currently proposed is some sort of closed primary for candidate selection: in other words, only enrolled party members would be eligible to vote in it. The common objections concern mechanical problems. For instance, since British parliaments have a maximum but not a fixed term and can be dissolved at any time, the primary election cannot be scheduled in advance, as it is in the United States. This is not a serious objection; in the event of a snap election, a special telescoped procedure could be used in those constituencies that had not already selected their candidates. A second objection, largely derived from American experience, is that it is difficult to envisage precisely how and by what means candidates would conduct their campaigns. The people who object on this ground are particularly

---

[28] Paterson, *The Selectorate.*
[29] Ibid.

concerned lest wealthy candidates secure an edge over the others. This objection seems very farfetched in view of the way trade unions elect their officers. Rival candidates must campaign and so must distinguish their attitudes from their rivals', and they do in fact succeed in doing so. In many cases it is the union that pays for their election addresses. A third objection is that a primary election would prejudice sitting M.P.s by putting them on a par with newcomers in the primary race.

The most practical suggestions for a party primary are those of the Hansard Society Commission. They propose that such primaries be required by law. Any candidate might stand for parliamentary election after receiving the due number of nominations, as at present; but a candidate would only be able to add a party political label after his name on the ballot if he lodged with the electoral registration officer a certificate from the constituency party stating that the following requirements had been complied with.

First, all registered members of the local party must have had the opportunity to vote by secret ballot, financed from public sources, on their choice of candidate; next, if only one candidate was named and was rejected on the ballot the entire process must be repeated until a suitable candidate was nominated; finally, the chief officer of the local party must be responsible for maintaining a list of members, available for public inspection at any time.

The commission went on to make the necessary exceptions. Sitting M.P.s would be protected; they would be exempted from these provisions unless 20 percent or more of the paid-up members of the party signed a declaration requiring an election to be held under the foregoing provisions. Next, if a snap election were called and the postal ballot would take too long to organize, party members might vote in person at local party headquarters or some other convenient place determined by the party.[30] Such machinery would open up candidate

Referendum and popular initiative. One must be very careful when one talks about referendums, because they come in many forms, each of which will entail profoundly different consequences. Furthermore, the names by which these different varieties are known differ from country to country. For the sake of clarity we shall employ our own terminology.

First of all, a distinction exists between constitutional referendums and legislative ones. The former applies to alterations in the text of a

---

[30] *Report of the Hansard Society Commission on Electoral Reform,* 1976, pp. 18–19. selection to the entire party membership.

constitution, the second to alterations to ordinary laws. Since Britain does not have a written constitution that is legally superior to ordinary laws, we make this distinction only to forget it in our subsequent terminology.

Next, some referendums are *mandatory* on the government (and/or legislature), others *advisory or consultative*. The results of the first must be acted upon by the government, those of the second are merely persuasive.

Third, where the laws prescribe that a body such as the government, or a group, or some other public institution *must* hold a referendum on some specified topic (for example, an alteration in the constitution or a treaty), that referendum is said to be *obligatory*. Where the law *permits* some body, institution, or group of electors to hold a referendum, that is called an *optional* referendum.

Finally, in some cases only the government is permitted to launch a referendum. We shall call these *referendums*, without further qualification. In other cases, however, regional councils or a given number of petitioners can launch the referendum. When a body of petitioners launches a proposal that some policy be enacted into law, it is called the *popular initiative*. On the other hand people may learn that the legislature has passed a law that they dislike. In that case they may launch a proposal that this law be repealed. This we shall call the *popular veto*.

Proposals for optional and obligatory referendums. As we have seen, a number of Conservatives have rediscovered the referendum and favor using it either to entrench a statute like a bill of rights or for other purposes.

At the same time, Britain is rapidly acquiring experience with referendums. During the 1970 general election both Heath and Wilson rejected any idea of holding a referendum on Britain's entry into the EEC. After the election (which the Conservatives won), Heath rapidly took the decision to adhere, while opinion in the Labour party hardened in opposition. During the passage of the European Communities Bill, in 1972, two Conservative antimarketeers, Neil Marten and Enoch Powell, put down an amendment requiring a consultative referendum before the country entered the EEC. The Labour party NEC, led by a prominent antimarketeer, Tony Benn, now came out in favor of this proposal. Shortly afterward the parliamentary leadership reversed itself and also endorsed the suggestion. In a division on the amendment in the Commons, 209 Labour M.P.s voted for the amendment and 63 abstained. The amendment was defeated by 235 votes to 284. Thenceforward the Labour party affirmed that if elected again, it would renegotiate the terms and then consult the people. This left open consultation by another general election, or referendum. After the Labour victory in October 1974 and the subsequent renegotiation, Prime Minister Wilson plumped for a referendum, although this was a constitutional innovation of the first order. He and two-thirds of his cabinet recommended that they accept the renegotiated terms. Two broad all-party movements were formed, for and against entry; and so the campaign in the referendum began. The device had been adopted by Benn and the Labour left because they thought the popular vote was strongly antimarket. It was adopted by Wilson because his party was split, and this was a convenient way of passing the buck, especially since the referendum was consultative, not binding. In the event the left was totally confounded; on a turnout of 64.5 percent, 67.2 percent voted yes to 32.8 percent voting no.

The referendum, hitherto rejected by almost all pundits and purists, now enjoyed a vogue. In December 1976, Callaghan's Labour government introduced its Scotland and Wales Bill into Parliament, proposing to endow these two regions with local Assemblies. The bill, exceedingly ill-drafted, was also politically very unpopular in the Commons. The government was able to save it from extinction only by accepting a demand that the bill should not become operative unless approved in referendums in Wales and in Scotland. The government had to withdraw this bill notwithstanding. In 1977 it introduced a modified version, as two separate bills, one for Scotland and one for Wales. These passed, with the referendum provision still remaining, but its conditions were subjected to an additional and stringent provision. The "yes" vote must not merely be greater than the "no" vote: it must amount to more than 40 percent of the total eligible electorate. The referendums were duly held on March 1, 1979. In Wales, on a 58.3 percent turnout, the "no" votes triumphantly beat the "yes" votes out of the field with 79.7 percent votes to 20.3 percent. In Scotland the "yes" vote was some 52 percent of the total votes cast; but in terms of the eligible electorate, it represented only 32.8 percent, as against 30.2 percent voting "no." The remainder did not vote at all. (The turnout was 62.9 percent.)

So, once again, the results of a referendum appeared to confirm that it was indeed a Conservative device.

This is the background to the Conservative party pamphlet, *The Referendum and the Constitution*.[31] It must be noted that the pamph-

---

[31] *The Referendum and the Constitution* (London: Conservative Publication Centre, 1978).

let itself states, "This paper is a contribution to Conservative thought for discussion and is not an official statement of Party Policy."

The report recommends what we have styled an obligatory referendum for certain items of major constitutional import, and optional referendums on any others. The chief proposal is that all bills relating to the abolition of the House of Lords, or the unity of the realm, or the constitutional status of the Crown, or (possibly) a bill of rights *must* be submitted to a referendum. A minimum proportion (40 percent is suggested) would have to vote affirmatively before the question was approved. If the question was the independence of Wales, Scotland, or Northern Ireland, however, a positive vote of 50 percent of the electorate would be required. This entrenchment of these fundamental constitutional provisions would be effected by Parliament enacting a Constitution (Fundamental Provisions) Bill.

In addition, however, the report advocates that the proposed bill should also include provision for the government of the day to hold referendums on "non-constitutional matters."

The proposals fall between two stools. On the one hand they confine the "constitutional issues" to far too narrow a range. On the other, they endow the government of the day with the option to hold referendums on anything else they care to name. As to the first, the effect of an obligatory referendum on the specified constitutional issues, especially with its thresholds of 40 percent or 50 percent of eligible voters, is of course an entrenching device. Government could not amend these measures unless a very high proportion of the electorate approved. As a Conservative device this does the trick. The point is that many other matters, like the legal status of trade unions or the use of retrospective legislation, are also constitutional. If a government chose to extend the law in either of these respects, why should not this referendum power be invoked? But conversely, if a government may call an optional referendum on these matters, or indeed on any matters at all, this enormously expands the power of the executive government, which is precisely what the device is being introduced to limit! It is highly significant that in Switzerland, the model of the direct democracy, there are *no* optional referendums; government cannot launch a referendum on any matter and at any time it chooses. As the comparative statistics show, optional referendums are nearly always the successful ones.[32] Obviously, governments would not launch them unless they thought they were going to win. It is true that sometimes things go wrong, as in the case of the 1979 Scot-

---

[32] David Butler and Austin Ranney (eds.), *Referendums* (Washington: American Enterprise Institute, 1978), p. 16.

217

land Act Referendum in Britain, but not usually. An optional referendum would not bypass the parties and the government of the day. It would not help the people to set their own agenda or to express their own view on what *they* themselves regarded as impertinently unrepresentative measures. On the contrary, it would reinforce the two-party system, confirm its closed nature, merely calling in the public as an ancillary, or, to change the metaphor, inviting it to become its own executioner.

Instead, what the antielitist proposes is the introduction of the twin devices: the popular initiative and the popular veto.

The popular initiative and the popular veto. For an example of the *popular initiative* we can turn to Switzerland. There, 100,000 citizens can demand the revision of the constitution. They may put down the full draft of the text of the proposed new article or clause, and in that case the federal government cannot change it, though it can put forward an alternative draft of its own. Alternatively citizens can put forward a general proposition only, and if this is carried the government must then draft it in legal form and resubmit it. In either case, the popular initiative is the trigger to the referendum. The fact that this only applies to constitutional provisions in Switzerland is of no importance in the British context: with equal facility the procedure can be applied to any kind of law, and that is what is suggested here. For Britain, the figure of 100,000 would have to be multiplied. If the respective electorates are taken into account, the comparable figure in Britain would be one million.

For examples of the *popular veto* we can turn to Switzerland or to Italy. In Switzerland, statutes can be challenged if within ninety days of their enactment a petition is signed by a mere 50,000 voters. Thereupon the law must be put to a popular referendum. The equivalent number of voters in the British context would be some 500,000.

In Italy, whose population is roughly the same as Britain's, 500,000 voters signing a petition can trigger a referendum for the abrogation of a law. No such referendum is permittted on money laws, or amnesties, or authorizations of treaty ratification.

To put these provisions into some perspective it is useful to see how many times the provisions have been invoked. In Switzerland, 1848–1978, the popular initiative (for constitutional amendment) has been used seventy-three times. It was successful in only seven instances. What we have called the popular veto has been invoked ninety-five times and has succeeded in thirty-four instances.[33]

---

[33] Ibid., p. 44.

In Switzerland, direct democracy is far more highly institutionalized than in any other country in the world, so these frequencies, such as they are, cannot be taken as indicators of what to expect if similar arrangements were approved in Britain. The Italian example might be more relevant. The first time the popular veto was used was in 1974, after 1,350,000 people had signed a petition calling for the abrogation of the 1970 act that permitted civil divorce. In the event, the supporters of the legislation (who had to vote "no" in order to *prevent* abrogation) carried the day by 19,093,000 votes to 13,188,184, in a turnout of 88.1 percent. The next occasion occurred in June 1978. By this date a very small party, the Radicals, whose chief platform is the extension of the civil liberties, had acquired a toehold in the Italian Parliament. This party has made the popular veto its chosen instrument. Originally, it demanded referendums to abrogate nine laws, but four proposals were struck down by the Constitutional Court. Under the Italian constitution the referendums are held unless appropriate amendments have already been passed by Parliament. In fact, the threat of the referendum was itself sufficient to provoke satisfactory amendment of no less than three of the designated laws. The most important of these was concerned with abortion. The Radicals had tabled their petition in the form of abrogating the existing antiabortion laws on the Italian statute book. As a result of their initiative Parliament approved an abortion law. It is fair to say that without this initiative, no such legislation would have been passed, given the opposition of the Roman Catholic Church. The incident provides an instance of how the device can break the parties' monopoly of issue definition.

In the event, therefore, only two laws came up for abrogation. The first was the law providing for the public financing of political parties and the second was certain articles in the Reale law on public order. The public voted three to one to retain the latter. On the former, the great parties, which of course favored public financing of their activities, had a narrow squeak. Although they campaigned against abrogation of the law, they succeeded by only 56.3 percent against 43.7 percent. The turnout was 88.1 percent.

In both Switzerland and Italy, the ground rules relating to the use of these initiatives and vetoes are laid down by a constitution which is the supreme law of the land and which in Italy is interpreted by the Constitutional Court. The equivalent enabling legislation in Britain would have to be an ordinary parliamentary statute. It would lay down under what conditions an institution or a number of voters could trigger a popular consultation to revoke an existing law or, alternatively, suggest one for enactment. It would specify what body would draw up the question to be asked. And, finally, it would list the policy areas in which the instrument could be used. It could either specify these matters, as the Conservatives proposed for their Constitution (Fundamental Provisions) Bill, or it could simply list the matters that could *not* be the subject of the consultation—not, that is, unless Parliament itself decided to amend the statue by admitting some new category of topic. Such a statute might thus confer on, say, a million voters a general power to trigger popular initiatives or vetoes except in the cases of treaties, foreign affairs, the budget, and equal protection of the laws. By the last is meant some such provision as a clause providing that no call for initiative or veto should be admissable under the act if its effect would be to abrogate the existing liberties of citizens of the United Kingdom by reason of their race, sex, religion, color, or political opinions, and so forth.

There are both ideological and constitutional objections to such a plan.

One ideological objection to the initiative (it does not apply so much to the veto) is that it could threaten the rights of minorities. It would make possible, for example, an initiative for an act for the forcible repatriation of non-white immigrant citizens of the United Kingdom. Parliament, it is rightly suggested, is much more tolerant and liberal in this matter—as it is on capital punishment also— than the electorate. Nor would it be sufficient to rejoin that the electors are in fact fair-minded enough to listen to argument and would reject the initiative in the end; even so, the minority would have been put to fear and humiliation while the matter was under discussion.

This objection would only be valid, however, if the enabling statute placed no restriction on the subject matter of popular initiatives. Insofar as it did, this is as much a guarantee that minorities will not be harassed or persecuted as the current situation. Of course, it might be open to a million electors to call for the abrogation of the schedule to this statue under the legal clauses providing for popular veto. This is, in fact, avoidable, but in any case a safeguard would exist if the referendum were advisory and not mandatory, and there is a good reason for this irrespective of the protection of minorities. In the first place some consultations speak with a forked tongue, like the ambiguous result of the Scotland Act Referendum of 1979. In the second place, nothing should be quite automatic in politics. Suppose the case where, as a result of popular initiative, the government was mandated to alter the law relating to the picketing of firms outside those directly involved in the dispute—a tactic that British trade unionists were still insisting on practicing this tactic. It would be vote took place at a time when a number of violently militant trade unionists were still insisting on practicing this tactic, it would be far wiser to allow the government some maneuver to persuade or even threaten them, rather than to force them into automatic confrontation.

Another ideological objection comes from those who maintain that in practice the popular initiative or veto is a reactionary instrument, that is to say one that would restrict public spending, destroy welfare legislation, bring back the noose and the birch, and so forth. The short answer is that the results of such popular consultations are mixed—sometimes liberal and progressive, sometimes not. On inspection, the device turns out to be ideologically neutral.[34]

The Conservative study group that drafted *The Referendum and the Constitution* did in fact consider both the popular initiative and the popular veto, but rejected them. As to the veto, which they say "has some attractions," their objections are that it would weaken "the executive authority or the power of parliament"; that if it could be triggered by half-a-million voters this would reduce Parliament's power to legislate, which would be undesirable; that government and Parliament should not "abdicate their responsibilities"; and finally, that there is no practical possibility of passing it through Parliament "at the present times."[35]

For any antielitists the short answers to such objections are that it is positively desirable that Parliament's power to legislate should be reduced, if the legislation embodies policies that the electorate has never positively endorsed and to which it stands opposed; that a weakening of the executive authority or the power of Parliament in such areas is the very object of the proposed reform; that there is nothing in it that necessarily compels Parliament and government to "abdicate their responsibilities" (whatever this may mean); and that there is a perfectly practicable way to get a measure passed through Parliament. Once the Conservative party wins an election, all it need do is to pass the necessary legislation. And it should not go unnoticed that while the pamphlet talks of reducing "the power of parliament," or, alternatively of "parliament abdicating its responsibilities," it is uncandid in that it never says what is manifest truth, that for Parliament one must nowadays read "majority party."

Even more firmly, the Conservative study group expresses its

---

[34] Butler and Ranney, *Referendums*, passim and especially, pp. 84–85 and pp. 224–25.

[35] *The Referendum and the Constitution.*

objections to the introduction of the popular initiative. In the first place, it affirms, it would "transform the whole basis of representative government in Britain." One answer is that the Italian experience proves this is not necessarily true. A better answer would be that, on the findings of the previous chapter, such a transformation is both desirable and necessary. A second objection is that it would be difficult to carry on government effectively if numerous decisions were made subject to votes by the people. But the decisions need not be so numerous as all that. Swiss statistics indicate a frequency of little more than one consultation a year—and that is in Switzerland, the ne plus ultra of this device; elsewhere it is comparatively rare. A third objection is that "we do not think it certain that government on that basis would necessarily be more popular than that based on proper debate and consideration by a representative assembly." This begs many questions, including just how representative is this assembly? and of whom? and for how long? A fourth argument is that if the initiative or veto impinged on tax powers or treaties, it could create immense practical problems. The short answer to this objection is that any sensible statute would exclude such items. The final argument is that the reform would be costly. *Costly?* And this, in a country that annually spends £60 billion? The estimated cost of the two 1979 referendums is only £12 million!

The plan would grant the voter two precious things that the present setup denies him. The first is the power of discrimination. At the moment the voter is called on to choose, under a disproportional arrangement, between two packages, each containing proposals he either detests or has not even heard of. Insofar as issues count at all in British elections, he votes for what in supermarkets are known as the "loss leaders."[36] Now and for the first time the voter would have the power to discriminate between the policies he wants and those he dislikes.

Whereas this gift would go to every elector, the second boon would go to only three-quarters of them; but that large proportion would receive the power of the vote itself. For as we know, in three-quarters of the constituencies, the outcome is foreclosed, whereas the voter who votes in a nationwide constituency, on a single issue, knows that his vote will count.

In the wider perspective, the popular initiative and the popular veto would correct the most serious of the malfunctions of the party

---

[36] In other words, for items priced below cost, and offered the customer in order to lure him into the store and get him to buy other goods on which the profit is more than reasonable.

system, its unrepresentativeness. The initiative and the veto permit voters themselves to help compile the national agenda, or, where this misrepresents their views, to modify it. It is not that the reform dispenses with the parties or the legislature. Far from it. On most of the issues likely to come up in these popular consultations, the parties themselves will have their own point of view and they will thrust themselves into the campaign. The reforms would not do away with parties at all; they would subject them to a long overdue critical discipline.

Conclusion: The Possibilities for Reform

1. Central to the likelihood of any reform is the fact that it must be approved by at least one major party, and, in respect of many specific reforms such as a primary (which requires legislation), by all of the parties. This considerably limits what, if anything, is likely to be achieved.

2. *The popular initiative* is the least likely to be introduced. The leadership of all the parties would fear it, partly as a dangerous rival, partly because it opens up such opportunities for organized pressures.

3. *The referendum*, at least in its advisory form, is quite a likely reform. There is nothing to prevent either of the two major parties from introducing a referendum bill and getting it passed if they command a parliamentary majority. Since such a referendum would only be called if the party leadership fancied they would derive some advantage from it, the likelihood that the device will become a recurrent feature is very high.

4. The introduction of *proportional representation* is unlikely. The two major parties are the beneficiaries of the present system and will retain it as long as they continue to benefit from it. The immediate prospect for the reform lies in one of two possibilities; that the next House of Commons is "hung," with the Liberals holding the balance and refusing to support either of the main parties except in return for proportional representation or, alternatively, so crushing defeat for the Conservative party that its M.P.s (currently a minority) who believe in this reform will become a majority in order, as they would see it, to try to stem the socialist tide just as the capitalist parties introduced proportional representation in Scandinavia, Belgium, and the Netherlands. The first of these alternative scenarios is the more unlikely, simply because the two major parties would not, in their present mood, care to barter away their long-term future for the sake of a temporary spell in office.

5. There remain the changes put forward by the left wing of the Labour party. Their inner-party reforms are quite likely to succeed. As we have seen many of the items in the program are already being carried, for example, the implantation of political advisers in the ministries or the threat to abolish the House of Lords. On the other hand, Lord Hailsham's demand for checks and balances will be pressed by the Conservatives. As all of these are within the legislative competence of the majority party in the Commons, they are likely to be enacted there. In that event a new dimension will be added to adversary politics: two contrasting views on the constitution will clash, the one striving to strengthen its party's hold on Parliament and the bureaucracy, the other trying to establish as many checks and barriers to this unbridled power as it can manage.

A Personal Postscript

As I look back on what I have written, I am left with an overriding conviction that for much of the time we have been dealing with *ritual*.

In appearance, choices are offered us at every political level. We have the right to choose between rival candidates, or, effectively, the right to choose between rival programs. If we are rank-and-file party members, we have the right to choose between alternative party policies. If we are elected M.P.s, we have the right to vote independently of our constituents and indeed any outside body, on legislative measures and on votes of confidence in the government of the day. And conversely, because we are offered these opportunities of choice, accountability exists. The ministry collectively and each minister individually depends on the support of his majority party, and this in turn depends on the votes of the public at the forthcoming general election.

In practice most choices are Hobson's choices. This is what makes them ritualistic rather than effectual, whether at the level of the electorate, the level of the party or the level of Parliament.

At the electoral level, our choice is effectively confined to the candidates of the two parties who, under our electoral arrangements, are the only ones who have a chance, and indeed in three-quarters of the constituencies only one candidate has a chance, so that the voter who votes for another candidate in a safe seat is engaging in purely ritual activity. Even if we have accomplished an effective act of local voting, however, the electoral system distorts and misrepresents the national outcome. In any event we are only called on to choose between two indivisible packets of policies, among which we have no power to discriminate, and which, when implemented by the victorious party, we have no power to veto. True, some observers prefer to say that we are not choosing between rival programs but between rival groups of politicians: it is not clear whether the proposition is supposed to be descriptive or normative or both, but we can no more discriminate between the members of each of the rival groups of politicians than we can between the rival manifesto-policies. There is no way we could have had Callaghan without Benn and Thatcher without Joseph. Other commentators try to amend this argument by saying that we are choosing between two party leaders. This is just as false. In 1955, Conservative voters may indeed be deemed to have voted for Sir Anthony Eden as Prime Minister, but in that case they certainly did not vote for Harold Macmillan who succeeded him in 1957, any more than Labour voters in 1974 voted for Callaghan, who succeeded Sir Harold Wilson in 1977. So, even if it be argued that our choice is in effect a choice between two rival parties in any of the senses mentioned above, it is largely ritualistic.

The same is true of another interpretation, namely that in voting we are choosing between "two general directions of policy." How can this be anything but ritual choice when, since 1964, each of the two main parties have reversed the policies on which they were elected within two years of taking office? Others again, forced to abandon fantasies like these, conclude hopefully that what we are really being called on to do at a general election is to pass judgment on the outgoing ministry. They make much of the importance attaching to the government's past record and to the cumulative and persuasive effect of a continuum of Commons debates. It is not cynical to reply that the public remember yesterday but forget the day before, and that a little sunshine and euphoria subinduced by economic manipulation works wonders with a government's popularity in its terminal (and only dangerous) moment. And in any case, how are we to pass an effectual judgment on each of the manifold measures the government has carried out when we are given only the choice of returning it to power or ejecting it?

If, turning now to the party organizations, we imagine ourselves as party members, our choices are equally ritualistic. The notion that we frame party policies or actively influence them is false. Parties were going concerns at the moment we adhered to them; they have their leaders and their policies at the time we join; and our choice is, once again, the blunt Hobson's choice of joining one party or the other, always in the spirit of "love me, love my dog." We are in fact very junior members of a long-established and perpetual corporation. If we are highly active we may become part of that tiny local circle that selects the candidate, but unless we are ambitious, we shall have no say in it. At the conference we shall be asked to make noises about the items of party policy put before us, but it will not be ourselves who invented them, and the likelihood that we can change or reject them is remote. Nor can we change our parliamentary leaders. British parties at any given moment are bands of leaders who possess a following, and as party members we shall be part of that following. There will indeed be some congruity between our opinions and those of the leadership. We would never have joined the party at all had there not been an elective affinity of this sort, and thereafter the congruence will be maintained by the leadership pursuing the law of anticipated reaction.

And even at the parliamentary apex—a disproportional electoral system artificially inducing the condition wherein one or the other of the two major parties is in undisputed control of the Commons—the vaunted control by the House over the executive is even more ritualistic than anything so far mentioned. Under majoritarian party control, parliamentary amendment of government measures is purely marginal,[1] it has no control over government finance and the twin doctrines of collective and individual responsibility of ministers, which were invented to subordinate the executive machine to the Commons, have ended up by shielding it. It was not until the 1974–1979 period, after the government lost its majority, that the Commons was able to impose constraints on the government's legislative policies, and even then despite fierce public unpopularity of the governing Labour party, the opposition was unable to thrust it from office until March 1979. The fate of the Scotland and the Wales Acts, 1979, provides a cautionary demonstration of the impotence of the House vis-à-vis even a minority government. These bills were notoriously unpopular in the Commons; they only reached the statute book by the ministry administering blandishment and threat to their sullen backbenchers. They were passed, however, for all the minority status of the government. In the event it was not the House that killed them, but the people of Wales and the people of Scotland voting directly on them in the referendums of March 1, 1979.

But the complicated rituals we have described are certainly not empty. They have two effects—instrumental and symbolic.

These rituals at the various political levels, produce an outcome. Sir Leo Amery formulated it as "a system of democracy by consent and not by delegation, of government of the people for the people but

---

[1] J. A. G. Griffith, *Parliamentary Scrutiny of Government Bills* (London: Allen and Unwin, 1976).

not by the people."[2] And, another observer describes the outcome as a "gyroscopic" process. This congruence of governmental policy and popular attitudes does not come about by the transmission of something called the public will through a choice of representatives who express it in assembly and control an executive that carries it out. The mechanism, rather, is that

> the Government decides the policies and promotes legislation as it thinks fit; if this is sufficiently popular it will secure electoral success and hence continuance; if it is outbid by the Opposition than policies will shift over to try and catch public opinion on another tack. It is because the Government *must attempt* to catch the wind of popular approval that it is democratic, not because it has secured an alleged endorsement of its actions beforehand. The electoral arrangements operate to keep policy initiative and decisions on a general line (like a gyroscope) by the constant threat of popular disapproval.[3]

Even if it is not optimal, this is not an unsatisfactory outcome. It is a far cry from the authoritarianism of marxist or fascist regimes and serves to distinguish them from what we call "liberal-democratic" states. Nor is it any less representative, and indeed is arguably more so, than the governmental arrangements in, say, France or the United States. It is not, however, the way in which the commonality of the British people see their form of government. It does not correspond to what they think they are doing, nor to what the rituals of electoral choice suggest to them they are doing. The common perception of the system is much better captured by, say, what Sir Ivor Jennings wrote in his *British Constitution*.[4] Its first chapter is characteristically entitled "Government by the People," and that chapter's two sections are headed "We, the People" and "The People's Choice." "Democracy as we understand it," he writes, "means that the people choose the rulers and the rulers govern according to the wishes of the people." The parties are based on "competing political principles" and therefore, in preferring one of them to the other, the "electorate not only prefers one government to another but prefers one line of policy to another. We have government by the people," he goes on, "not merely because the people exercise a choice freely and secretly at intervals, but also

---

[2] Sir Leo Amery, *Thoughts on the Constitution* (Oxford: Oxford University Press, 1947), pp. 20–21.

[3] L. Tivey, "The System of Democracy in Britain," in Roger Benewick and Robert E. Dowse (eds.), *Readings in British Politics and Government* (London: University of London Press, 1968), p. 49. Emphasis added.

[4] Ivor Jennings, *The British Constitution* (New York: 1941).

because it follows from the fact that the whole machinery of government—the House of Lords in part excepted—is keyed to public
opinion."[5]

This is a myth. Anybody who has read this book can see that.
But it is the operative myth of the British system of government. If the
majority of electors ever think about what they are doing as between
parties and elections, it is something of this kind. But of course, what
we think we are doing is one thing and the objective outcome of our
activity may be quite another; and so it is in this case. Yet as long as
most people in the country do vaguely believe that this is what they
are about when they play the role of electors or party members, the
ritual we have described performs another function apart from its
instrumental one, and this function is vital; it performs the function of
legitimation. For, as Vilfredo Pareto never ceased to observe, the truth
or falsity of a proposition bears no relationship to its power to move
men to social action. This was a function of belief, not of truth. And
indeed, he further observed, in respect to this very same myth of
popular sovereignty:

> Social stability is so beneficial a thing that to maintain it
> it is well worth while to enlist the aid of fantastic ideals and
> this or that theology—among the others, the theology of
> universal suffrage—and be resigned to putting up with cer-
> tain actual disadvantages. Before it becomes advisable to
> disturb the public peace, such disadvantages must have
> grown very serious; and since human beings are effectively
> guided not by the skeptical reasonings of science but by
> 'living faiths' expressed in ideals, theories such as the divine
> right of kings, the legitimacy of oligarchies, of "the people,"
> of "majorities," of legislative assemblies, and other such
> things, may be useful within certain limits, and have in fact
> proved to be, however absurd they may be from the scientific
> standpoint. . . .[6]

The political parties, performing (well or badly) the functions described in Chapter 5, are essential motors of the system of representative parliamentary democracy. It could not function without
them—unsurprisingly for it is their creation. Insofar as they throw
open membership to the general public, even if the general public does
not respond, insofar as they then put forward their chosen candidates,
insofar as they compete with each other for office, and insofar as the

---

[5] Ibid., pp. 209, 212, 229.
[6] Vilfredo Pareto, *The Mind and Society* (New York: Dover, 1963), para. 2184. Cf.
the common-law maxim: *Communis Error Facit Jus.*

one that wins takes office—so they offer to the public simulacra of choice and accountability, and their supreme justification is that in this way they serve the myth that legitimizes government in the eyes of the governed.

But they do so at a cost and, it is my conviction, a wholly unnecessary cost.

> Elective autocracy although not necessarily the worst form of government, is not good enough. It is a guarantee against bloody revolution and effective in preventing the government from systematically ignoring the interests and flouting the wishes of the governed. It avoids the worst abuses and makes the government responsive to large shifts of opinion. But it cannot discriminate finely enough to take account of the individual, to remedy his grievances or carry out his ideas. . . .[7]

It cannot discriminate for three reasons. In the first place, party members cannot discriminate between the potential candidate who represents one tendency in his party and another potential candidate representing another. Next, the general public can, effectively, only chose between two major parties. And third, they cannot discriminate between individual policies offered by any one of these two parties. The competition of parties, essential to the operation of representative government in any industrialized state is in Britain too blunt and the prize of office too absolute. The elector must acquire the power to finetune his choices.

A party's candidates should be the choice of all its members, not of a handful; this entails a statute obliging parties to conduct primary elections. In general elections, the safe seats must be swept away, and the parties must receive parliamentary seats in accordance with the size of their electoral vote. This signifies a more proportional system of representation, since this alone permits the elector an effective choice between more than the two major parties. If, as one might expect, this leads to minority or coalition governments in the House of Commons, this will by the same token strengthen the Common's power to discriminate vis-à-vis the executive, on legislation and the way it is being carried out.

Even these changes will not of themselves correct the proven tendency of governments to misrepresent the views of their followings inside and outside Parliament, and as we have demonstrated these followings are by no means representative of public opinion at large.

---

[7] John R. Lucas, *Democracy and Political Participation* (London: Penguin, 1976), p. 200.

So, in either case, some policies are enacted against the wishes of the people and others that conform to those wishes are not enacted. The foregoing changes must be complemented by the two radical innovations mentioned in the last chapter; that is the popular initiative and the popular veto. A duly specified number of petitioners should have the right to trigger a referendum to abrogate a statute they dislike, and likewise the power to trigger a referendum on proposals they wish to see enacted.

The practitioners of politics have become professionals, and to all intents and purposes they are operating a closed shop. It is time to break it open. "How can it be a closed shop," some will rejoin, "where any citizen is free to become a member of a political party and so join it?" The fact is that only a few people have either the time or the inclination to match the furious *libido dominandi* of the activists and turn themselevs into full-time or even part-time politicians simply to prevent the full-time or part-time politicians from doing things they disapprove of. And why should they? When I engage an attorney to act for me, do I have to become a full-time attorney as well, just to stop him from doing things I dislike? Not at all! I engage him to save my time and convenience, but I reserve the right to instruct him when he is doing things I do not care for. Likewise with politicians. These were the folk who used to say that "experts should be on tap and not on top." Now that the politicians have in their turn become experts, it is time to say it of them also. They claim to exist to serve the public. Very well. Let us make it so.

BIBLIOGRAPHY

Alderman, Geoffrey. *British Elections—Myth and Reality*. London: Batsford, 1978.

Almond, Gabriel, and Coleman, John. *The Politics of the Developing Areas*. Princeton: Princeton University Press, 1960.

Almond, Gabriel, and Powell, Bingham. *Comparative Politics*. Boston: Little Brown, 1966.

Alt, John; Crewe, Ivor; and Svarlik, Bö. "Angels in Plastic." *Political Studies*, September 1977.

Amery, Sir Leo. *Thoughts on the Constitution*. Oxford: Oxford University Press, 1947.

Bacon, Roger, and Eltis, Walter. *Britain's Economic Problem: Too Few Producers*. London: Macmillan, 1976.

Benewick, Roger, and Dowse, Robert. *Readings in British Politics and Government*. London: University of London Press, 1968.

Benewick, Roger, and Smith, Trevor. *Direct Action and Democratic Politics*. London: Allen and Unwin, 1972.

Berrington, Hugh Bayard. *Backbench Opinion in The House of Lords 1945–1955*. Oxford: Pergamon, 1973.

Birch, Anthony. *Representative and Responsible Government*. London: Allen and Unwin, 1964.

Birch, Anthony. *Political Integration and Disintegration in the British Isles*. London: Allen and Unwin, 1977.

Blackstone, Sir William. *Commentaries on the Law of England*. London: 1825.

Blank, Stephen. *Industry and Government in Britain: The Federation of British Industry in Politics 1945–1965*. London: Saxon House, 1973.

Blewett, Neal. *The Peers, the Parties and the People: the General Elections of 1910*. London: Macmillan, 1972.

Blondel, Jean. *Voters, Parties and Leaders*. London: Penguin, 1974.

Blumler, Jay; Gurevitch, Michael; and Ives, Julian. *The Challenge of Election Broadcasting*. Leeds: Leeds University Press, 1978.

Bogdanor, Vernon, and Skidelsky, Robert. *The Age of Affluence, 1951–1964*. London: Macmillan, 1970.

Brittan, Samuel. *The Economic Consequences of Democracy*. London: Temple Smith, 1977.

Bromhead, Peter. *Britain's Developing Constitution*. London: Allen and Unwin, 1974.

Budge, Ian; Crewe, Ivor; and Farlie, Dennis (eds). *Party Identification and Beyond*. London: John Wiley, 1976.

Budge, Ian, and Farlie, Dennis. *Voting and Party Competition*. London: John Wiley, 1977.

Burke, Edmund. *Letter to Sir Hercules Langrishe Bart MP*. London: Rivington, 1808.

Butler, David. *The British General Election of 1951*. London: Macmillan, 1952.

Butler, David. *Coalitions in British Politics*. 2nd ed. London: Macmillan, 1978.

Butler, David, and Kavanagh, Dennis. *The British General Election of February 1974*. London: Macmillan, 1974.

Butler, David and Kavanagh, Dennis. *The British General Election of October 1974*. London: Macmillan, 1975.

Butler, David, and King, Anthony. *The British General Election of 1964*. London: Macmillan, 1965.

Butler, David, and Kitzinger, Uwe. *The 1975 Referendum*. London: Macmillan, 1976.

Butler, David, and Pinto-Duschinsky, Michael. *The British General Election of 1970*. London: Macmillan, 1971.

Butler, David, and Ranney, Austin. *Referendums*. Washington D.C.: American Enterprise Institute, 1979.

Butler, David, and Rose, Richard. *The British General Election of 1959*. London: Macmillan, 1960.

Butler, David, and Sloman, Anne. *British Political Facts 1900–1975*. London: Macmillan, 1975.

Butler, David, and Stokes, Donald. *Political Change in Britain*. 2nd ed. London: Macmillan, 1974.

Chisman, Forrest. *Attitude Psychology and the Study of Public Opinion*. Pennsylvania State University Press, 1976.

Coates, Ken. *Democracy in the Labour Party*. Nottingham: Spokesman, 1977.

Cook, Chris, and Ramsden, John. *Trends in British Politics Since 1945*. London: Macmillan, 1978.

Crewe, Ivor; Fox, Tony; and Alt, Jim. "Non-Voting in British General Elections 1966–Oct. 1974." *British Political Sociology Yearbook*. Vol. 3. London: Croom, Helm, 1977.

Crewe, Ivor; Svarlik, Bö; and Alt, Jim. "Partisan De-Alignment in Britain, 1964–1974." *British Journal of Political Science*, vol. 7, part 2, April 1977.

Crossman, Richard. *The Diaries of a Cabinet Minister*. London: Hamish Hamilton and Jonathan Cape, 1975.

Crouch, Colin, ed. *British Sociology Yearbook*. Vol. 3. London: Croom, Helm, 1977.

Cyr, Arthur. *Liberal Party Politics in Britain*. London: Calder, 1977.

Dahl, Robert. *Political Oppositions in Western Democracies*. New Haven: Yale University Press, 1976.

Dalyell, Tam. *Devolution—The End of Britain?* London: Cape, 1977.

De Smith, S. A. *Constitutional and Administrative Law*. London: Penguin, 1971.

De Vigny, Alfred. *Grandeur et Servitude Militaire*. Paris: Germain, 1965.

Dittrich, Karl, and Johansen, Lars. *A Preliminary Note on Voter Turnout*. The European University Institute, 1978.

Epstein, Leon. *Political Parties in Western Democracies*. London: Pall Mall Press, 1967.

Finer, Samuel Edward. *Anonymous Empire*. 1st ed. London: Pall Mall, 1958. 2nd ed., 1966.

Finer, Samuel Edward. *Adversary Politics and Electoral Reform*. London: Wigram, 1975.

Forester, Tom. *The Labour Party and the Working Class*. London: Heinemann, 1974.

Gilmour, Sir Ian. *The Body Politic*. London: Hutchinson, 1969.

Gilmour, Sir Ian. *Inside Right*. London: Quartet Books, 1978.

Goodhart, C., and Bhabsali, R. "Political Economy." Political Studies. Vol. 18 (1970).

Grant, Wynn, and Marsh, David. *The C.B.I.* London: Hodder and Stoughton, 1977.

Griffith, John. *Parliamentary Scrutiny of Government Bills*. London: Allen and Unwin, 1976.

Hailsham, Lord. *The Dilemma of Democracy*. London: Collins, 1978.

Haines, Joe. *The Politics of Power*. London: Hodder and Stoughton, 1977.

Hatfield, Michael. *The House the Left Built*. London: Gollancz, 1978.

Hayter, Dianne. *The Labour Party: Crisis and Prospects*. Fabian Tract 451, 1977.

Heffer, Eric. *The Class Struggle in Parliament*. London: Gollancz, 1973.

Holland, Philip, and Fallon, Michael. *The Quango Explosion*. London: Conservative Political Centre, 1978.

Hooson, Emrys. *The Case for a Bill of Rights*. London: Liberal Publication Department, 1977.

Kavanagh, Dennis, and Rose, Richard. *New Trends in British Politics*. London: Sage, 1977.

Kimber, Richard, and Richardson, Jeremy. *Campaigning for the Environment*. London: Routledge, 1974.

Kimber, Richard, and Richardson, Jeremy. *Pressure Groups in Britain*. London: Dent, 1974.

King, Anthony. *British Members of Parliament: A Self Portrait*. London: Macmillan, 1974.

King, Anthony. *Britain Says Yes: The 1975 Referendum on the Common Market*. Washington D.C.: American Enterprise Institute, 1977.

Lloyd, Trevor. *The General Election of 1880*. Oxford: Oxford University Press, 1968.

Lucas, John. *Democracy and Political Participation*. London: Penguin, 1976.

Lumley, Roger. *White Collar Unionism in Britain*. London: Metheun, 1973.

Mackintosh, John. *The Government and Politics in Britain*. 4th Ed. London: Hutchinson, 1977.

Martin, Colin, and Martin, Dick. "Decline of Labour Party Membership." *The Political Quarterly*. 48, no. 4 (1977).

McKenzie, Robert, and Silver, Allan. *Angels in Marble*. London: Heinemann, 1968.

McKie, David, and Cook, Chris. *Election '70*. London: Quartet Books, 1970.

McKie, David, and Cook, Chris. *The Guardian/Quartet Election Guide*. London: Quartet Books, 1974.

Mellors, Colin. *The British MP*. London: Saxon House, 1978.

Miller, William. *Electoral Dynamics in Britain Since 1918*. London: Macmillan, 1977.

Milligan, Steven. *The New Barons: Union Power in the '70s*. London: Temple Smith, 1976.

Minkin, Lewis. *The Labour Party Conference*. London: Allen Lane, 1978.

Muller, William. *The 'Kept Men': Trade Union Representation in the British House of Commons 1874–1975*. London: Harvester Press, 1977.

Neumann, Sigmond. *Modern Political Parties*. Chicago: University of Chicago Press, 1956.

Nicholas, Herbert. *The British General Election of 1950*. London: Macmillan, 1951.

Norton, Philip. *Conservative Dissidents. Dissent within the Conservative Party, 1970–1974*, London: Temple Smith, 1979.

Norton, Philip. *Dissension in the House of Commons, 1945–1974*. London: Macmillan, 1975.

Pareto, Vilfredo. *The Mind and Society*. New York: Dover, 1963.

Paterson, Peter. *The Selectorate*. London: Macgibbon and Kee, 1967.

Penniman, Howard. *Britain at the Polls: The Parliamentary Election of 1974*. Washington D.C.: American Enterprise Institute, 1975.

Pulzer, Peter. *Political Representation and Elections in Britain*. 2d ed. London: Allen and Unwin, 1972.

Punnett, R. Malcolm. *Frontbench Opposition*. London: Heinemann, 1973.

Ranney, Austin. *Pathways to Parliament*. London: 1975.

Richie, Alistair, and Hoggart, Simon. *The Pact*. London: Quartet Books, 1978.

Robertson, David. *A Theory of Party Competition.* London: John Wiley, 1976.

Rogaly, Joe. *Parliament for the People.* London: Temple Smith, 1976.

Rokkan, Stein, and Lipset, Seymour. *Party Systems and Voter Alignments.* London: Collier, Macmillan, 1967.

Rose, Richard, ed. *The Problem of Party Government.* London: Penguin Books, 1974.

Rose, Richard, ed. *Electoral Behaviour: A Comparative Handbook.* New York: Free Press, 1974.

Rose, Richard, ed. *Studies in British Politics.* 3d ed. London: Macmillan, 1976.

Rose, Richard. *Politics in England Today.* London: Faber, 1974.

Rush, Michael. *The Selection of Parliamentary Candidates.* London: Nelson, 1969.

Russell, Alan. *Liberal Landslide: The General Election of 1906.* Hamden, Connecticut: Archon Books, 1973.

Russell, Trevor. *The Tory Party.* London: Penguin, 1978.

Schoen, Donald. *Enoch Powell and the Powellites.* London: Macmillan, 1977.

Seymour-Ure, Colin. *The Political Impact of the Mass Media.* Beverly Hills: Sage, 1974.

Shanks, Michael. *Planning and Politics.* London: Allen and Unwin, 1977.

Shipley, Peter. *Revolutionaries in Modern Britain.* London: Bodley Head, 1976.

Smith, Trevor. *Anti-Politics, Consensus Reform and Protest in Britain.* London: Knight, 1972.

Spiegelberg, Richard. *The City.* London: Quartet Books, 1973.

Taylor, Robert. *The Fifth Estate: Britain's Unions in the Seventies.* London: Routledge, 1978.

Tunstall, Jeremy. *Media Sociology.* London: Constable, 1970.

Wallington, Peter, and McBride, Jeremy. *Civil Liberties and a Bill of Rights.* London: Cobden Press, 1976.

Wilson, Harold. *The Governance of Britain.* London: Weidenfeld and Nicolson and Michael Joseph, 1976.

Party Publications
  Labour Party
    Annual Conference Reports
  Conservative Party
    The Campaign Guide, 1950 through 1977
    Annual Conference Reports

Miscellaneous Publications
    The Public View (New International, 1977)
    Report on Electoral Reform (The Hansard Society Commission, 1976)
    Gallup Political Index

Government Publications
    Report of the Committee on the Civil Service (Fulton, Vol. 1, CMND 3638, 1968)
    Royal Commission on the Constitution (Kilbrandon, CMND 5460, 1973)
    Report of the Committee on Financial Aid to the Political Parties (Houghton, CMND 6601, 1976)
    Final Report of the Royal Commission on the Press (Macgregor, CMND 6810, 1977)
    11th Report from the Expenditure Committee Session 1976–77: The Civil Service (HC 535-1, 1977)
    First Report from the Select Committee on Procedure 1977–78 (HC 588-1, 1978)

APPENDIX

TABLE A1
General Election Results, 1945–1970

	Total Votes	M.P.s Elected	Candidates	Unopposed Returns	% Share of Total Vote	Average % Vote per Opposed Candidate
1945. Thu., 5 Jul[a]						
Conservative	9,988,306	213	624	1	39.8	40.1
Liberal	2,248,226	12	306	—	9.0	18.6
Labour	11,995,152	393	604	2	47.8	50.4
Communist	102,780	2	21	—	0.4	12.7
Common Wealth	110,634	1	23	—	0.4	12.6
Others	640,880	19	104	—	2.0	15.4
Elec. 33,240,391 Turnout 72.7%	25,085,978	640	1,682	3	100.0	—
1950. Thu., 23 Feb						
Conservative	12,502,567	298	620	2	43.5	43.7
Liberal	2,621,548	9	475	—	9.1	11.8
Labour	13,266,592	315	617	—	46.1	46.7
Communist	91,746	—	100	—	0.3	2.0
Others	290,218	3	56	—	1.0	12.6
Elec. 33,269,770 Turnout 84.0%	28,772,671	625	1,868	2	100.0	—

1951. Thu., 25 Oct					
Conservative	13,717,538	321	4	48.0	48.6
Liberal	730,556	6	—	2.5	14.7
Labour	13,948,605	295	—	48.8	49.2
Communist	21,640	—	—	0.1	4.4
Others	177,329	3	—	0.6	16.8
Elec. 34,645,573 Turnout 82.5%	28,595,668	625	4	100.0	—
1955. Thu., 26 May					
Conservative	13,286,569	344	—	49.7	50.2
Liberal	722,405	6	—	2.7	15.1
Labour	12,404,970	277	—	46.4	47.3
Communist	33,144	—	—	0.1	4.2
Others	313,410	3	—	1.1	20.8
Elec. 34,858,263 Turnout 76.7%	26,760,498	630	—	100.0	—
1959. Thu., 8 Oct					
Conservative	13,749,830	365	—	49.4	49.6
Liberal	1,638,571	216	—	5.9	16.9
Labour	12,215,538	258	—	43.8	44.5
Communist	30,897	—	—	0.1	4.1
Plaid Cymru	77,571	—	—	0.3	9.0
SNP	21,738	1	—	0.1	11.4
Others	124,64	—	—	0.4	11.0
Elec. 35,397,080 Turnout 78.8%	27,859,241	630	—	100.0	—

(Table A1 continues on the next page.)

TABLE A1 (continued)

	Total Votes	M.P.s Elected	Candidates	Unopposed Returns	% Share of Total Vote	Average % Vote per Opposed Candidate
1964. Thu., 15 Oct						
Conservative	12,001,396	304	630	—	43.4	43.4
Liberal	3,092,878	9	365	—	11.2	18.5
Labour	12,205,814	317	628	—	44.1	44.1
Communist	45,932	—	36	—	0.2	3.4
Plaid Cymru	69,507	—	23	—	0.3	8.4
SNP	64,044	—	15	—	0.2	10.7
Others	168,422	—	60	—	0.6	6.4
Elec. 35,892,572	27,655,374	630	1,757	—	100.0	—
Turnout 77.1%						
1966. Thu., 31 Mar						
Conservative	11,418,433	253	629	—	41.9	41.8
Liberal	2,327,533	12	311	—	8.5	16.1
Labour	13,064,951	363	621	—	47.9	48.7
Communist	62,112	—	57	—	0.2	3.0
Plaid Cymru	61,071	—	20	—	0.2	8.7
SNP	128,474	2	20	—	0.2	14.1
Others	170,569	—	31	—	0.6	8.6
Elec. 35,964,684	27,263,606	630	1,707	—	100.0	—
Turnout 75.8%						

1970. Thu., 18 Jun

Conservative	13,145,123	330	628	—	46.4	46.5
Liberal	2,117,035	6	332	—	7.5	13.5
Labour	12,179,341	287	624	—	43.0	43.5
Communist	37,970	—	58	—	0.1	1.1
Plaid Cymru	175,016	1	36	—	0.6	11.5
SNP	306,802	1	65	—	1.1	12.2
Others	383,511	6	94	—	1.4	9.1
Elec. 39,342,013	28,344,798	630	1,837	—	100.0	—
Turnout 72.0%						

[a] Result announced 26 July 1945.

SOURCE: David Butler and Anne Sloman, *British Political Facts, 1900–1975* (London: Macmillan, 1976).

TABLE A2
The May 1979 Election Results

	Total Votes	% of Votes	% of Electorate	Seats Gained[e]	Seats Lost[e]	Seats
Conservative	13,698,720 (10,429,094)	43.9 (35.7)	33.3 (26.0)	61	6	339 (276/284)[f]
Labour	11,504,958 (11,468,618)	36.9 (39.3)	28.0 (28.6)	11	51	268 (319/308)
Liberal	4,313,784 (5,346,704)	13.8 (18.3)	10.5 (13.3)	0	3	11 (13/14)
SNP	504,297 (839,617)	1.6 (2.9)[c]	1.2 (2.1)	0	9	2 (11)
Plaid Cymru	132,544 (166,231)	0.4 (0.6)[c]	0.3 (0.4)	0	1	2 (3)
Official Unionist	254,578[b]	0.8[c]	0.6	0	2	5 (7)
Democratic Unionist	70,975[b]	0.2[c]	0.2	2	0	3 (1)
SDLP	126,325 (154,193)	0.4 (0.5)[c]	0.3 (0.4)	0	0	1 (1)
UUUP	39,856[b]	0.1[c]	0.1	0	0	1 (1)
UU	36,989[b]	0.1[c]	0.1	0	0	1 (1)
Independent (NI)	22,398 (32,795)[a]	0.1 (0.1)	0.1 (0.1)	0	0	1 (1)
Speaker	27,035					1 (1)
National Front	191,706 (113,843)	0.6 (0.4)	0.5 (0.3)	0	0	0 (0)
Others	297,520 (292,792)	0.9 (1.0)	0.7 (0.7)	0	2[d]	0 (0/2[d])
Total poll	31,221,685 (29,189,104)					

Note: Overall Results and State of the Parties (Figures in brackets refer to October 1974 results): Total electorate 41,093,262 (40,072,-971); Turnout 76.0% (72.8). Overall swing, 5.2% Labour to Conservative; 74 seats changed hands.

[a] Excluding Independent votes outside N. Ireland.

[b] OUP, DUP, UU & UUUP candidate stood as UUU in 1974. Their total vote was 407,778 (1.4% of votes, 1.0% of electorate).

[c] SNP won 17.3% of the votes cast in Scotland; PC 8.4% in Wales. In N. Ireland OUP won 36.6% of the votes cast. DUP 10.2%, SDLP 18.2%, UUUP 5.7%, and UU 5.3%.

[d] Scottish Labour Party.

[e] Seats gained or lost compared with the seats held at dissolution. There were 30 by-elections in the lifetime of the last Parliament.

[f] The first figure in brackets shows the number of seats won in October 1974; the second figure is the number held at dissolution. Where there is only one figure there was no change.

Source: The BBC Guide to Parliament (London: BBC, 1979), p. 112.

5751138.

GEMCO